D. H. Lawrence and the Devouring Mother

In memory of Robert J. Ruderman

D. H. Lawrence and the Devouring Mother

The Search for a Patriarchal Ideal of Leadership

Judith Ruderman

Duke University Press
Durham, N.C.   1984

© 1984 Duke University Press, all rights reserved

Printed in the United States of America on acid-free paper

Permission to quote from D. H. Lawrence's work granted by Laurence Pollinger Ltd. and the Estate of Frieda Lawrence Ravagli.

Library of Congress Cataloging in Publication Data
Ruderman, Judith, 1943–
  D. H. Lawrence and the devouring mother.

  Includes bibliographical references and index.
  1. Lawrence, D. H. (David Herbert), 1885–1930—Criticism and interpretation.   2. Family in literature.
  3. Mothers in literature.   4. Fathers in literature.
  5. Matriarchy in literature.   6. Patriarchy in literature.   7. Leadership in literature.   8. Sex role in literature.   I. Title.
  PR6023.A93Z858   1984   823'.912   84-7987
  ISBN 0-8223-0598-4

Contents

Acknowledgments   vii

Abbreviations   ix

Prologue   3

1. Clytemnestra's Victory: Lawrence's Theories on Matriarchalism   5
2. Lawrence's Pollyanalytics: *Psychoanalysis and the Unconscious* and *Fantasia of the Unconscious*   22
3. In Flight from Matriarchy: *The Lost Girl*   37
4. Sanctions from the Animal World: *The Fox*   48
5. Over the Border: *The Ladybird* and *England, My England*   71
6. "The Italian Brutal Way": *Aaron's Rod*   90
7. A Lesson in Disillusion: *Kangaroo*   104
8. The Outlaw Hero: *The Boy in the Bush*   115
9. The American Experience: *Studies in Classic American Literature*, "The Woman Who Rode Away," *St. Mawr*   127
10. Rekindling the Father-Spark: *Movements in European History* and *The Plumed Serpent*   142

| 11. | Blessed are the Powerful: The Last Works | 154 |
| 12. | The Symbolic Father and the Ideal of Leadership | 173 |

Notes 189

Index 205

Acknowledgments

This book evolved over several years; many invaluable guides aided its progress.

To Elgin Mellown of Duke University I credit the wise and patient tutelage that resulted in my doctoral dissertation on *The Fox*, the germ of this book. Susan and Allen Dyer read the manuscript in its various stages and provided the intellectual stimulation and the warm friendship to encourage and improve it. Alan Stern and Donald Rosenblitt were especially helpful with the final chapter. To these readers and the other, more "official" ones, I give thanks for their attention and criticism.

All the Duke University librarians, most notably Emerson Ford, have facilitated my research. In addition, the Humanities Research Center at the University of Texas in Austin and the Morris Library at Southern Illinois University in Carbondale graciously acceded to my requests for materials relating to *The Fox* and *The Lost Girl*.

My typists were Dedra Staples, Anna Stinson, and Marisa Johnson. Bob Mirandon of the Duke Press kept me on track with the details of editing and indexing. All of these efficient people helped to keep me sane. My two teenagers, Lee and Marjory, helped to keep me insane, which is all right, too.

This book is dedicated to the memory of my husband, Bob Ruderman, who did not live to see its completion. I cannot encapsulate what he meant to me, and so I shall not try. I know that Bob would be proud of what follows; I'm not sure about D. H. Lawrence. Perhaps somewhere in the Great Beyond they're discussing it now.

Abbreviations

    A *Apocalypse* (Cambridge: Cambridge University Press, 1980)
  AR *Aaron's Rod* (New York: Viking Press, Compass Books, 1961)
  BB *The Boy in the Bush* (New York: Viking Press, Compass Books, 1972)
  CB *D. H. Lawrence: A Composite Biography*, 3 vols., ed. Edward Nehls (Madison: University of Wisconsin Press, 1957–59)
  CD *The Captain's Doll*, in *Four Short Novels of D. H. Lawrence* (Harmondsworth: Penguin Books, 1976)
  CL *The Collected Letters of D. H. Lawrence*, 2 vols., ed. Harry T. Moore (New York: Viking Press, 1962)
  CSS *The Complete Short Stories of D. H. Lawrence*, 3 vols. (New York: Viking Press, Compass Books, 1961)
"EC" "Enslaved by Civilization," in *Phoenix II: Uncollected, Unpublished, and Other Prose Works by D. H. Lawrence*, ed. Warren Roberts and Harry T. Moore (New York: Viking Press, Compass Books, 1970)
  EP *Education of the People*, in *Phoenix: The Posthumous Papers of D. H. Lawrence*, ed. Edward McDonald (New York: Viking Press, Compass Books, 1972)
  EtP *Etruscan Places* (New York: Viking Press, 1933)
"F" "The Fox," reprinted in *A D. H. Lawrence Miscellany*, ed. Harry T. Moore (Carbondale: Southern Illinois University Press, 1959)
  F *The Fox*, in *Four Short Novels of D. H. Lawrence* (Harmondsworth: Penguin Books, 1976)
  FLC *The First Lady Chatterley* (New York: Dial Press, 1944)
  FM Manuscript of *The Fox*, unpublished
  FU *Fantasia of the Unconscious*, in *Psychoanalysis and the Unconscious and Fantasia of the Unconscious* (New York: Viking Press, Compass Books, 1960)
"IP" "Introduction to These Paintings," in *Phoenix: The Posthumous Papers of D. H. Lawrence*, ed. Edward McDonald (New York: Viking Press, Compass Books, 1972)

JTLJ *John Thomas and Lady Jane* (New York: Viking Press, 1972)
K *Kangaroo* (New York: Viking Press, Compass Books, 1960)
L *The Ladybird*, in *Four Short Novels of D. H. Lawrence* (Harmondsworth: Penguin Books, 1976)
LCL *Lady Chatterley's Lover* (New York: Bantam Books, 1968)
LG *The Lost Girl* (Cambridge: Cambridge University Press, 1981)
MD *The Man Who Died*, in *St. Mawr and The Man Who Died* (New York: Random House, Vintage Books, 1953)
"M" "Matriarchy," in *Phoenix: The Posthumous Papers of D. H. Lawrence*, ed. Edward McDonald (New York: Viking Press, Compass Books, 1972)
MEH *Movements in European History*, ed. James Boulton (Oxford: Oxford University Press, 1971)
PS *The Plumed Serpent* (New York: Random House, Vintage Books, 1954)
PU *Psychoanalysis and the Unconscious*, in *Psychoanalysis and the Unconscious and Fantasia of the Unconscious* (New York: Viking Press, Compass Books, 1960)
R *The Rainbow* (New York: Viking Press, Compass Books, 1961)
"RL" "The Risen Lord," in *Phoenix II: Uncollected, Unpublished, and Other Prose Works by D. H. Lawrence*, ed. Warren Roberts and Harry T. Moore (New York: Viking Press, Compass Books, 1970)
"RP" "The Reality of Peace," in *Phoenix: The Posthumous Papers of D. H. Lawrence*, ed. Edward McDonald (New York: Viking Press, Compass Books, 1972)
SCAL *Studies in Classic American Literature* (New York: Viking Press, Compass Books, 1964)
SL *Sons and Lovers* (New York: Viking Press, Compass Books, 1958)
SM *The Symbolic Meaning: The Uncollected Versions of Studies in Classic American Literature*, ed. Armin Arnold (Arundel: Centaur Press, 1962)
SS *Sea and Sardinia* (London: Heinemann Phoenix, 1956)
St.M *St. Mawr*, in *St. Mawr and the Man Who Died* (New York: Random House, Vintage Books, 1953)
"T" "The Thimble," in *Phoenix II: Uncollected, Unpublished, and Other Prose Works by D. H. Lawrence*, ed. Warren Roberts and Harry T. Moore (New York: Viking Press, Compass Books, 1970)
T *The Trespasser* (London: Heinemann Phoenix, 1955)
TG *Touch and Go* (London: C. W. Daniel, 1920)
TI *Twilight in Italy* (London: Heinemann Phoenix, 1956)

VG *The Virgin and the Gipsy* (New York: Bantam Books, 1968)
WL *Women in Love* (New York: Viking Press, 1948)

D. H. Lawrence and
the Devouring Mother

Prologue

From "Manifesto," by D. H. Lawrence

She touches me as if I were herself, her own.
She has not realized yet, that fearful thing, that I am the other,
she thinks we are all of one piece.
It is painfully untrue.

I want her to touch me at last, ah, on the root and quick of
    my darkness
and perish on me, as I have perished on her.

Then, we shall be two and distinct, we shall have each our
    separate being.
And that will be pure existence, real liberty.

Till then we are confused, a mixture, unresolved, unextricated
    one from the other.
It is in pure, unutterable resolvedness, distinction of being,
    that one is free,
not in mixing, merging, not in similarity.
When she has put her hand on my secret, darkest sources, the
    darkest outgoings,
when it has struck home to her, like a death, "this is *him*!"
she has no part in it, no part whatever,
it is the terrible *other*,
when she knows the fearful *other flesh*, ah, darkness unfathom-
    able and fearful, contiguous and concrete,
when she is slain against me, and lies in a heap like one outside the
    house,
when she passes away as I have passed away,
being pressed up against the *other*,
then I shall be glad, I shall not be confused with her,
I shall be cleared, distinct, single as if burnished in silver,
having no adherence, no adhesion anywhere,

one clear, burnished, isolated being, unique,
and she also, pure, isolated, complete,
two of us, unutterably distinguished, and in unutterable con-
    junction.

Then we shall be free, freer than angels, ah, perfect.

1. Clytemnestra's Victory: Lawrence's Theories on Matriarchalism

In 1965, George Ford remarked only semifacetiously that "no doubt the time will come when the critic of Lawrence will be able to attract attention to his wares only by arguing that *Kangaroo* or *Aaron's Rod* is his finest piece of full-length fiction."[1] Fortunately, almost twenty years after Ford's prediction that time has not yet come. Critics are still clear-eyed about Lawrence's failings as an artist, although some are "justifying" *Kangaroo* (1923) as an un-novel, and *Aaron's Rod* (1922) as a picaresque novel.[2] But the importance of these novels and others like them to the Lawrence canon has not yet been properly assessed.

In the middle years, or third phase, of his writing career, D. H. Lawrence drew his characters in search of the superior individual whose leadership would inspire them to greatness. Commentary on Lawrence's interest in the relationship between a leader and his followers has undergone a change in formulation since the author's death. Some early critics set Lawrence's treatments of power in a personal, biographical perspective, and none of them identified one portion of the canon as a "leadership phase." John Middleton Murry, for example, in his 1931 *Son of Woman*, discussed *Aaron's Rod* in terms of Lawrence's frustrated homosexuality.[3] Aldous Huxley lambasted Murry's approach as an "essay in destructive hagiography"[4] and defined the imperatives for the second stage of Lawrence criticism, which began with a revival of interest in Lawrence in the 1950s. By that time the spate of memoirs had let up, and another generation, studying Lawrence from a distance, sought to place his work in the appropriate philosophical, historical, and political perspectives. These critics saw that Lawrence had passed through a phase of being convinced of the necessity for submission by the masses to a superior individual; and Harry T. Moore, in his 1951 biography of Lawrence, was probably the first critic to label this conviction the "leadership ideal."[5]

F. R. Leavis attempted in his 1955 *D. H. Lawrence: Novelist* to maintain a balance between personal and social commentary, even as he stressed the latter; Leavis understood that biographical considerations are requisite to an understanding of both the content and the tone of Lawrence's art.[6] In contrast, in a book published the same year as Leavis's, Mary Freeman deliberately and painstakingly avoided biographical considerations in favor of a broad study of Lawrence's ideas, one of which she described as "leadership."[7] In the following decade, such critics as Eugene Goodheart, Ernest Tedlock, George Ford, and Keith Sagar, while not discounting biography, stressed Lawrence's ideological affinities with other artists and philosophers and examined Lawrence's ideal of leadership in terms of these affinities.[8] According to their critical approach, which prevails today, Lawrence articulated his ideal of leadership in *Aaron's Rod* and *The Ladybird*, both written in 1921, carried it to its logical culmination in *The Plumed Serpent*, published five years later, and abandoned it thereafter.

Within the political context of these critical assumptions, Lawrence did indeed move away from his ideal of leadership. As early as *Women in Love*, written and revised between 1916 and 1919, Lawrence had expressed society's need for "a man who will give new values to things, give us new truths, a new attitude to life, or else we shall be a crumbling nothingness in a few years; a country in ruin" (*WL*, 45). In the postwar years of 1921 and 1922, Lawrence showed his characters in desperate search of this man of authority; and in 1925 he embodied his ideal of leadership in an elaborate religious and political system. In 1928, however, he remarked in a letter: "The hero is obsolete, and the leader of men is a back number.... The leader-cum-follower relationship is a bore. And the new relationship will be some sort of tenderness, sensitive, between men and men and men and women, and not the one up one down, lead on I follow, *ich dien* sort of business" (*CL*, II, 1045). These remarks, and the "new relationship" depicted in *The Escaped Cock* and *Lady Chatterley's Lover* (originally called *Tenderness*), have caused Harry T. Moore to say, with the majority of critics, that by 1927 Lawrence "had given up the leadership ideal which had characterized his third writing phase."[9]

This critical approach to Lawrence's leadership period is, I believe, inadequate. It is distinguished by three characteristics: the focus on only three works of this period, the novels *Aaron's Rod*, *Kangaroo*, and *The*

Plumed Serpent; the reliance on a political viewpoint to explain these novels; and the generalization from these three sources to the period as a whole. The resulting emphasis on political power rather than on domestic love relationships in these novels has led to the belief that the novels and the phase they constitute were alien to Lawrence's enduring concerns, and that consequently Lawrence repudiated or outgrew them.[10] The error is one of emphasis, for political programs in and of themselves never interested Lawrence: it was the element of "bullying" in socialism, fascism, or democracy that concerned him. "Bolshevism is one sort of bullying, capitalism another: and liberty is a change of chains," remarks one Lawrence spokesman, Don Ramón (*PS*, 78); in another place, Lawrence states in his own voice that fascism is "only another kind of bullying" (*MEH*, 317). This concern with bullying that one finds in all the works of Lawrence's third writing phase is of a piece with the stress on domination—and particularly on maternal domination—in both his earlier and later works. Study of the Lawrence canon indicates that the period characterized by the ideal of leadership was in fact a natural outgrowth of what came before, and that Lawrence never turned away from it. To the contrary, the works of this period are to a great extent quintessential Lawrence.

A widespread case of misplaced psychological emphasis in the study of Lawrence has contributed to an incomplete and inaccurate reading of the leadership period. From 1930 to the present, writers who have discussed D. H. Lawrence's psyche have either deliberately or offhandedly shown a marked oedipal bias, looking toward mother-love to explicate Lawrence's work. The only significant differences in their approach arise from their differences of opinion about two separate but related issues: whether Lawrence retained his obsessional love for his mother or grew away from it, and whether this mother fixation was emotionally and artistically crippling or emotionally and artistically ennobling. While Witter Bynner pinpoints Lawrence's "deep trouble" as an inability to progress out of the mother-worship stage, Martin Green finds a positive value in Lawrence's lifelong commitment to what he calls "matriarchalism."[11] David Cavitch analyzes Lawrence's sexual fears, especially as they come to a head in his American period, in terms of an unresolved Oedipus complex: the son's fear of the castrating father-rival and his failure at identifying with that figure. Only by giving up the sex act, Cavitch says, was Lawrence able to exorcise "the horror that had possessed his soul."[12] Most critics, however, see in Lawrence's work evidence that the author grew away from the refined Lydia Beardsall Lawrence and toward an acceptance of the dark sexuality represented by the coalmining father.

In an unpublished doctoral dissertation entitled "Psychological Analysis of Literary Productions as a Revelation of Personality," Harold McCurdy presents the most thorough treatment of the oedipal issue. McCurdy differentiates between Lawrence's fictional characters who are associated with darkness, sexuality, animals, and the earth (McCurdy tags them as type b-characters) and those who are associated with blondness, industry, and society (type c-characters). Admitting that his schema is limited, McCurdy nevertheless infers from the increasing power of the type b-characters, modeled on John Arthur Lawrence, as well as "from the increasing restriction of the child-mother relation, that Lawrence originally hated his father and loved his mother and later began reversing his attitudes."[13] Daniel Weiss's well-known *Oedipus in Nottingham* also delineates Lawrence's gradual progression to an acceptance of the father-principle he had repudiated in *Sons and Lovers* (although Weiss believes that the force of Lawrence's anti-oedipalism suggests its opposite, the continuance of his mother-love).[14] Even George Ford's *Double Measure*, which avoids psychological jargon, assumes that Lawrence outgrew his Oedipus complex and shifted his allegiance from his mother to his father; as a result, in Ford's words, "Persephone becomes Circe" in Lawrence's fiction.[15]

Harry T. Moore deliberately repudiates the Freudian emphasis. In an admirable attempt to prevent the reduction of Lawrence's work to a single principle, Moore dismisses the Oedipus complex as irrelevant to an understanding of Lawrence's work after *Sons and Lovers*. He agrees with the opinion of Father Jarrett-Kerr, as expressed in *D. H. Lawrence and Human Existence*, that this novel records and resolves the Oedipus complex, the assumption being that elopement with Frieda Weekley signified the author's maturity into full genital sexuality.[16] But Moore may have thrown out the baby with the bathwater in his desire to free Lawrence studies from a psychological catchphrase; for when Moore denies the presence of a mother fixation in works after 1913, he denies only Lawrence's incestuous urges toward his mother and leaves untouched the question of Lawrence's continued need for, and hostility toward, a mother's care. This viewpoint, like its oedipal counterpart, is inadequate because Lawrence's work throughout his career and especially in his leadership period shows evidence of unresolved pre-oedipal conflicts beneath the oedipal overlay.

These pre-oedipal conflicts are manifested in strongly dyadic relationships—those involving chiefly two people, mother and child—rather than the oedipal triangle that includes the father. Freud himself considered the pre-oedipal attachment to the mother to be of utmost importance only in the development of the female ("On Female Sexuality" [1931]). But psychoanalytic theorists since Freud have broadened the concept of fixation to the mother to include the more primitive stages in any child's life, when attachment to the mother, and ambivalence toward this attachment, is a matter of the child's physical and psychic needs for sustenance. Erich Fromm, for one, declares unequivocally that "the pre-Oedipal attachment of boys and girls to their mother is in my experience by far the more important phenomenon, in comparison with which the genital incestuous desires of the little boy are quite secondary. I find that the boy's or girl's pre-Oedipus attachment to mother is one of the central phenomena in the evolutionary process and one of the main causes of neurosis or psychosis."[17]

Many theorists now emphasize that before the point of desiring the mother incestuously, and fearing castration as a result of this desire, the male child shares with the female child a desire to merge with the caretaker mother and a fear that his dependency on her will destroy him. The child's pre-oedipal dilemma is that his need for the mother's nurture and protection stimulates a desire to return to the womb, but this regressive dependency means that the child will in effect die, having been annihilated by the devouring, engulfing mother.

In *Childhood and Society* (1950), Erik Erikson specifically delineates the issues of conflict in the pre-oedipal phase, which Freud divided into two stages, the oral and the anal. The first or oral stage establishes the individual's lifelong trust or mistrust in the world, the attitude originating in the child's faith in the mother's availability and competence to minister to his needs, as well as in his own ability to cope with his urges to bite and to devour. Even under the best of circumstances the child feels cut off from the mother and maintains into adulthood a lasting regret for their lost oneness. The second or anal stage of psychic development, paralleling the physical maturation of the eliminative organs, establishes the tension between two modes of behavior, holding on or letting go, either of which may involve creative or destructive attitudes: to hold may mean to take care of or to restrain unduly; to let go may mean to relax one's grip or to unleash harmfully. The child already possesses a basic faith or lack of faith in existence. He now experiences a true sense of choice, his problem being to learn how to exercise his autonomous will in the face of the doubt and shame instilled in him by the controlling outside forces of (in Western culture) the parents, and more specifically the mother. Oedipal concerns do not appear until the third or phallic stage, when the child fixes sexually on a single, unrealizable goal and experiences guilt for doing so. The crux of this third stage is the conflict between the child's initiative and the inappropriateness of his goal rather than the conflict between dependence and independence that came to a head in the anal period, in acts of defiance.[18]

The pre-oedipal tension between the desires for merger and for separation, and the fear of the mother as an ego destroyer, may lead to the child's perceiving the mother as a wild animal who will eat him up. To Erikson, following Freud, the child sees the mother as an agent of destruction because he has projected onto her his own urge to devour. But Joseph C. Rheingold, in *The Mother, Anxiety, and Death* (1967), surveys the literature supporting his theory that the devouring nature of the mother actually inheres in the mother herself. Freud, discussing the pre-Oedipus, noted in passing that "it is impossible to say how often this dread of the mother draws countenance from an unconscious hostility on her part, which the child divines."[19] Rheingold's own experience led him to surmise that the urge to murder her child, along with the urge to succor, is present to some degree in every mother; moreover, he says, "the clearest impression of the filicidal impulse is gained from a study of women during pregnancy, in the course of delivery, and in the puerperium. . . . The castrative impulse appears later." Dreams of patients in psychotherapy reveal what the waking mother would deny: for example, a woman three weeks postpartum recounts a dream in which she turns into a wild beast, leaps at her daughter, and tears open her throat.[20] That D. H. Lawrence also recognized maternal destructiveness is suggested by his remarks in a letter to Lady Cynthia Asquith in 1918: "I feel I am all the time rescuing my nephew and niece from their respective mothers, my two sisters; who have jaguars of wrath in their souls, however they purr to their offspring. The phenomenon of motherhood, in these days, is a strange and rather frightening phenomenon" (*CL*, I, 554).

Lawrence's own readings in the psychoanalytic theory of his times supported his intuitive view of the "strange and rather frightening phenomenon" of motherhood. In autumn 1918 he read Jung on mother-love, having borrowed the book from a psychoanalyst friend. Although he does not specify the work, the nature of his remarks about it points to *The Psychology of the Unconscious*, translated into English in 1915 and published in 1916. Here Jung deals with the incest wish as symbolic of the child's primitive desire to return to the protection of the mother's womb; with the conflict between the child's wish for security and his need for independence; and with the child's perception of the mother figure (the "mother-imago") in her dual capacity as sustainer and destroyer. Prompted by his reading of Jung, Lawrence reflected on motherhood in a remarkable letter to Katherine Mansfield, in November 1918, in which he set down the ideas that underpin his leadership works:

> This mother-incest idea can become an obsession. But it seems to me there is this much truth in it: that at certain periods the man has a desire and a tendency to return into[21] the woman, make her his goal and end, find his justification in her. In this way he casts himself as it were into her womb, and she, the Magna Mater, receives him with gratification. This is a kind of incest. It seems to me it is what Jack [John Middleton Murry] does to you, and what repels and fascinates you. I have done it, and now struggle all my might [*sic*] to get out. In a way, Frieda is the devouring mother. It is awfully hard, once the sex relation has gone this way, to recover. If we don't recover, we die. But Frieda says I am antediluvian in my positive attitude. I do think a woman must yield some sort of precedence to a man, and he must take this precedence. I do think men must go ahead absolutely in front of their women, without turning round to ask for permission or approval from their women. Consequently the women must follow as it were unquestioningly. I can't help it, I believe this. Frieda doesn't. Hence our fight. (*CL*, I, 565)

The juxtaposition in this letter of the "devouring mother" concept with the male leadership edict supports the observation made by Herbert Howarth that "whoever has been mother-overwhelmed may grow to advocate the male ascendency."[22]

Lawrence's own mother fixation and the nature of the earliest, pregenital relationship between all mothers and their children are the central concerns of Lawrence's career, more important to an understanding of his works than the heterosexual, genital love relationship for which they are commonly known. Lawrence has a propensity for seeing double in his treatment of female characters, so that women tend to appear in pairs in many of his works: one thinks of Miriam and Clara in *Sons and Lovers*, Ursula and Gudrun in *Women in Love*, Louisa and Mary in "The Daughters of the Vicar," March and Banford in *The Fox*, Carlota and Teresa in *The Plumed Serpent*. Because these pairs often split neatly between the sexual and the spiritual aspects, one may ascribe their presence to Lawrence's puritanical upbringing, which caused him to see a woman either one way or the other (although of course Lawrence learned this pairing device from his literary ancestors as well, such as Hardy and George Eliot). Lawrence stands his early training on its head when he portrays the sexual, full-blooded woman offering man physical and psychic renewal, and the spiritual, weak-blooded woman offering only death. Although this view partially explains some or even all of the pairs, it fails to take into account the author's more important, if more subtle, emphasis on his female characters' attitudes toward their role in the love relationship. This emphasis cuts across the sexual-spiritual axis and often results in characters being treated as positive or negative aspects of the Magna Mater. When considering Gudrun, for example, one might keep in mind Lawrence's letter to Katherine Mansfield, the woman on whom Gudrun is modeled, in which he speaks of his friend as Magna Mater, both fascinated and repelled by her lover's dependence on her. In the novel, Gudrun incorporates aspects of the "bad mother," she who encourages her child's dependence on her and then, feeling that dependence a drag on her freedom, wishes to commit infanticide: "Was she his mother? [Gudrun asks, of Gerald]. . . . Ooh, but how she hated the infant crying in the night. She would murder it gladly. She would stifle and bury it, as Hetty Sorrell did" (WL, 446).

The mother-child relationship in Lawrence's works becomes more —not less—pronounced in the years after his elopement with Frieda Weekley, for the circumstances of his life threw him more and more on what he called the "tender mercies" of others (CL, I, 581; AR, 225). Paul Delany has most thoroughly charted the course of Lawrence's life between 1914 and 1918 and should be consulted for a full accounting of Lawrence's fortunes in the years of the Great War.[23] It is sufficient here to note that several matters conspired toward bringing Lawrence's reactions against women to a fever pitch, and that the first stirrings of his urge toward male leadership in the social and political realms should be dated at 1915, with the banning of *The Rainbow*, the dashing of his hopes for acceptance of his art, and his placement in a position of extreme dependency on those more powerful than he. These personal crises occurred in the context of a crisis mentality on England's home front, as the war reinforced Lawrence's innate tendencies to polarize others as "friends" or "enemies" and to regard life as a battle.[24]

As early as 1915, but especially in the years between 1917 and 1925, Lawrence came to be ever more dependent upon the women who cared for him, and his hostility toward them increased as a result. Poor in pocket but rich in imagination, Lawrence used his fiction to express his feelings and to assert his independence. For example, one can gauge Lawrence's reaction to Lady Ottoline Morrell's playing hostess at Garsington by Birkin's mockery of Hermione in the Breadalby portions of *Women in Love*. Lawrence's ambiguous relationship with Lady Ottoline gains clarity when viewed from the pre-oedipal perspective of the child's ambivalence toward the caretaker mother. In 1915 Lawrence was uneasy at Greatham, where he felt like only a long-term guest of the Meynell family,[25] and accepted Lady Ottoline's offer of permanent lodging at Garsington at nominal rent; however, he was not totally happy about the prospect: "If I had a house and home [he wrote to Lady Ottoline], I should become wicked. I hate any thought of possessions sticking on to me like barnacles, at once I feel destructive. And wherever I am, after a while I begin to ail me to go away."[26] A rise in the contractors' costs for renovating the building provided a handy excuse for both parties to break off the arrangement, with Lawrence sighing his relief to a friend: "Thank heaven we shall get out of the Lady Ottoline cottage" (*CL*, I, 333). Ottoline's decorating ideas for the cottage, antithetical to Lawrence's taste, had already provided him a warning of her tendency to exert her prerogatives as owner.[27] Accordingly, in *Women in Love*, Hermione's furnishing of Birkin's rooms at the mill indicates her overbearing motherliness and explains Birkin's later refusal, when he commits himself to Ursula, to be smothered by things ("Chair").

In 1916 and 1917 Lawrence lived cheaply on the west coast of England, in a spartan cottage he had chosen and decorated himself. But after his expulsion from Cornwall, under suspicion as a spy for the Germans, he once again had to rely on others for shelter and support. He often rented or borrowed a cottage in Berkshire owned by Margaret Radford, an upper-class woman whose family had been friends of the Lawrences since 1915. At this cottage, surrounded by gorgeous countryside, Lawrence began to gain a measure of peace. How enraging, then, was Margaret Radford's practice of reappropriating her home, frequently at short notice. Equally enraging to Lawrence's mind was the characteristic effusive sweetness with which she intruded on his privacy. He chafed at his dependence on Margaret Radford in his letters of 1918 to 1920 (*CL*, I, 548–608). And he recorded in the various versions of *The Fox*, produced between 1918 and 1921, not only his increasing hostility toward this landlady but also his fantasy of revenge.

A third important landlady was Mabel Dodge Sterne (later Luhan), doyenne of the Taos art colony in New Mexico. After reading Lawrence's travel book called *Sea and Sardinia*, she entreated him to come to the United States to do for New Mexico what he had done for Sardinia: that is, to capture its spirit of place. After some initial resistance Lawrence did travel to New Mexico and wrote essays on it collected in *Mornings in Mexico*. But his imagination was stimulated as much by Mabel herself as by her country. The cabin with which she provided him proved to be too close to her own: he moved to Questa because there was "too much Mabel Sterne at Taos" (*CL*, II, 729). He also penned a concise and scathing portrait of his former *padrona*: "very 'generous,' wants to be 'good' and is very wicked, has a terrible will-to-power, you know—she wants to be a witch and at the same time a Mary of Bethany at Jesus' feet" (*CL*, II, 730). Readers (including Mabel herself) of the 1924 story "The Woman Who Rode Away" generally agree that Lawrence had Mabel's demise in mind when he showed the American protagonist about to be stabbed in the heart for the good of society. Certainly Mabel Dodge joins the others in the catalogue of "devouring mothers" in Lawrence's life, those two-faced women whose nurture of him Lawrence felt to be deadly.

No list of Lawrence's "devouring mothers" is complete without Frieda, the only woman he actually called by that term. The Lawrences' marriage was never a placid affair, in part because Frieda's desire to see her children conflicted with Lawrence's need for her single-minded attentions to him. His letters from the beginning of their relationship make note of Frieda's anguish for her children left behind in England, and of the toll that these children were taking on the couple's attempts to become closer (*CL*, I, 170, 172). The poetry of *Look! We Have Come Through!* also denounces "[t]he mother in you, fierce as a murderess . . . / Yearning toward England, towards your young children, / Insisting upon your motherhood, devastating" ("She Looks Back"). As Lawrence complained of "this drawn sword of the children" between Frieda and him, and of the "pretty bad—half-healed cuts" they got from it (*CL*, I, 205), Frieda reacted to an early version of *The Rainbow* and *Women in Love* by exclaiming to Edward Garnett that "they [Ella and Gudrun, the sisters] are *me*, these beastly, superior arrogant females! Lawrence *hated* me just over the children, I dare say *I* wasn't all I might have been, so he wrote this!" (*CL*, I, 207). With the decline of the Lawrences' fortunes in the years of the Great War, the marriage grew increasingly tempestuous and Lawrence's references to Frieda's children become increasingly vitriolic.[28] It must be noted here that Lawrence's own wish to have children by Frieda—"I don't care how soon" (*CL*, I, 120)—was never to be fulfilled.

Second only to Frieda's children, the phenomenon that caused the most trouble in the marriage, from Lawrence's point of view, was his illness of 1918–19. Caught in the great influenza epidemic, Lawrence was deathly ill for several months and had to rely almost entirely on his wife, who, though sick herself at this time, always had greater resources of flesh and basic good health to combat infirmity. In 1920, in his essays on education (written originally in 1918, though that first version is lost), Lawrence expressed his disdain for servants: "A servant moving about me, or even anybody moving about me, doing things for me, is a horrible drag on my freedom. I feel it as a sort of prostitution. *Noli me tangere.* It is our motto as it is the motto of a wild wolf or deer. I want about me a clear, cool space across which nobody trespasses" (*EP*, 649). No doubt he had in mind, when he wrote those words, his recent and utter dependency upon his wife, which repeated the pattern established by his mother during his sickly childhood. The solicitous attentions of his sister Ada during this adult illness, and his removal to the midlands country where he grew up, must have contributed further to his feelings of being reduced to a state of helpless dependency; indeed, Ada Lawrence Clarke had leased the cottage in Derbyshire for her brother entirely at her own expense.[29] Already angry at Margaret Radford for her on-again, off-again welcoming of him to her Berkshire home, Lawrence was uncomfortably sensitive to the ministrations of the women about him—but especially to those of his wife and mainstay. Thus he struck out at Frieda in letters to his friends:

> I am a wretched object like a drowned ghost creeping downstairs to tea—properly hate my condition, I can tell you. I suppose I'll get strong enough any day to slap Frieda in the eye, in the proper marital fashion. At present I am reduced to vituperation.[30]
>
> I am not going to be left to Frieda's tender mercies until I am well again. She really is a devil—and I feel as if I would part from her forever—let her go alone to Germany, while I take another road. For it is true, I have been bullied by her long enough. I really could leave her now, without a pang, I believe. The time has come to make an end, one way or another. If this illness hasn't been a lesson to her, it has to me. (*CL*, I, 581)

Of course, Lawrence did not part from Frieda forever, because he needed her nurturing as much as he resented it. Hadn't he admitted to Ernest Collings in 1913, "It is hopeless for me to try to do anything without I have a woman at the back of me" (*CL*, I, 179)? He got well, but his extended illness was in fact a lesson to him, a reinforcement of his lifelong mistrust and hatred of "tender mercies." Surely the tale that Lawrence wrote shortly after this illness, "Hadrian" (published in 1920 as "You Touched Me"), records Lawrence's own feelings when it relates how the sickly father, Mr. Rockley, "seemed to have a strange desire, quite unreasonable, for revenge upon the women who had surrounded him for so long, and served him so carefully" (*CSS*, II, 407).[31]

Lawrence's sense of being "bullied" by Frieda may not be the fantasy of an overly sensitive, even paranoid personality, for it accords with one modern psychoanalytic view of maternal destructiveness: as Joseph Rheingold says, "It is notorious that certain kinds of solicitous mothering conceal hostile feelings for the child, and even the genuinely nurturant mother is not without a degree of adverse effect."[32] Although Lawrence had no difficulty in recognizing the destructive elements in his wife's nurturing, others have ignored or denied Frieda's status as a "devouring mother." To Catherine Carswell, Lawrence's first meeting with Frieda Weekley meant that "never again would he be mothered by any woman. He would even put behind him that first mothering that had meant more than anything else to his youth."[33] Hillis Miller, deducing from Lawrence's novella *The Fox* Lawrence's concept of the ideal woman, finds her to be "a sort of transformed Frieda, . . . a woman who is able to escape from repression into a vital sexual relation with a man without trying to mother him."[34] Yet some observers have seen that it was precisely Frieda's motherliness that may have appealed to Lawrence, and that its value to him was not unmixed. Bertrand Russell has written that "Lawrence was an essentially timid man who tried to conceal his timidity by bluster. His wife was not timid. . . . Under her wing he felt comparatively safe."[35] Frieda's wingspread grew more ample as time went on, and Lawrence grew ever thinner; Lawrence's friend Koteliansky (familiarly known as Kot) has supplied an imaginative interpretation of these facts that corresponds with the author's own view of his wife: "If [Frieda] disappeared Lawrence would be saved, because she is devouring him bit by bit, gradually, permanently. We had a few more quarrels and she shed profuse tears, but, I think, she weeps only to benefit her digestion, after which she eats with an increased appetite and gusto."[36] Even those more sympathetic than Kot to Frieda Lawrence tended to describe the marriage in fascinatingly oral terms: Katherine Mansfield wrote to Lady Ottoline that Lawrence was lost, "like a little gold ring in that immense German Christmas pudding which is Frieda and with all the appetite in the world we cannot eat our way through Frieda to find him. One simply looks and waits for someone to come with a knife and cut her up into the smallest pieces that L. may see the light and shine again."[37] That someone would be D. H. Lawrence himself.

Lawrence's need for nurturance, his hatred of the dependency on others that this need dictated, his desire to assert his adulthood and to revenge himself on the "devouring mothers" in his life —all these personal concerns became linked in Lawrence's mind and art to society's problems in the chaotic years during and after World War I. As the men went off to war, leaving the women at home to take on traditionally male occupations and responsibilities, profound changes occurred in the male-female relationship. These changes were deeply threatening to Lawrence, with his need to assert male dominance over (strong) females. Women in trousers, women lobbying for the vote, women conducting trams and running farms—all were, to him, signs of society's decay. When his American agent, Robert Mountsier, asked Lawrence to write an article on the takeover of male jobs by women on the home front, Lawrence explained in terms of the "devouring mother" his reason for declining the assignment:

> in the tearing asunder of the sexes lies the universal death, in the assuming of the male activities by the female, there takes place the horrible swallowing of her own young, by the woman. . . . I am sure woman will destroy man, intrinsically, in this country. . . . I am sure there is some ghastly Clytemnestra victory ahead, for the woman. . . . My way is elsewhere. It is not I who will stay to see Medea borne up on a chariot in heaven. That belongs to the tearing asunder, of which I have had enough. I am going now out of this Sodom.[38]

Lawrence had always been interested in the intimate relations between parents and children and men and women, but during the war he linked the perversion of these relationships to the decline of England and sought a new Eden—he called it Rananim, from the Hebrew words *Ranenu tsadakim*, or "Let the righteous rejoice"—in which the proper relationships could be established. His efforts at this time to leave for America were thwarted by the authorities; stuck in England for the duration, he reflected time and again on the meaning for society not only of woman's straying out of "her place" but also of the more fundamental elevation of femaleness to a ruling principle.

One can chart Lawrence's movement from the personal and domestic realms to the societal and political in his works after 1913, for instance in the essays on Italy eventually published together as *Twilight in Italy* (1916). The first version of one essay, "The Theatre," published in *The English Review* for 1913, centers on Lawrence's opinions of Italian play productions and holds philosophical speculations to a bare minimum. But in the final version, Lawrence's attendance at a production of *Hamlet* stimulates his reflection first on the modern-day reversal of the poles of male dominance–female submission and then on the historical process that underlies this reversal. The audience itself causes Lawrence to remark that "the women triumph. . . . The male spirit, which would subdue the immediate flesh to some conscious or social purpose, is overthrown. The woman in her maternity is the lawgiver, the supreme authority. The authority of the man, in work, in public affairs, is something trivial in comparison. . . . And this is why the men must go away to America. It is not the money. It is the profound desire to rehabilitate themselves, to recover some dignity as men. . . ." (*TI*, 58–59). As for the play itself, Hamlet's self-consciousness and his failure to avenge his father signify to Lawrence not only that character's inability to *be*—to be the King and the Father in his own self—but also the degeneration of all of western society in its movement away from an earlier, better way of life. That way was patriarchal and aristocratic: "The whole Greek life was based on the idea of the supremacy of the self, and the self was always male. Orestes was his father's child, he would be the same whatever mother he had. The mother was but the vehicle, the soil in which the paternal seed was planted" (*TI*, 69). Although Orestes's matricide provokes his mother's avengers, the Furies, Orestes is exculpated because of the patriarchal principle on which his society was constructed. Still, the Furies have killed something in Orestes—his sense of kingliness as a male—and therefore, to Lawrence, the Orestes story records the first glimmer of a society organized around the principle of matriarchalism: a "Clytemnestra victory," as his letter to Mountsier phrases it. The woman will rule, and in her rule she will substitute the political system of democracy for that of dictatorship, and the religion of Christianity for paganism.

"[A]ccording to his idea of fulfilment," Lawrence writes, "man establishes the whole order of life" (*TI*, 69). If a person believes that his greatest fulfillment comes in self-fulfillment, and the greatest virtue is pride in the self and its activities, then he will seek a religion that emphasizes self and a ruler who represents the best self of that society. The Middle Ages saw the rise of the opposite view, that one's greatest fulfillment comes in self-abnegation and the greatest virtue is humility; the grand kings and popes and Jesus the King were gradually replaced as sources for inspiration by the infant Jesus on his mother's lap, "helpless, at the mercy of the world" (*TI*, 71). Thus Lawrence, himself susceptible to "tender mercies," sees an infantile dependency problem at the heart of modern Christianity. The Renaissance completed this transformational process, extending it into the state with the rule of Elizabeth the Queen:

as Lawrence explains in a later essay, "Shakespeare's whole tragic wail is because of the downfall of the true male authority.... It fell with Elizabeth. It was trodden underfoot with Victoria" (*SCAL*, 98). Without a kingly "best self" for one's consumption (a queenly "best self" being, for Lawrence, a contradiction in terms), the way to Cromwell and Parliament has been cleared, and the dynamic life principle is no longer "For the King" but rather "'For the good of my neighbor,' or 'For the good of the people,' or 'For the good of the whole'" (*TI*, 72).

In the years of World War I, Europe was shaken by the Bolshevist revolution in Russia, and from 1919 to 1921 Lawrence had opportunities to observe firsthand the fascist surges in Italy. He was also in Australia at the time when the Australian Communist party was founded (1922), and when many in that country were sympathetic to fascist attitudes (though Fascism achieved no formal political recognition in Australia). His short stay in Australia and his later, longer one in the United States showed him a fiercely egalitarian democracy at work. Lawrence's fear and hatred of merging with the woman caretaker, responses developed early in life and recorded in his first novel, *The White Peacock* (1911), influenced the development of his political theory—if anything so diffuse and uncodified can be called a theory—as he expressed it directly in his nonfiction and obliquely in his fiction. That is, his negative attitudes toward democracy and the socialist movement that was for him but one step down the road from democracy, as well as his protofascist leanings, were conditioned by his attitude toward the "devouring mother." The early versions of Lawrence's studies in American literature show a stubborn preoccupation with woman in her maternal role. That the final versions replace the Magna Mater with American democracy signifies not that Lawrence had switched targets between 1917 and 1922 but rather that the two targets were, for him, related. This relation is spelled out in Lawrence's final essay on Walt Whitman:

> The great merge into the womb. Woman.
> And after that, the merge of comrades: man-for-man love.
> And almost immediately after this, death, the final merge of death.
> There you have the progression of merging....
> So that if the new Democracy is to be based on the love of comrades, it will be based on death too. (*SCAL*, 169)

For Lawrence, democracy is deathly because it kills the proud and inviolate self: the all-men-equal guide to life does no more than reduce the superior to the level of the inferior and bring out the basest qualities in the latter. As for socialism, Lawrence's letters as late as 1922 pay lip service to this ideal, but his only full-blown fictional portrait of the bolshevist is Jim Bricknell in *Aaron's Rod*, a man who desperately needs a woman's love to sustain him; by implication, Bricknell's political outlook is a mere extension of his psychological weakness into another, larger realm. In *Kangaroo*, the Lawrence-hero rejects the socialist principles of Willie Struthers, despite his attraction to them, precisely because they require a bonding together of mates with the glue of love and trust and because they ignore "the inevitable necessity of each individual to react away from any other individual, at certain times" (*K*, 201).

Interestingly, in *Mutterrecht* [*Mother Right*] (1861), a work that Lawrence seems not to have read, the anthropologist J. J. Bachofen also draws a connection between the matriarchal principle and democracy. In fact, the early socialists—Marx, Engels, Bebel, and others—drew on Bachofen's work, and upon this principle, for their formulation of and justification for their belief in communalism. Yet the views of Bachofen, his followers (such as Robert Briffault, in *The Mothers* [1927]), and those who arrived at similar conclusions independently of Bachofen (L. H. Morgan, in *Systems of Consanguinity and Affinity* [1871] and *Ancient Society* [1877]) are diametrically opposed to Lawrence's.[39] Besides believing that the *Oresteia* depicts the transition from a matriarchal to a patriarchal society (and not the other way around, as Lawrence believed), Bachofen is of the firm opinion that the matriarchal values are superior to the patriarchal:

> The relationship through which mankind has first grown into civilization which is the beginning of the development of every virtue and of the formation of the nobler aspects of human existence is the matriarchal principle, which becomes effective as the principle of love, unity, and peace. . . . The idea of the universal brotherhood of man is rooted in the principle of motherhood, and this very idea vanishes with the development of a patriarchal society.[40]

Lawrence seems to have read none of these authors but Marx. He arrived at his theories on matriarchalism not in reaction to the scholarly work of others but rather from years of ruminating upon his own mother fixation and upon the "kind of incest" that he himself had committed. Disagreeing with the idea that there is a separation between the man who suffers and the artist who creates (to use T. S. Eliot's famous phraseology), Lawrence expressed his feelings about the mother figures in his life in work after work. Psychological considerations toward which

Lawrence himself was drawn help to explain the increasing violence in his works during the leadership period. For whether they consider a mother's threat of destruction to originate in the mother or in the child, psychoanalysts agree that the child's fear of being destroyed by the mother leads to a rage to destroy her—to commit matricide. Although acts of matricide are uncommon, a person has access to equivalents of matricide[41] that unleash hostility while keeping the actual wish repressed. In D. H. Lawrence's works after 1920 or so, a central concern is with the means of combatting the "devouring mother"; the violence reveals a modern-day Orestes committing what he thinks is justifiable homicide in an effort to return the patriarch to his rightful throne.

In the period between 1915 and 1925, Lawrence integrated his views about the parent-child and male-female relationships with his search for the patriarchal political organization that would restore western society to health. What follows in this study is an attempt to reconsider in the light of this integration the three novels—*Aaron's Rod*, *Kangaroo*, and *The Plumed Serpent*—by which the leadership period is commonly, and almsot exclusively, known; to examine two other novels of the period, *The Lost Girl* and *The Boy in the Bush*, that are either largely ignored or else treated as works quite apart from the leadership period; to consider the nonfiction as important statements on the ideal of leadership; and to review in relation to this ideal the short novels or novellas written during these years. The leadership works, it is to be hoped, will never be considered Lawrence's finest; but in an analysis of them one may hope to find reasons for what Eliseo Vivas calls "the failure and the triumph of [Lawrence's] art."[42] One may hope as well to assess the importance of these works to an understanding not only of Lawrence and his times but also of the exigencies to which we today have been led in our own efforts to cope with the breakdown of hierarchical values.

2. Lawrence's Pollyanalytics: *Psychoanalysis and the Unconscious* and *Fantasia of the Unconscious*

Like other twentieth-century British writers, D. H. Lawrence felt the need to recreate a mythology that would simultaneously explain and enrich a world stripped of meaning by the rationalism of the Enlightenment. Many scholars recognize that although the work of W. B. Yeats and Robert Graves can stand alone, without reference to their cosmologies, the enigmatic images used by these writers gain clarity when seen in the perspective of the worldviews set down in *A Vision* and *The White Goddess*. Yet few pay careful attention to D. H. Lawrence's two books on psychology, written between 1919 and 1921: *Psychoanalysis and the Unconscious* and *Fantasia of the Unconscious*. Readers who overlook these works may be taking their cue from Lawrence himself, who said that he called his second treatise *Fantasia* "to prevent anybody tying themselves [*sic*] into knots trying to 'understand' it," and who extolled its merits only to the extent of being "satisfied with it for what it is" (*CL*, II, 670, 672). Perhaps readers are too embarrassed and confused by Lawrence's fervent discussions of "plexuses" and "ganglia"—discussions that do not agree with standard descriptions of human anatomy—to use Lawrence's "science" as metaphor and apply it to his fiction.[1]

The foreword to *Fantasia of the Unconscious* may explain why Lawrence relegated his treatise to second rank: "The novels and poems are pure passionate experience," he explains, whereas these "pollyanalytics" are mere inference abstracted from experience. Yet Lawrence goes on to say that "art is utterly dependent upon philosophy": one must be clear about one's metaphysics, which Lawrence defines as "what the heart really believes in, after all," in order to live life fully and create good art (*FU*, 57). The act of setting down, in these psychological studies, what his heart really believed in undoubtedly gave Lawrence a clearer sense of purpose during his leadership phase, helping him to define the ideal society whose establishment passionately engaged him. Students of Lawrence's work might profitably react to these theories on psychology with the mix of skepticism and involvement that Lawrence himself expressed toward Mme. Blavatsky's theosophical writings: he characterized her *Secret Doctrine* as "[i]n many ways a bore, and not quite real. Yet one can glean a marvelous lot from it, enlarge the understanding immensely."[2] Indeed, all of Lawrence's leadership fiction rests on the ideas spelled out in these treatises, and much of the fiction is not comprehensible without reference to these ideas.

Lawrence had been interested in human psychology for several years, but not until December 1919, shortly after his removal from England, did he announce his intention of doing something on psychoanalysis for periodical publication. By the end of January the "six little essays on Freudian Unconscious" were completed, and on 24 March 1920 Lawrence had got them back from the typist. They were not published as articles, as planned, but rather came out in book form in May 1921, as *Psychoanalysis and the Unconscious*—a title adapted, no doubt, from Jung's *Psychology of the Unconscious*.

Lawrence intended the six essays comprising his book as an intensive study of the nature of the unconscious mind, but one must not look to them for the order and clarity of a scientific treatise. Rather, Lawrence approaches his subject intuitively (as he himself says, in his foreword to *Fantasia*) and proceeds to characterize the unconscious by a repetitive, circular, and sometimes contradictory accumulation of concepts, gathered from sources as disparate as St. John the Evangelist and Sir James Frazer and recombined with characteristic Lawrentian gusto. To read *Psychoanalysis and the Unconscious* is to be reminded of the poet-physician George Groddeck, whose *Book of the It* (1923), equally outrageous and entertaining, is similar in both subject matter and methodology to Lawrence's psychology works.[3]

Unlike Groddeck, however, Lawrence wanders far afield of basic psychoanalytic principles. *Psychoanalysis and the Unconscious* begins by lambasting Freud for the view of the unconscious that he and his followers perpetrated on mankind: "Gagged, bound, maniacal repressions, sexual complexes, faecal inhibitions, dream-monsters" (*PU*, 5). Lawrence scoffs at Freud's promise to cure neuroses by bringing these horrors up into the light of mental consciousness, since making conscious the unconscious has not in fact achieved the goal of mental health. Therefore, Lawrence continues, the psychoanalysts are drawn to an inevitable moral dilemma: if the incest-desire, in which almost every complex is rooted, remains unabated even after the conscious mind's repressions are lifted, then this desire is actually the norm, and inhibitions of it are the cause of neurosis. Lawrence balks at this conception of an innate incest-craving, and at the idea of psychoanalysts bringing their patients to the practice of incest "as a duty even." For the choice offered by Freud, as Lawrence mistakenly saw it while writing his essays, was clear-cut: either incest or insanity.

Determined to combat what seemed to him an ineluctable extension of Freud's views, Lawrence denied the incest-craving altogether as a component of the unconscious and affirmed its opposite, what might be called the incest-aversion. From the American psychoanalyst Trigant Burrow he took the cue that the unconscious contains not repressed sexual desires but merely the repressed *ideas* man has of sex.[4] The incest-craving as Lawrence defines it is only a conclusion that a man logically draws if he finds his marital relation unsatisfactory; his sexual passions being unfulfilled by his wife, he ties these passions to the deepest emotional connection he has known—the link with his mother. Then, instinctively, he revolts against this idea of incest and represses it, so that in secret it begins to guide his actions. No doubt Lawrence was attempting to draw such a picture of the incest process when, years later, he portrayed the impotent Clifford Chatterley obtaining perverse sexual satisfaction from his nurse, Mrs. Bolton.

Lawrence congratulated Freud for focusing on the problem of incest, but he felt that Freud's analyses could not help humankind to cure neuroses. In essence, Lawrence wrote his essays on psychology precisely in order to define scientifically the "kind of incest" that he wrote of incessantly and obsessively in his letters, poetry, and narrative prose—a pre-oedipal, pre-genital desire to merge with the caretaker mother—and, by this definition, to provide ammunition for use in combating the "devouring mother" and her perversion of life.

To Lawrence the real nature of the unconscious is "a very different affair from that sack of horrors which psychoanalysis would have us believe is the source of motivity. The Freudian Unconscious is the cellar in which the mind keeps its own bastard spawn" (*PU*, 9). The Lawrentian unconscious is announced simply but conclusively as the uniqueness of every individual. New life arises out of nowhere at the moment of conception, for the nature of the child cannot be explained completely by reference to the natures of the parents. Science, working on the basis of cause and effect, is powerless to determine the nature of the unconscious, since individuality is itself causeless. Thus Lawrence bids his readers abandon the intellectualization of Freud and adopt a religious attitude toward the subject. In effect, he gives his own version of the virgin birth, with each child a miraculous creation whose essence is defined in relation to neither the biological father *nor* the mother.

Having set forth his opponents' views in the first two essays of *Psychoanalysis and the Unconscious*, Lawrence begins in the third to describe the workings of the unconscious mind as he sees it. He insists that the unconscious is not an abstraction but rather a scientifically verifiable, tangible reality; and his stress on the inextricable connections between psyche and soma—not unlike Freud's—becomes immediately evident as Lawrence locates the primal seat of human consciousness beneath the navel of the fetus, in the solar plexus. After the infant's birth, he says, "the great first-mind of the abdomen" urges the child toward reconnection with its mother, which it enjoyed in the womb; the infant recaptures the primal unity during the act of nursing at the mother's breast. Yet the very striving toward unity stimulates a repulsion from unity, toward separation. The infant's shrill screams, accompanied by a stiffening of the backbone, arise from activity of the lumbar ganglion located in the spinal nerve system; the child kicks free from the womb's domination and asserts its proud singleness. The act of urination is as it were a battle cry, signalling repudiation of the tie to the mother. Thus ingestion can be equated with assimilation of the mother, and excretion with rejection of her. Both functions, and the centers from which they arise, are centripetal, relating the external world back to the self.

Once a polarity is set up between the two centers, a new degree of consciousness, hitherto essentially dormant, comes awake above the diaphragm, in the breast. Knowledge gained on this upper plane is not mental, but neither is it subjective or centripetal. Through activity of the cardiac plexus the child becomes aware not of the mother's connection to him, but of the mother herself, as a separate and awesome person, and of the child's connection to her. This kind of knowledge is pictured in Lawrence's short story "The Blind Man," when Maurice Pervin traces with his fingers the lineaments of Bertie Reid's face; for "from the cardiac plexus goes forth that strange effluence of the self which seeks and dwells upon the beloved, lovingly roving like the fingers of an infant or a blind man over the face of the treasured object, gathering her mould into itself and transferring her mould forever into its own deep unconscious psyche" (*PU*, 31). The source of devotional love, or what Lawrence calls "objective emotion," the cardiac plexus acts centrifugally, relating the self to the external world.

In recoil from the activity of the cardiac plexus, the thoracic ganglion of the shoulders measures the gulf between lover and beloved, discriminating between self and other so that the self does not merge with the other and lose its identity. Lawrence calls this discrimination "objective knowledge." Now a complex, nonmental circuit has been set up within the individual: the solar plexus works toward incorporating the object into the self, the cardiac plexus toward merging the self with the object; in counterpoint, the lumbar ganglion works toward self-realization, and the thoracic ganglion toward recognition of otherness. In short, on each plane of the human body, above and below the diaphragm, there are two modes of consciousness, one ventral and the other dorsal: a "sympathetic" striving toward unison and a "voluntary" striving toward separation. The horizontal division, marked by the diaphragm, and the vertical division, marked by the front and back of the human body, form "the cross of all existence and being" (p. 44). And without this polarity between modes, there is no possibility of creative development (p. 24).

Lawrence probably knew full well that standard medical discussions of neuroanatomy at the time included the lumbar and thoracic ganglia in the sympathetic (known today as autonomic) nervous system rather than in the voluntary system. He had, after all, asked a friend associated with the field for a description of the nervous system, complete with map (*CL*, I, 553). But in matters scientific and otherwise, Lawrence was never one to be hamstrung by the "facts"—facts were to be played with and imaginatively extended so that the truth might be arrived at. To Lawrence, the truth of psychological development was that the child seeks and needs a balance between the desire for merger (which he considered a function of the sympathetic centers) and the desire for independence (a function of the voluntary centers). Grounding his theory in neuroanatomy, Lawrence may have posed more questions than he answered, especially for the orthodox neuroanatomist or psychoanalyst of his time; but he also indicated the innate and polarized nature of the urges toward merger and separation.

Because no child or parent exists in a vacuum, the complex circuit within an individual relates to the complex circuits within other individuals. Through this door enters the question of morality, so important to Lawrence, and which he thought orthodox science unable to handle. Lawrence finds "a new moral aspect to life" in the fact that if one does not keep his plexuses and ganglia in balance he will disturb the precarious balance within other people. The following pronouncement sets up a guideline for parents and teachers in the rearing and education of children: "The essence of morality is the basic desire to preserve the perfect correspondence between the self and the object, to have no trespass and no breach of integrity, nor yet any refaulture in the vitalistic interchange" (p. 28). The emphasis in this pronouncement, as in all of Lawrence's work, lies in preserving the integrity of the unique individual. For without a strong sense of self, a person longs to—indeed must—identify with another, and this merging of identities, which Lawrence defines as incest, further weakens the individual psyche as it drains the loved one of his or her vitality.

One can escape neurosis, then, by keeping the poles of the unconscious in balance, and it is at this task that the mind, or mental consciousness, can be of service. The brain develops last in the growth of the child, and acts merely as a telegraph transmitter, printing off static concepts from the living flux of dynamic consciousness. But the brain or mind may act as a tool by providing humans with the means to recognize their deviations from the life-path. "This is the use of the mind—a great indicator and instrument. The mind as author and director of life is anathema" (p. 49). In this manner, Lawrence dismisses the rationalist position of Freud; for Freud said that the primacy of the id must be challenged by the ego, while Lawrence believed that childhood spontaneity must never be stifled.

Most readers of *Psychoanalysis and the Unconscious* received the essays then, as they recieve them today, with open derision or embarrassed silence. This unfavorable critical reaction stimulated Lawrence to try once again to convince others of the truth of his theories. Almost all of *Fantasia of the Unconscious*, Lawrence's second attempt to supersede Freud, was written in Germany in the late spring and early summer of 1921; the original title was *Psychoanalysis and the Incest Motive*. The foreword was finished in Taormina, Sicily, on 8 October; and Lawrence had corrected the entire work by the middle of the month. By 5 November he had sent the manuscript to Thomas Seltzer, his American publisher at the time.

Most of the ideas in *Fantasia of the Unconscious* are restatements of concepts from a series of essays on education written a few months after the completion of *Psychoanalysis and the Unconscious*. Lawrence had begun *Education of the People*, which he intended for the *Times Literary Supplement*, in November 1918; but, like the first draft of the essays on psychoanalysis, it was not accepted for that publication. From four essays (never published and now lost) the work expanded, in June 1920, into 116 holograph pages, or 143 pages of typescript. Although Stanley Unwin had expressed interest in bringing out the book, nothing came of it. Instead the ideas found their expression in *Fantasia of the Unconscious*, written a year later.

Education of the People ostensibly concerns itself with the inadequate educational system in England and the means of rectifying that inadequacy. "If ever there is a poor devil on the face of the earth it is the elementary school-teacher," Lawrence sighs (*EP*, 589), drawing no doubt on his own unhappy experiences at the Davidson Street School in Croydon in 1911. Lawrence gave some of his experiences and probably all of his feelings to Ursula in *The Rainbow* and made Birkin a school inspector in *Women in Love*; in these education essays, he recommends a hierarchical system that puts real (as opposed to token) power in the hands of the school administrators to right the wrongs of society. According to Lawrence, the state runs its schools on the false notion of equality among its pupils, just as it runs its politics and its industries: in these modern times, everything is devoted to the "trades-unionistic, strike-menacing truckshunters" of the world (*EP*, 588). In what Lawrence calls a "true democracy," however, "[a]s the leaves of a tree accumulate towards its blossom, so will the bulk of mankind at all times accumulate towards its leaders" (*EP*, 609). Education of the people must mean different things to different people, depending upon their own innate capabilities.

The central concept of this book comes in the central essay, number six among the twelve. The impetus behind the writing of these essays on education is shown to be the mother's miseducation of her children from earliest childhood, long before they enter school. Modern mothers, says Lawrence, are responsible for the fact that schoolchildren are automatons without a spark of creative individuality left in them, and modern schools perpetuate the problem with curricula designed to substitute self-conscious, mental frictions for true knowledge gained darkly from the lower, unconscious centers. Lawrence progresses from the proletariat and "the old ideal of Equality" (*EP*, 600) to the need for "the very summit of the supreme judge and utterer, the first of men" (*EP*, 610) via the "devouring mother," who stifles her child's development. Only lengthy quotation from this section can impart the full force of Lawrence's fury:

> How to begin to educate a child. First rule, leave him alone. Second rule, leave him alone. Third rule, leave him alone. That is the whole beginning....
>
> ... Leave his sensibilities, his emotions, his spirit, and his mind severely alone. There is the devil in mothers, that they must try to provoke *personal* recognition and *personal* response from their infants....

2. Lawrence's Pollyanalytics 29

... There should be a league for the prevention of maternal love, as there is a society for the prevention of cruelty to animals. ...

... And why? Not for any thrilling Freudian motive but because our now deadly idealism insists on idealizing every human relationship, but particularly that of mother and child. Heaven, how we all prostrate ourselves before the mother-child relationship, in all the grovelling degeneracy of Mariolatry! Highest, purest, most ideal of relationships, mother and child!

... A mother is to a high degree, alas, mentally conscious of her own self, her own exaltedness, her own mission, in these miserable days. And she wants her own mental consciousness reciprocated in the child. The child must *recognize* and respond. Alas, that the child cannot give her the greatest smack in the eye, every time she smirks and yearns for recognition and response. If we are to save the ultimate sanity of our children, it is *down with mothers*! *A bas les mères*!

Down to the right level. Pull them down from their exalted perches. No more of this Madonna smirking and yearning. No more soul. A mother should have ten strokes with the birch every time she "comes over" with soul or yearning love or aching responsibility. Ten hard, keen, stinging strokes on her bare back, each time. Because White Slave Traffic is a cup of tea compared with yearning motherlove. It should be knocked out of her, for it is a vice which threatens the ultimate sanity of our race.

... But with the cunning of seven legions of devils and the persistency of hell's most hellish fiend, the cooing, clapping, devilish modern mother traduces the child into the personal mode of consciousness. She succeeds, and starts this hateful "personal" love between herself and her excited child, and the unspoken but unfathomable hatred between the violated infant and her own assaulting soul, which together make the bane of human life, and give rise to all the neurosis and neuritis and nervous troubles we are all afflicted with. (*EP*, 620–25)

A cure for these mother-caused diseases is suggested in Lawrence's offhand remark that the great races, such as the ancient Romans, had no mothers (a reference to Romulus and Remus, suckled by a she-wolf), while the weak races, such as Christians, have no father (*EP*, 632). Lawrence would soon elaborate upon this idea in *Fantasia of the Unconscious*. Here, in *Education of the People*, he exhorts his readers to take upon themselves the responsibilities for their own destinies: "Break clean away from this old yearning navel-string of love. ... Break it, and be born!

Fall apart into your own isolation; set apart single and potent in singularity forever" (*EP*, 634).

Once again Lawrence's emphasis is on the necessity for space between people, or, in psychoanalyst Margaret Mahler's phrase, on the psychological birth of the human being.[5] He uses a favorite metaphor as he advises parents that "there must be no trespass into the solitariness. . . . Do not be afraid, either, to *drive* him into his own soul's inviolable singleness. A child will trespass. It is born nowadays with an irritable craving to trespass into the nature of the mother. Nay, the parent-child relationship in these nervous days resolves itself into one series of trespasses across the confines of two natures, till there is some unholy arrest" (*EP*, 638–39). The concept of trespassing had a special resonance for Lawrence. In his first novel, *The White Peacock* (1911), the gamekeeper Annable catches the young trespassers and lectures them against poaching; the second novel is entitled *The Trespasser* (1912), and deals with the breakdown of Sigmund's self—his private space—as he is engulfed by a "devouring mother" whom he calls "Hawwa—Eve—Mother!" (*T*, 60). In the Lawrence canon, trespassing quickly became a psychological outrage, the encroachment on a person's inner territory. Lawrence's hatred of the enveloping, encroaching female parent—the trespasser par excellence—lay behind his distaste for democracy, mass man, humans in the aggregate, and led him to search for the alternate political system that he prescribed in *Fantasia of the Unconscious*.

In *Fantasia of the Unconscious*, Lawrence's attitude is defensive and his tone at times flippant, as he attempted to anticipate and thus forestall inevitable criticism. The foreword advises the reader that he or she is "quite free to dismiss the whole wordy mess of revolting nonsense, without a qualm" (*FU*, 54); the epilogue remarks, "I hope you say Amen! along with me, dear little reader: if there be any dear little reader who has got so far" (p. 222). But Lawrence was perfectly willing to say Amen! all by himself, for he was utterly committed to the ideas he elaborated on in this sequel to *Psychoanalysis and the Unconscious*, published by Martin Secker (without the epilogue) in London in September 1922, and by Thomas Seltzer in New York the following month.

These ideas were not essentially different from those in *Psychoanalysis and the Unconscious*, but the emphasis placed on them changed significantly. In *Fantasia* Lawrence revises his attack against Freud, because "what Freud says is always partly true"; the attribution of a sexual motive to all human activity, rather than the nature of the unconscious, is now the main source of their disagreement. Lawrence asserts that a greater impulse even than sex is "the desire of the human male to build a world" (*FU*, 59–60). The proper coordination of the male and the female principles is the subject of the fifteen essays comprising this treatise.

Psychoanalysis and the Unconscious stresses the primal connection between mother and child, but in *Fantasia*, following the lead of *Education of the People*, Lawrence took pains to tip the scales in the other direction, toward the father. The navel may indicate the child's connection with the mother but within the solar plexus lies the "father-spark" that connects the infant just as firmly, if less obviously, to the father:

> For true it is that the one bright male germ which went to your begetting was drawn from the blood of the father. And true it is that that same bright male germ lies unquenched and unquenchable at the centre of you, within the famous solar plexus. And furthermore true it is that this unquenched father-spark within you sends forth vibrations and dark currents of vital activity all the time; connecting direct with your father. You will never be able to get away from it while you live.
>
> The connection with the mother may be more obvious. Is there not your ostensible navel, where the rupture between you and her took place? But because the mother-child relation is more plausible and flagrant, is that any reason for supposing it deeper, more vital, more intrinsic? Not a bit. Because if the large parent mother-germ still lives and acts vividly and mysteriously in the great fused nucleus of your solar plexus, does the smaller, brilliant male-spark that derived from your father act any less vividly? By no means. It is different—it is less ostensible. It may be even in magnitude smaller. But it may be even more vivid, even more intrinsic. So beware how you deny the father-quick of your self. You may be denying the most intrinsic quick of all. (*FU*, 70)

Too frequently, according to Lawrence, modern mothers act out what he terms the "Northern" mode of cardiac plexus love, or devotional worship, as opposed to the "Southern," sensual mode of the solar plexus (Lawrence had already depicted these two ways of loving in *The Lost Girl*, written the year before, in which the appropriately named Miss Frost exemplifies the Northern mode and Ciccio the Southern [see next chapter]). Mothers bully their children by such "refined punishments of the spiritual mode" as "pained but resigned disapprobation" (*FU*, 89). Indeed, the mother's living and loving almost exclusively from her sympathetic centers leads to the gross underdevelopment of the child's voluntary centers of independence, so that he of necessity is bound forever to her. Lawrence explains in *Education of the People* that "[t]he proud volitional centres of the lower body, those which maintain a human being integral and distinct, these have collapsed, so that the whole individual crawls helplessly and parasitically from the sympathetic centres, to establish himself in a permanent life-oneness with another being, usually the mother. And the mother, too, rejoices in this horrible parasitism of her child, she feels exalted, like God, now she is the host of the parasite" (*EP*, 639). To break this "horrible circle" Lawrence advocates whipping and beating about the shoulders and buttocks, sites of the thoracic and lumbar ganglia, even with "stinging rods." In *Education of the People*, Lawrence advises the mothers to take this action; but in *Fantasia of the Unconscious* he has given up on the mother and is looking toward the father. In order to develop healthily, the child needs a *father* to counteract the smothering, stultifying effects of the mother's characteristic means of parenting, by spanking the child and thereby activating its ganglia and helping the move toward independence. A father's love, like the father-spark, may be less obvious than a mother's, but it is "ultimately on the remote but powerful father-love that the infant rests, in a rest which is beyond mother-love. For in the male the dominant centres are naturally the . . . centres of responsibility, authority, and care" (*FU*, 87–89). *Fantasia of the Unconscious* boldly states a Lawrentian truism (and extremism) pictured obliquely in all the leadership fiction: that the father's mode of parenting is superior to the mother's, and that it holds the key to regeneration of society at large.

Fantasia's discussions of the "father-spark" might be viewed as the author's acceptance of his own father, whom he had ignored or repudiated long ago in deference to the refined Lydia Beardsall Lawrence, and also as a last-ditch, all-out attack against his mother. Indeed, the autobiographical content of Lawrence's psychology theories becomes especially apparent in *Fantasia of the Unconscious*, in which Lawrence, like Freud before him, makes psychological generalizations from his own introspection and experience. The connection between the great nerve centers and the health of the body (for each organ has its source in a nerve center) is illustrated by tuberculosis, which Lawrence maintains is caused by an overactive cardiac plexus. The mother who makes her child too loving, in the devotional sense, must take responsibility for his ultimate derangement and death. Lawrence's own case of tuberculosis did not become evident until the mid-1920s, and he was loath to call the disease by name even then; but from the age of two weeks he was beset with such upper respiratory illnesses as bronchitis, pneumonia, and the common cold. No doubt he had his own frail health in mind when he railed against maternal overprotectiveness.

Then, too, Lawrence probably had his own family situation in mind when he elaborated upon the correlate to maternalism, the incest-desire. The word *incest* was part of Lawrence's original title for this work, and the concept is of utmost importance to it. Lawrence here clarifies the derivation of incest, left vague in the previous set of essays, by fixing blame for the incest-craving on the parent, more specifically on the mother, for whom Lawrence reserves his most hysterical outbursts. Because of the polarity within the individual between the upper and lower planes, intense spiritual love for a parent prematurely arouses the deeper sensual centers that would normally awaken at puberty: these are the hypogastric plexus and the sacral ganglion (complemented on the upper plane by the cervical plexus and the cervical ganglion). *Psychoanalysis and the Unconscious* does not concern itself with adult sexuality, for Lawrence's purpose in those essays is to uncover the dynamics of child-consciousness that underpin adult behavior. In *Fantasia*, however, Lawrence denies Freud's concept of infant sexuality, stating that although sex in terms of gender is present from birth, sex in terms of coition is the outcome of the metamorphosis of child into adult. In "*spiritual* incest, more dangerous than sensual incest, because it is more intangible and less instinctively repugnant," the child has no outlet for his awakened sexuality because a child's relations with his parents exist only in the first four modes of consciousness. So instead of being polarized with an external electrical circuit, the child becomes polarized within himself, obsessed with his own sexuality. The result is masturbation and other "mild sex perversions" (*FU*, 153–55).

Further, Lawrence says, the incestuous devotion felt for the parent by the child prevents any later satisfactory love relationship. In *Sons and Lovers* the highly autobiographical Paul Morel recognizes that his mother "bore him, loved him, kept him, and his love turned back into her, so that he could not be free to go forward with his own life, really love another woman" (*SL*, 345). Because a man tied to his mother cannot make a good husband to his wife, she in turn will look to her own sons for fulfillment. Lawrence terms this process "the viciousest of circles." The circle begins with the fact that "not one single breath does a baby draw, free from the imposition of the pure, unselfish, Botticelli-holy, *love-will* of the mother" (*FU*, 173). The circle must be broken by utter concentration on "the one lesson worth learning at last": that is, "my soul is my own. It shall not be violated" (p. 177). The importance of this lesson is underscored by the fact that Lawrence does not bury it in the treatise, like a gem to be extracted after much hard digging and careful sifting; rather, he devotes to it a single, succinct (three-page) essay entitled "Litany of Exhortations."

A marriage between individuals—"an equilibrium, a pure balance of two single beings:—as the stars balance each other," to quote Birkin in *Women in Love* (*WL*, 168)—counterposes a woman's emotional nest-guarding to a man's authoritative pioneering; for Lawrence believed that women by nature have their positive charge in the sympathetic centers of the belly and breast, whereas men by nature act from the volitional centers of the backbone and shoulders. When a man approaches maturity, at about age thirty-five (Lawrence was thirty-five at the writing), he must step beyond fulfillment in marriage and embrace responsibility for the world's future, putting his wife "under the spell of his fulfilled decision." In fact, the great purpose of coition is to refresh the blood of the participants, especially so that the renewed male will set out to renew the world. The night is the time for coition and for sleep, the day for purposive activity (*FU*, 210).

Lawrence thus affirms what he calls the moon-principle (for *Fantasia* makes "a sudden lurch into cosmology, or cosmogony" [p. 53]), associated with woman, water, darkness, anticommunalism, and sex; but he subordinates the principle to that of the sun, associated with man, fire, light, culture, and world change. By so doing he provides, he believes, a corrective to psychoanalysis, for "when Freud makes sex accountable for everything he as good as makes it accountable for nothing" (p. 61). This from the Lawrence who was commonly known for his "dirty books"—or in more genteel terms, for his paeans to the sex act.

Toward the close of *Fantasia* the author tentatively defines the true goal of manhood. Earlier in the treatise, in chapters six through eight, he broached the subject of a chosen few who would assume responsibility for the masses in some future society. To this end, using ideas worked out in his unpublished education essays, he outlined the ideal educational process, in which most children are never taught to read and write and no children are permitted to cerebrate before age fourteen. Now, in the final essay, Lawrence asserts that every individual male can best fulfill himself by trusting and serving a supreme leader; the tacit assumption is that every individual female can best fulfill herself by cooking and cleaning for an individual male. But Lawrence is not addressing himself to women, or to their appropriate roles. He speaks most directly to himself, at a critical juncture of his life, when he makes this recommendation: In touch with the lower, sensual centers through coition with a blood-polarized female (for the puritanical Lawrence, who abjured both masturbation and sex in the daytime, also abjured promiscuity), the purposive male should set forth to passionate and creative activity with and for a superior individual. One is reminded of Robert Browning's companion poems "Meeting at Night" and "Parting at Morning," in which "the two hearts beating each to each" give way at dawn to "the need of a world of men for me." Lawrence's dichotomy between the world of man and woman and the world of men marks his refutation of Freud's notion that all nonsexual activities are mere sublimations of the sex drive.

Lawrence seems to have overlooked the discrepancy between his theory that women are "charged" naturally in their sympathetic centers and his complaint that they tend to smother their children. Works like *Sons and Lovers* suggest that Lawrence realized how deadly it is for a woman to be limited to the care of home and children, and how this deadliness might lead to the very smothering of children (and husbands) that he excoriates. But in his later, leadership works, Lawrence firmly and unapologetically places woman in her narrow realm. To many women today who work eight hours outside the home—often returning at night to start the meals and clean up—the notion that their function as wives centers on the recharging of their husband's batteries, so that the men can go out again the next morning to do important manly tasks, must appear quaint when it doesn't offend and infuriate. But to many men and women in this last part of the twentieth century, Lawrence's ideas do not seem outmoded; indeed, the notion that home is "woman's place," and that any stepping out of it disrupts the natural order, still exerts the powerful force of myth.[6]

In his psychological treatises Lawrence emphasized the pure isolation of the individual as both the mysterious first cause of being and as the antidote to the incest-desire. But in *Fantasia of the Unconscious*, in reaction to the "devouring mother," he drew toward the perilous conclusion that to entrust one's consciousness to another, "superior" individual will lead one to personal fulfillment. The thin line between fulfillment and annihilation, whether physical or psychic, manifests itself in the jarring discrepancy between means and ends to be found in many of Lawrence's leadership works, in which, as John Stoll puts it, "the leader completes himself through the social order, which he embodies, only by dominating the lesser individuals who comprise it, by bullying them on behalf of the dark gods."[7] The difference between a "devouring mother" and a dominating leader begins to blur before the reader of Lawrence, as it blurred for Lawrence himself at times. What is clear is that Lawrence's strictures about leadership of society by a strong man were based on his beliefs about the proper relationships among family members. His purpose in his second treatise on psychology was to show how the problems of society at large begin in the mother-centered first society of most individuals in this modern age. The child's connection with the father, or the child's acceptance of the "father-quick" in himself, is what Lawrence offered as the salvation of humankind: this is what he meant by the principle of lordship that his leadership novels are all about. Becuse the mother-dominated household is the springboard from which Lawrence produced the works of his leadership period, one can trace a direct path from *The Lost Girl*, which depicts the invidious rule of the Magna Mater, to *The Plumed Serpent*, which restores the Pater Magnus to his rightful throne.

3. In Flight from Matriarchy: *The Lost Girl*

The Lost Girl, published in 1920, was the only Lawrence novel to win an award: the £100 James Tait Black prize. Arnold Bennett spoke highly of the work at the time, and critics since have tended to characterize and also to damn it as Bennett-like rather than Lawrentian. Graham Hough, for one, condemns *The Lost Girl* as "the dullest and least characteristic Lawrence.... without any of the passionate psychological preoccupations that had lifted Lawrence's earlier books out of their setting."[1] Although Hough's views may be extreme, the novel today is little known by anyone other than a Lawrence scholar and is certainly not accorded major status by the critics. Whether the novel as novel is any good may justifiably be debated still—after all, even the accepted and enshrined Lawrence novels have their share of detractors. But whether it is Lawrentian may no longer be questioned. For in spite of its naturalistic atmosphere, *The Lost Girl* shows the same "passionate psychological preoccupation" with maternal destructiveness that marks the entire Lawrence canon.

Like many of the leadership works produced in Italy between 1919 and 1921, *The Lost Girl* had been brewing in Lawrence's mind for many years. In fact, the novel took its impetus from the George Cullen family in Eastwood, Nottinghamshire, Lawrence's hometown, and is bound up in many ways with the Lawrences themselves. The novel's beginnings may be traced to the earliest version of *Sons and Lovers*, then called *Paul Morel*. Lawrence worked on this novel at home during Lydia Beardsall Lawrence's last illness in 1910, when Flossie Cullen was her nurse; in the months following his mother's death, as he worked on *Paul Morel*, Lawrence continued to think of Miss Cullen and inscribed her copy of *The White Peacock* as follows: "To Flossie Cullen in gratitude to her, for her rare kindness to my mother."[2] This draft of the novel combines elements of the Cullens' lives with those of the Lawrences and the Chamberses: for example, the Miriam character is present, but she is clearly based on Flossie Cullen (the name changed here to Staynes) as well as Jessie Chambers. For the Staynes governess, a major character in this version, Lawrence drew on the Cullen governess, who had helped him with his own schoolwork; but in his story she marries the minister who had courted Mrs. Morel, the Lydia Lawrence figure.[3] These and other complicating aspects of the story were eliminated after Lawrence showed the manuscript to Jessie Chambers in the autumn of 1911: she recommended that Lawrence remain true to what he knew best—his own family—for reasons both artistic (the novel would seem less forced) and psychological (Lawrence could work through his mother fixation).[4]

But the Cullens continued to occupy Lawrence's thoughts, no doubt because he saw a common thread running through the two families, so he continued to write about them. An unpublished fragment beginning, "My mother made a failure of her life . . ." dating from 1912, is concerned primarily with the Cullens (here called the Culverwells), although elements of the Lawrence biography are mixed in: the mother's feeling of superiority and of marrying beneath her; the death of an older sibling in London. In fact, the back of the tenth leaf of the manuscript bears the title "*Sons & Lovers*".[5] In December 1912 or January 1913, shortly after finishing *Sons and Lovers* as we know it today, Lawrence started over with a novel he called *The Insurrection of Miss Houghton*, now firmly centered on the Cullens. He abandoned the project after four months and two hundred pages (the manuscript does not survive) and took it up again only after World War I: he wrote to Martin Secker in December 1919, "I am waiting for MS of a novel three parts done, *Mixed Marriage*, which I left in Germany before the war" (*CL*, I, 602). In February 1920, after finishing *Psychoanalysis and the Unconscious*, Lawrence received the manuscript (delayed because of a postal strike) and began to push toward its completion, but in March he "scrapped" it and began again. In two months he had completely rewritten the novel.[6] The Cullens' story, as Lawrence saw it, took a decade to achieve its final, published form and gave expression to Lawrence's deepest concerns. What he shows imaginatively, under the guise of fiction, in *The Lost Girl*, he discusses analytically, if not dispassionately, in *Fantasia of the Unconscious*, which he took up when this novel was done: that the mother-dominated household is the cause of neuroses from the smallest to the largest levels of society.

The Lost Girl is a novel about growing up and away from one's parents into an independent adult life. Although the protagonist is female, she undergoes the same crises of development as Paul Morel, and for similar reasons, most important of which is the domination of the mother in the absence of the father. The desire for merger with the mother conflicts with the need for separation, and no father figure is available during the formative childhood years to aid the movement into independence. The first chapter of *The Lost Girl* is a kind of prolegomenon to that novel, for it suggests how the heroine, now named Alvina Houghton, came to be lost in the first place. The reasons for Alvina's "lostness" vary with one's perspective; and, in fact, alternative explanations are offered in the novel.[7] But neither fictional character nor literary critic has pointed to a most important cause of Alvina's troubles: her lack of a father.

To be sure, Alvina has a nominal father, James Houghton, and in a certain sense the author shows a wry affection toward him. However, the first chapter—'The Decline of Manchester House'—records the many ways in which Alvina's father abdicates his leadership responsibilities and, in effect, abandons his daughter from early babyhood. Because James is always busy with one impractical financial scheme or another, Miss Frost, the governess, "imperceptibly [takes] into her hands the reins of domestic government" (*LG*, 7); and Miss Pinnegar, the manager of Houghton's work-girls, develops "a curious ascendancy" over her boss in matters of business (p. 12). James says little about his lack of status, seemingly indifferent or resigned to it, until, in his seventies, he lashes out at Alvina when she tries to take charge of him in his last illness: "Leave me alone! Will you leave me alone! Hectored by women all my life—hectored by women—first one, then another. I won't stand it—I won't stand it—" (p. 172). James Houghton's belated self-assertion does little to help either himself or his daughter: he dies the following day, leaving Alvina unprovided for in the psychological as well as the financial sense. For she too has been "hectored by women" all her life. Even the most passive woman in the household—Alvina's mother, Clariss—has in her invalidism manifested a hectoring feminine willfulness. Suffering from heart trouble, she cannot tolerate violence of any sort or degree, and she cultivates daintiness and gentility in her only child. Lawrence shows greater harshness toward Alvina's mother than toward her father, having created Clariss's illness to express her "obstinate self-importance" and her unfulfilled expectations of being made happy (pp. 43–44). Clariss effectively rules the roost from her sick bed, for she has a kindred spirit in the governess, Miss Frost; and James in his dreamworld allows Miss Frost to take a parent's charge of Alvina.

Miss Frost's characteristic mode of parenting is forcefully illustrated when Alvina tries to make up her mind about marrying Alexander Graham and going with him to Australia. The matter is of central importance, for in Lawrence's fiction a common test of a child's maturity is the decision not merely to leave the nest but also to go off with a mate to a foreign land. Everyone in the Houghton household opposes the union, but it is Miss Frost who effectively circumvents it by arousing Alvina's feelings of guilt:

> "I feel you don't love him, dear. I'm almost sure you don't. So now you have to choose. Your mother dreads your going—she dreads it. I am certain you would never see her again. She says she can't bear it—she can't bear the thought of you put there with Alexander. It makes her shudder. She suffers dreadfully, you know. So you will have to choose, dear. You will have to choose for the best. . . . Don't trust me, dear, don't trust what I say," poor Miss Frost ejaculated hurriedly, even wildly. "Don't notice what I have said. Act for yourself, dear. Act for yourself entirely. I am sure I am wrong in trying to influence you. I know I am wrong. It is wrong and foolish of me. Act just for yourself, dear—the rest doesn't matter. The rest doesn't matter. Don't take *any* notice of what I have said. I know I am wrong." (pp. 25–26)

After this "piece of indecent trickery of the spiritual will," as Lawrence calls it in *Fantasia* (*FU*, 91), Alvina certainly cannot act for herself; instead she acts for her mother and for Miss Frost, who require her dependence on them for their own sense of identity.

If Alvina had had a father worth his salt, she could have resisted Miss Frost's maternal bullying; for the father's role in the child's development, as we have seen, is to stimulate the urge toward independence and thus to counteract the smothering effects of a mother's love. Lawrence characterizes the sort of love shown by Miss Frost as the "Northern" mode, arising from overactivity of the cardiac plexus and involving devotional worship. Miss Frost's name unsubtly hints at the "northern" aspects of her northerliness, but in case there is any doubt about the matter, Lawrence spells out that "her very breeding had that Protestant, northern quality, which assumes that we have all . . . the same divine nature" (*LG*, 45–46). This northern quality is an enormous burden to Alvina: "It is doubtful which shadow was greater over the child: that of Manchester House, gloomy and a little sinister, or that of Miss Frost, benevolent and protective. Sufficient that the girl herself worshipped Miss Frost: or believed she did" (p. 20). Alexander Graham—with his "cruel, compact teeth," his dark skin and "dark blood," and the probability "that never, never would he make any woman's life happy" (p. 22)—offers Alvina what Lawrence in *Fantasia* calls the "Southern" mode of love, a "lower" kind, arising from the solar plexus. As the governess herself recognizes, "it was a question of heart against sensuality. Miss Frost tried and tried to wake again the girl's loving heart" (p. 33); and, with the weight of twenty-odd years of instruction behind her, she necessarily succeeds.

Miss Frost's seemingly benevolent protectiveness seduces Alvina into the view that Alexander is only a "little man, . . . a terrible outsider, an inferior, to tell the truth" (p. 24)—a situation repeated in *The Fox* (1921), when Banford convinces March that Henry Grenfel is just a boy, and an intruder into their cozy domestic relationship (see chapter four). But Alvina has more spunk than March, and her force of will propels her out of Manchester House and into a six-month training period as a maternity nurse in Islington. Once she is geographically separated from Miss Frost, and engaged in an occupation that focuses her attention on the mother-child connection, Alvina seeks complete emotional separation and decides that it is "time for Miss Frost to die" (p. 36). Thereafter she appears to maintain with Miss Frost their old, loving relations, but in actuality Alvina is "almost coldly independent" (p. 45). Miss Frost, who has always been subject to bronchitis, finally develops pneumonia and dies, a victim of ailments that, according to *Fantasia*, result from an overactive cardiac plexus: a too-loving heart. It is as if she has been willed to death by Alvina, as Grenfel in *The Fox* wills that Banford be crushed by a tree.

But domineering mothers abound in *The Lost Girl*, as in a nightmare; no sooner is one slain than another arises to take her place. Alvina's dependency problem has not been solved, for gradually Miss Pinnegar takes over Miss Frost's role. Alvina had believed that Miss Pinnegar was different from Miss Frost, since "she never made you feel for an instant that she was one with you. She was never even near. She kept quietly on her own ground, and left you on yours. And across the space came her quiet commonplaces—but fraught with space" (p. 45). Yet, when Alvina is so stunned by her father's acquisition of a cinema that she cannot eat her dinner, Miss Pinnegar bids her eat in a way that makes her sound "short, almost like Miss Frost. Oddly like Miss Frost." (p. 98); and thirty-year-old Alvina dutifully picks up her fork. Miss Pinnegar only *seems* to leave space: as far back as the maternity nurse episode, when she says in Alvina's defense, "Well, really, if she wants to do it, why, she might as well try," Lawrence comments ominously, "And, as often with Miss Pinnegar, this speech seemed to contain a veiled threat" (p. 30). From years of tutelage in a mother-dominated household, Lawrence was extremely well schooled in niceties of speech that mask hostile and aggressive interdependencies. Miss Pinnegar unmasks herself when, after James's death, Alvina decides to join a traveling stage show as a pianist, a rather compromising endeavor for a proper Woodhouse spinster; Miss Pinnegar simply assumes that Alvina is out of her mind and needs someone—namely, Miss Pinnegar—to take charge of her life: "You need to be looked after," she says (p. 217). Alvina flees the benevolent despotism of her mother-friend, and with it the cocoonlike protection of Woodhouse as a whole.

But Alvina merely exchanges one matriarchal society for another when she joins the traveling company. Madame Rochard, who heads the troupe, acts as a "wonderful mother" to the actors, busily sewing and cooking for them and generally looking after their needs. When Alvina first meets her, called in to diagnose her illness before her scheduled performance at James Houghton's theater, Madame is being attended by two of her "boys," Max and Louis, who are devastated to the point of tears by her fever. Advised to take to her bed, Madame worries about fulfilling her matronly duties: "'Tonight,' she moaned, 'I shan't be able to see that the boys' rooms are well in order. They are not to be trusted, no. They need an overseeing eye'" (p. 125). She worries, too, that their Indian act, in which she plays the part of the squaw Kishwégin, will fail without her: "'Children—they are all children!' wailed Madame. 'All children! and so, what will they do without their old *gouvernante*? My poor *braves*. What will they do without Kishwégin?'" (p. 133). Her "wonderful" motherliness, therefore, has as its negative aspect the belief that these grown men are singularly incapable of acting on their own. Like the other *gouvernante*, Miss Frost, and like Miss Frost's doubles, Clariss Houghton and Miss Pinnegar, Madame Rochard is what *Fantasia* labels "queen of the earth, and inwardly a fearsome tyrant. She keeps pity and tenderness emblazoned on her banners. But God help the man whom she pities. Ultimately she tears him to bits" (*FU*, 134).

Of the troupe, Max and Louis are so devoted to Madame that they may be said to worship her: while she sleeps, they repeatedly cross themselves and drop to their knees before her bed "as before an altar" (*LG*, 147). Like Mr. May, the manager of Houghton's Picture Palace, Max and Louis take their places in the long procession of Lawrence's male characters who adore the Madonna figure: Mr. May is said to like "the *angel*, and particularly the angel-mother in woman. Oh—that he worshipped" (p. 104). This kind of "northern" love renders Mr. May unfit for a normal, sexual relationship with a woman, and even though Lawrence treats

3. In Flight from Matriarchy 43

this gentleman's marital problems somewhat comically (pp. 102–3), the repetitiveness of the issue in Lawrence's novels and the factual discussion of it in *Fantasia of the Unconscious* indicate the seriousness with which Lawrence considered it.[8]

The alternative to Max and Louis's devotion to Madame is offered by the two other members of the troupe, Geoffrey and Ciccio, especially the latter. While Max and Louis hover anxiously over their sainted mother-figure, Geoffrey sits "blowing the smoke down his nose, while Ciccio callously [lights] another cigarette"; when Madame's fever mounts, "the young men [are] all extremely uncomfortable. . . . Only Ciccio [keeps] the thin smile on his lips, and [adds] to Madame's annoyance and pain" (pp. 124–25). Madame is extremely sensitive to Ciccio's recalcitrance and tells Alvina that of all her boys, Ciccio especially needs her "overseeing eye" (p. 125). Ciccio, in turn, is "on" to Madame's maternal dictatorship. He notes, in answer to Alvina's question about what Madame does, that "she does it all, really. The others—they are nothing—what they are Madame has made them." In answer to the question about why the troupe loves Madame so intensely, Ciccio responds simply, "We like her—we love her—as if she were a mother" (p. 137). Exactly how much Ciccio himself likes this relationship is made clear a moment later, when the seemingly dull-witted man waxes suddenly profound on this issue:

"Have you a mother and father?" [Alvina asked.]
"I? No! . . . They are dead."
"And you wander about the world—" she said.
He looked at her, and made a slight, sad gesture, indifferent also.
"But you have Madame for a mother," she said. He made another gesture this time: pressed down the corners of his mouth as if he didn't like it. Then he turned with the slow, fine smile.
"Does a man want two mothers? Eh?" he said. . . .
"I shouldn't think so," laughed Alvina. He glanced at her to see what she meant, what she understood.
"My mother is dead, see!" he said. "Frenchwomen—Frenchwomen—they have their babies till they are a hundred—"
"What do you mean?" said Alvina, laughing.
"A Frenchman is a little man when he's seven years old—and if his mother comes, he is a little baby boy when he's seventy. Do you know that?"
"I didn't *know* it," said Alvina.
"But now—you do." (p. 139)

Alvina, of course, has spent a lifetime of conflict between her desire to please the women she has been devoted to and her desire to cut free from these women and assert her independence. Her life's pattern repeats itself when, in spite of Ciccio's tacit warning, she attaches herself to yet another domineering mother-figure by accepting initiation into the theatrical "tribe" of the Natcha-Kee-Tawara Indians. The ceremony is a farce: the participants have been drinking large quantities of wine and Alvina's "Indian" name of Allaye is a ribald joke—which she does not comprehend—referring to Ciccio's sexual access to her. But Madame is deadly serious when she has all her followers repeat certain key concepts: "We Have No Lawgiver Except Kishwégin. We Have No Home But the Tent of Kihswégin" (pp. 199–200). After holding her customary court, requiring her troupe to come forward and kiss her fingers, Madame unites Alvina-Allaye and Ciccio-Pacohuila in tribal marriage. But Alvina is unable to find her home "beneath the wings of Pacohuila" as long as she and Ciccio live like babies beneath the smothering wings of Kishwégin. As she had once fled Manchester House Alvina now flees the Natcha-Kee-Tawara, taking again a position as maternity nurse in another town.

Here begins an affair that curiously and ironically seems to invert the pattern of mother-child relationships established in the novel: no longer is Alvina the child dependent upon a mother whom she seeks to please; instead, she herself becomes the divine mother adored by a child-slave. The child in question is an unlikely one indeed: a fifty-four-year-old doctor, tall and beefy, with a blustering manner. Dr. Mitchell bullies his patients by insisting that he and he alone knows what is good for them, but his dominating and willful behavior is soon revealed as an attempt to cover up, or perhaps to compensate for, his inner lack of security. The doctor's stomach is said to be "as weak as a baby's" (p. 256) and thus he provides in this novel another physical manifestation of a psychic impairment. Before long, Dr. Mitchell begins to dote on Alvina. When he shows her his grand home he is so delighted by her admiration that he feels himself capable of falling at her feet and kissing them ecstatically. He contemplates "the treat of his life: hanging around the woman he had made his wife, following her about, feeling proud of her in his house, talking to her from morning till night, really finding himself in her" (p. 261). His first thought at the idea of having children with Alvina is that "a child would take her away from him" (p. 262). His pathetic, infantile relationship with Alvina therefore fits the definition of incest that Lawrence offered in the 1918 "devouring mother" letter, in reference to

Middleton Murry's relationship with Katherine Mansfield and to his own with Frieda (*CL*, I, 565).

On the one hand, Alvina does receive Dr. Mitchell with gratification. At first she had disliked him, but when he begins to fawn on her she "liked him much better, and even saw graceful, boyish attractions in him. There was really something childish about him. And this something childish, since it looked up to her as if she were the saving grace, naturally flattered her and made her feel gentler toward him." (*LG*, 259). But if Alvina is tempted by the knowledge that "of course he'd adore her" (p. 265), she also feels Dr. Mitchell's demanding love as a kind of weight upon her. Their relationship reaches its crisis when the doctor, incensed by Alvina's obstinate refusal to say yes or no to his marriage offer, shoves her violently against a wall, then falls on his knees before her "like a child" and begs her over and over again, "Love me! Love me!" (pp. 267–68). The incident shows clearly his immature need for Alvina's nurturing as well as his hostility toward her because of the power over him that his very need grants her. It is only to extricate herself from this painful situation, and from his smothering embrace, that Alvina accepts Dr. Mitchell's ring, which Lawrence has him place symbolically above the mourning ring that had been Miss Frost's. Both Dr. Mitchell and Miss Frost wish to engage Alvina in a mother-child dependency that stifles growth; Dr. Mitchell's desires are the complement to Miss Frost's: "He wanted her to be there. That was his greatest craving. He wanted her to be always there. And so he craved for marriage: to possess her entirely, and to have her always there with him, so that he was never alone. . . . She could see the hysterical little boy under the great authoritative man" (pp. 270–71).

Obviously Dr. Mitchell is not the "Dark Master" upon whom Alvina had ruminated some years earlier, in Woodhouse (p. 48). In 1919, Lawrence's escape from England and from his matriarchal past gave him a new direction for his fiction: the swarthy Italian whom Alvina eventually marries is Lawrence's first extended portrait of the dark god that came to dominate his work in the leadership period. Did a Ciccio figure play a role in the earlier versions of the story, whose manuscripts seem to have disappeared? Lawrence's remark in 1920—that he was waiting for a novel entitled *Mixed Marriage*—suggests this possibility, although Alvina Houghton's prototype, Flossie Cullen, did not run off with a dark and dangerous foreigner but rather married the doorman at the local theater and moved away only so far as the north of England.[9] Perhaps a fragment of a novel on Robert Burns (published in *CB*, I, 184–95), begun and abandoned in December 1912, provides a clue about the nature of the hero in *The Insurrection of Miss Houghton*. Lawrence stated that he would "do [Burns] almost like an autobiography" (*CL*, I, 167); indeed, the hero, Jack Haseldine—"He was swarthy and ruddy, his dark eyes were full of fire and laughter" (*CB*, I, 194)—lives on Haggs farm like the real-life Chamberses and may be an idealization of Jessie Chambers's brother Alan, to whom Lawrence felt very close ("I have always been fond of [Burns], as a sort of brother" [*CL*, I, 169]). No mother appears in the Haseldine household, and the mother of Mary Renshaw, Haseldine's girlfriend, has been dead for five years. The penultimate scene in the fragment takes place in a tavern, where bearded and grimy working men are holding court, and where Haseldine is "something of a king among the men." L. D. Clark surmises that in the Burns novel, Lawrence was portraying his own wished-for father—strong, vital, and dominating (indeed, there are as many dominating fathers in this fragment as there are mothers in *The Lost Girl*). Noting that *The Lost Girl* was originally started immediately after the Burns work was dropped, and assuming that this version contained the Ciccio that we know today, Clark comments that "Ciccio also has traits in common with Jack Haseldine to satisfy the compulsion to fictionalize the father."[10]

It may well be that the first Ciccio, if such a character existed, was only a rudimentary figure of a dark god, a mere shadow of his later self. Certainly the central characters in the early fragment beginning, "My mother made a failure of her life. . . ." bear little resemblance to their final embodiments in *The Lost Girl*: the father, eleven years younger than his wife, is an opportunist and a bounder; the mother is sensitive and honorable; the governess, called Miss Neill, and the shop manager, a Miss Venner, hold house and home together with their wisdom and their strength. These characterizations probably reflect Lawrence's early attitudes toward the prototypes. For example, he was quite close to Miss Wright, the Cullens' governess, who helped him with his high school lessons. But Lawrence most decidedly did not pay a "quiet tribute" to Miss Wright in *The Lost Girl*, as Harry T. Moore remarked;[11] on the contrary, his changing of her name to Miss Frost, his depictions of her subtle manipulations of Alvina, and his implied comparison of her relationship with Alvina to that between Alvina and Dr. Mitchell all indicate a change of attitude toward the caretaker mother. No doubt the Ciccio figure changed as well, becoming stronger and more dominant than his counterpart, if one existed, in the first versions—becoming, in other words, a fictionalized father.

Katherine Mansfield disliked *The Lost Girl*, remarking that in it Lawrence had denied his humanity and reduced his people to "animals on the prowl" (*CB*, II, 51–52). Lawrence recognized this element in his work. Although Alvina denies the charge that Ciccio is a mere animal and calls him "something else" (*LG*, 283), at other times she wonders if he is "just stupid and bestial" (p. 179). She marries Ciccio and goes off with him to live in a primitive region of southern Italy, surrounded by ancient gods; presumably they have left behind the "northern," smothering atmosphere of England and the various maternal figures who have sought to entrap them there: now that they have come south, Alvina is even repulsed by the grape hyacinths because they remind her of the many-breasted Artemis. But the success of the mixed marriage is not assured. Alvina occupies as tenuous a position among the people of Pescocalascio as among the tribe of the Natcha-Kee-Tawara (in fact, Ciccio still calls her Allaye). She is pregnant as the story ends, a many-breasted Artemis herself. The reverence tendered her by Ciccio and his uncle contains the same elements of repulsion and hatred that Alvina feels toward the hyacinths; further, Alvina senses that Ciccio's benevolent sentimentalism toward her masks his unconscious desire for her death (pp. 330, 336). These attitudes suggest a fear of the "devouring mother."

Alvina is, in a sense, Lawrence himself: from his earliest conception of her she was bound up with Paul Morel. Having always "banked hard on her independence" (*LG*, p. 240), as Lawrence banked on his, Alvina feels herself annihilated by Ciccio's love; this "Dark Master" threatens to crush her spirit. Ciccio, in turn, needs to keep a part of his life separate from Alvina, and excludes her from his "masculine" activities in the piazza. The central problem in the novel—the tension between the desire for merger or union and the desire for separation or independence, originating in the mother-child relationship—remains unresolved in the relationship between husband and wife. The decline of Manchester House as outlined in chapter one, caused by the father's dropping the reins of leadership, is expanded upon in the course of this novel and comes to symbolize the decline of England—even Europe—itself.[12] Lawrence tempers his pessimism with a note of hope: Alvina's unborn child and a projected journey to America after Ciccio's return from war offer promise for a future life in which the proper balance in human relationships will be achieved. But the novel ends with a question mark, like many works of the leadership period, with the characters looking outside of Europe, as Lawrence himself did, for the promised land called Rananim.

4. Sanctions from the Animal World: *The Fox*

Tracking D. H. Lawrence's *Fox* takes one across several years and three countries in the formative stages of Lawrence's leadership period. Lawrence wrote the first version of *The Fox* in the late autumn of 1918, after having discussed his plans for the story with Katherine Mansfield. After finishing this "rather odd and amusing" work (*CL*, I, 568), he sent Miss Mansfield the story to read and pass along to their agent.[1] Several months later Lawrence wrote to Pinker that "the letter about shortening the story, with the enclosure from Vivian Carter [journalist and editor of the *Bystander*, a popular magazine, from 1908 to 1916] came yesterday.... I would rather do the cutting myself"; a second letter, dated the same day, states, "I send *The Fox* by return. I wish I could have cut more—but I simply can't, without mutilating the story."[2] The story appeared in *Hutchinson's Story Magazine* (vol. iii., no. 17, pp. 477–90) in November 1920.[3] Lawrence revised *The Fox* again in November 1921, when he was living in Taormina, Sicily, and preparing to leave Europe in search of his Rananim. He had in his possession at that time the 1918 version of *The Fox* that he had requested and received from Pinker a month after severance of their business relationship in January 1920;[4] he also had the copy of *Hutchinson's Story Magazine* that his British publisher had sent him almost one year later. Between October 1921 and January 1922 Lawrence expanded his short stories "The Mortal Coil" and "The Thimble" (also requested from Pinker) into *The Captain's Doll* and *The Ladybird*, which he intended for publication with a new version of *The Fox* in a volume of novellas. On 16 November 1921 he wrote to a friend in Ceylon, who was importuning him to visit there, "I have put a long tail to 'The Fox,' which was a bobbed short story. Now he careers with a strange and fiery brush. I hope you will read him sometime, because then you will see that I am not really drawn Buddhawards, but west" (*CL*, II, 678).⁵ With further changes, the Taormina *Fox*, complete with "tail," ran serially in the American magazine *The Dial* from May through August 1922.⁶

Since its first public appearance as a novella, *The Fox* has encountered contradictory reactions. F. R. Leavis praised the novella for "the unambiguous clarity with which it presents its theme";⁷ but most critics seem to agree with the assessment of the anonymous reviewer in *The Spectator*, who, after recounting the plot of *The Fox*, admitted that "actually the story is very strange."⁸ In fact, there is much disagreement about the author's intentions and the story's meaning, not to mention the impact of the "message" on the reader.⁹ The differences of opinion about *The Fox* point up ambiguities not only in the work itself but also in the larger leadership period of which it is a part.

Although most critics read *The Fox* as a love story about adult men and women, the work is curiously nonsexual in the genital sense. In neither the 1918 first draft, the 1920 publication, nor the 1921 expansion does Henry Grenfel really desire a wife or Ellen March a husband; even so, the two are irresistibly drawn to one another in a powerful if ambivalent relationship. This relationship, because it derives from Lawrence's own (though partly unconscious) relationship to women, is not immediately apparent. Perhaps the common assumption is that the fox (Grenfel), symbolic of vital sexual forces, overwhelms the sterile intellectual forces represented by Jill Banford. This reading leads naturally to an explanation of the novella's uncertain ending as a realistic appraisal of the old values of England obstinately opposing the new belief in the vital self.¹⁰

D. H. Lawrence apparently intended his novella to present this conflict between the blood and the intellect, for he built his creed on "a belief in the blood, the flesh, as being wiser than the intellect. We can go wrong in our minds, but what our blood feels and believes and says, is always true" (*CL*, I, 180). Yet certain aspects of *The Fox* do not fit neatly into this schema. Henry Grenfel first sets his sights on March chiefly because he wants a home, and then he proceeds to calculate the best manner in which to win her. Moreover, the querulous Banford is described as "warm-hearted" (*F*, 129), a "warm and generous soul" (p. 115) with "natural warmth and kindliness" (p. 126); in fact, Lawrence made her a more sympathetic character in the 1921 revision of the story, when he added such descriptions to the text. He also tempered the reader's elation at her death by describing her smashed head as "a mass of blood, of horror," and by reducing her body to an "it" (p. 174). Surely the author reveals more than ideology in *The Fox*, for the story is more complex than a mere assertion of blood over intellect. The mother-child relationships among the characters, rather than the theme of sexual salvation, may account for the novella's uncertain tone.

More than two decades ago the psychoanalyst Edmund Bergler noted the importance of the pre-oedipal and pre-genital mother fixation in *The Fox*. Writing about the nature of the relationship between March and Banford, as he observes it from a clinical perspective, Bergler states that Lawrence has instinctually presented a classic lesbian configuration in the connection between the two women: although they appear to be enacting husband-wife roles, in actuality they are perpetuating a mother-child dependency. The subtle antagonism between the two women masquerades as a conflict between the "masculine" figure (March) and the "feminine" figure (Banford) because this conflict more readily admits of conscious recognition than the actual conflict: the pre-oedipal relationship between mother (Banford) and child (March). March's replacement of Banford with Henry Grenfel results in no satisfactory marriage because her connection with Grenfel is based on the same childish needs that drew her to Banford in the first place. Both Grenfel and Banford rob March of her independence, and hence of her life; the fox, like Jill Banford, destroys rather than regenerates. To quote Bergler, "Lawrence ingeniously hints that the fox, the devourer of chickens, symbolizes the 'devouring' mother; we know that the fear of being devoured has priority in the 'septet of baby fears.'"[11]

Bergler's article deals in the main only with the relationship between Banford and March, but the aptness of Bergler's emphasis is pointed up by Lawrence's description of his wife as a "devouring mother" (*CL*, I, 565) and of his sisters as wild beasts (*CL*, I, 554). As Bergler suggests, the same ambiguity in the relationship between March and Banford clouds the relationship between March and the fox, and later between March and Henry Grenfel. Although most critics recognize March's ambivalence toward the fox, they see the animal as a clear-cut masculine symbol. To be sure, Lawrence gives support for this theory: the fox is a dog-fox (p. 148);[12] his phallic tail and nose both fascinate and repel Ellen March (pp. 148–49). Translated into genital terms, March is the virginal female who simultaneously desires and fears sexual intercourse. In fact, the story contains numerous images of open (female) spaces locked up against intruders: the hen house; the little English houses (p. 146); the hole in the barn that must be stopped up to keep out the rats (p. 234); March's tightened mouth and firmly crossed knees (pp. 121, 136). In contrast to these closed spaces, March's eyes dilate receptively and it is through her eyes that the fox penetrates in his mystical union with her.

Henry Grenfel, by killing the fox and thereby replacing him (both are compared to a snake, also a phallic symbol [pp. 116, 146]), enables March to act out her sexual fantasies with a real man.

Hillis Miller voices the usual psychological view of these sexual relationships when he states that "the problem which all of Lawrence's characters face is the problem of how to escape the locked room of the mother fixation, from a love which inevitably destroys the lover. The escape into a relation between man and woman which avoids the destructivity of transferred mother-love is to be attained only with the utmost difficulty." Miller labels this classic Lawrentian predicament man's "Oedipal situation," and he asserts that in *The Fox* Henry Grenfel is the "perfectly adjusted male" who awakens March's repressed femininity and, by killing the symbol of that repression (Banford), brings March to fulfillment.[13] In biographical terms, Henry Grenfel is seen by many as the savior of Woman, a figure much like D. H. Lawrence himself when he rescued Frieda from her unsatisfying marriage to Ernest Weekley.[14] However, if Grenfel is the "perfectly adjusted" savior, one wonders why he is unable to provide Ellen March with a more satisfactory marriage than the one she experienced with Jill Banford.

Interestingly, the first draft of the story, written in 1918, ends with the assertion that March is "curiously happy," living on an instinctual level with her husband. When Lawrence published a slightly cut version of the story in November 1920, he made the ending even more conclusive by changing "She suffered when he was gone, and he suffered in going" to "March suffered when he was gone, but it is doubtful if he suffered in going."[15] When Lawrence revised again, in the autumn of 1921, he changed the character of Grenfel even more, further de-emphasizing his lostness and confusion and building upon his shrewdness and his calm. Yet in counterpoint to Grenfel's evolution toward self-confidence, between 1918 and 1921, Ellen March moves toward refusal of his mastery in the final published version of the story. Even in 1919 Lawrence had changed March's reaction to the fox from "She did not so much think of him: she was possessed by him" to "she was possessed by a desire to defeat him—to outmatch him." And in the proposal scene, March's acquiescence to Grenfel's wish evolves from "Yes—yes" (1918) to "Yes—If you like" (1919) to "Oh I can't" (1921). In short, the surer Grenfel becomes of himself, the more Ellen March resists him. The complexity of their relationship—as of that between March and Banford—might best be viewed not from the oedipal, or genital, perspective, but as a manifestation of the pre-oedipal "marriage bond" between mother and child.

Ellen March has a clear need to remain a child, and to sleep snugly in Grenfel's shelter (*F*, 125), but this need alternates with her fear of being absorbed again by the womb. In fact, March's resistance to Grenfel is the note on which the story draws to a close, and Lawrence expresses this resistance in terms of the nursery: "She looked round at him, with the strained, strange look of a child that is struggling against sleep" (p. 179). Earlier in the story March's recognition that the fox spells annihilation takes the form of dreams: in one, Banford lies in her wood-box coffin, covered with fox fur (March has already told Grenfel that *she* will never wear fox fur); in another, the fox bites March's wrist and burns her mouth. When the former dream comes true, and Banford is slaughtered by the fallen tree, March is reduced to childish weeping—Lawrence twice refers to her tears as childish—that signals her capitulation to the dominant power. Lawrence also gives a visual indication of March's submission: she sinks to her knees, reduced to the level of a child, and looks up to Grenfel both literally and figuratively (p. 174).

March's dream of the fox's burning brush comes true in a fashion when Grenfel kisses her searingly on the mouth with a "quick, brushing kiss" (*F*, 140). This dream, in which the fox appears "yellow and bright like corn," is cited by John Vickery to support his view of the phallic animal's salvation of the lost girl: from Frazer's *The Golden Bough*, Vickery learned that during the harvest season the man who gleans the last ear of corn is sometimes termed the Fox and is honored by a dance that evening with the maidens.[16] The fact is, however, that in many more of the examples provided by Frazer (whom Lawrence had read), both the last ear of corn and the person who harvests it are called the "corn-mother," the "Great Mother," the "Old Woman," the "Old Wife," or some variant thereof.[17] Lawrence's fox might also be a corn-mother, for it appears in March's dream as a principle of fertility. Yet it also has sharp teeth that draw blood, and a burning brush that might be glossed with Frazer's description of foxes with burning torches attached to their tails as punishment for having destroyed the crops.[18] Grenfel as the fox exerts a power over March that she both desires and fears: in anthropological terms, he is her totem animal. And, to quote Frazer, totemism "appears to be mainly a crude, almost child-like attempt to satisfy the primary wants of man."[19] This anthropological primitivism of spirit-worship rather than god-worship corresponds to the psychological primitivism of the pre-oedipal and pre-genital origins of *The Fox*. That is to say, the dynamics of March's relationship with Grenfel are oral and nutritional rather than genital and sexual.[20]

4. Sanctions from the Animal World 53

If Henry Grenfel is a "devouring mother" to Ellen March, March in turn is a "devouring mother" to Grenfel. As Lawrence conceived the character of Grenfel in 1918, the salient feature of his personality was his need for security. When Lawrence revised *The Fox* in 1921, he underplayed this need, emphasizing instead Grenfel's "foxiness": he changed Grenfel's initial reaction to March from confusion to calm and added sentences throughout that mention Grenfel's cunning. Grenfel's attraction to the security offered by Bailey Farm evolves subtly from "And suddenly, he wanted to stay here permanently, to have this place for his own" (1918) to "And suddenly he decided to stay here permanently, to have this place for his own" (1920) to "And he thought to himself, it would be a good thing to have this place for his own" (1921). The thought of marrying March to gain the farm enters him first "like a bullet" (1918), later "wickedly" (1920), and finally "shrewdly" (1921). Further, in place of a discussion about Grenfel's desire to own the farm so that he can be master, Lawrence in 1921 inserted a treatise on how to win the battle between the sexes. All these changes tend toward the elimination of Grenfel's little-lost-boy quality.

Yet even in the final version, Grenfel is attracted to March not so much because she is a mysterious woman but because she is a mother figure. After he shoots a rabbit, Henry muses, "Why not marry March? . . . Why not indeed? It was a good idea. . . . What if she was older than he? It didn't matter. When he thought of her dark, startled, vulnerable eyes, he smiled subtly to himself. He was older than she, really. He was master of her" (*F*, 130). The age difference between March and Grenfel certainly does matter; in fact, therein lies most of her appeal to him. Significantly, in the first version of the story March's age is thirty-three, Frieda's age when Lawrence married her. Although Lawrence changed March's age to "not yet thirty" in 1921—under the assumption, perhaps, that a great discrepancy in their ages reduces the credibility of the love affair—he also added Grenfel's thoughts, quoted above, about their age difference. This addition, of course, has the effect of underscoring the importance of something that Grenfel rather cavalierly discounts.

Grenfel wants to marry this symbolic mother in part so that he can have someone to nurture and support him: he tells her, "I should like to feel I'd got somebody there, at the back of me, all of my life" (*F*, 161). But another aspect of his desire for her is his wish to revenge himself for her domination. His attraction to March's "soft, white breasts" parallels her attraction to the soft, white underbelly of the fox (pp. 155, 148), but his attraction, like hers, is balanced by a fear of being dominated. March's verbal assaults make Grenfel feel childish; and when she resists his advances he wonders why he wants her: "But he did want her. . . . And he was convulsed with a youth's fury at being thwarted" (p. 152). The fact that this supposed phallic symbol of a man-fox is frequently described as a cub and a puppy (pp. 123, 124, 137, 139, 170), not to mention a child, suggests the need for a closer look at his relationship with women.

Henry Grenfel's conflicting impulses of attraction to and repulsion from Ellen March repeat the psychological pattern of ambivalence toward the "devouring mother," whose nurturing and support rob the child of his independence. Grenfel's relationship with Jill Banford may also gain clarity from the pre-oedipal perspective, for ambivalence toward the mother figure explains why Lawrence made Banford both more hospitable and more dangerous in the final version of *The Fox*. Hillis Miller, in his article on *The Fox*, notes in passing the "minor" recurrence in Lawrence's stories of "the older woman, a kind of mother-ogress, who destroys or tries to destroy her son or daughter" by dominating him and keeping him a child;[21] but Miller does not see that this figure appears at the center of *The Fox*, in the person of Jill Banford.

Unlike the characters of Grenfel and March, which show development between the first draft and the magazine publication of *The Fox*, the character of Jill Banford changes significantly only in the expanded version of the story. In a sense Banford *is* the final expanded version, for the "tail" that Lawrence added to the short story is concerned with her influence on March and with Grenfel's attempts to fight that influence. Banford's role in the novella is as ambiguous as it is prominent, for Lawrence was very careful to make her a rather sympathetic figure even as Grenfel perceived her to be a threat to his existence. In the Lazarus manuscript (first draft), Lawrence mentions Banford's "natural warmth and kindliness" and her "sisterly attention" to Grenfel ("F," 41). In the Taormina typescript, after the notation that Ellen March was attending to the fowls, Lawrence adds in his own hand that "then she flew into the village on her bicycle to try and buy food. She was a hospitable soul"; but he crosses out "then she" and inserts the word *Banford*—it is Banford, not March, who is to be the "hospitable soul" (*FM*, 23). Again, when the women decide to let Grenfel stay on for a while, Lawrence inserts the following exchange between Banford and Grenfel:

> "It's no bother, if you like to stay. It's like having my own brother here for a few days. He's a boy like you are."
> "That's awfully kind of you," the lad repeated. "I should like to stay, ever so much, if you're sure I'm not a trouble to you."

"No, of course you're no trouble. I tell you, it's a pleasure to have somebody in the house besides ourselves," said warm-hearted Banford. . . .

"Well, then," he said, "I should love it, if you would let me pay my board and help with the work."

"You've no need to talk about board," said Banford. (*FM*, 24–25)

The nature of Banford's charitableness is that she thinks of Grenfel as a boy who needs her protection. Moreover, in order to protect her own relationship with March, she must emphasize Grenfel's immaturity, both to reassure herself that he poses no serious threat to her and to convince March of his unimportance. Banford's influence on March is so pronounced that she is able to make her friend share this vision: March thinks of Grenfel as "such a long, red-faced, sulky boy! That was all he was" (*F*, 143).

According to the psychoanalyst Joseph Rheingold, the negative aspect of maternalism "tends to elude emphatic perception by men, for masculine aggressivity is characteristically overt and direct. The lack of recognition of the subtle sadism of women is one of the imperfections of our knowledge of feminine psychology and therefore of the husband-wife and mother-child relationships."[22] In *The Fox*, Lawrence depicts the "warm-hearted" Banford's attempts to undermine the Grenfel-March relationship by tears, hysterics, and bitter invectives. Thus Lawrence recognizes a woman's covert means of aggression, and her hostility toward her child. March and Banford together, in league against Grenfel, suggest the dual nature of the "devouring mother," whose love destroys as it nourishes. Grenfel is dependent on the women for shelter—especially on Banford, who owns the farm—but the manner in which they shelter him would destroy his dignity and delay maturity.

Kingsley Widmer has called Banford March's "negative self,"[23] and in essence Banford does represent the dangerous aspect of the Magna Mater. Grenfel thinks of her breasts, unlike March's, as being tiny and made of iron, symbolically withholding nourishment (*F*, 155); when he challenges her dominance he perceives her transformation from a sympathetic hostess to a witch crouched by the fire (p. 163). A few months before writing this novella, Lawrence attended a puppet show in Sicily and ended his travel book *Sea and Sardinia* with a description of that performance: while the boys in the audience shout gleefully as the ugly witch marionette burns in her castle, Lawrence somewhat ruefully notes that only little boys believe that the "old, ghastly woman-spirit can be vanquished" (*SS*, 203). In *The Fox*, Lawrence took his own little-boy revenge, for Henry Grenfel's murder of Jill Banford might well be seen as a fantasized retaliation against the "devouring mother" whose attempts to keep him dependent on her make Grenfel feel insignificant and "small" to the point of extinction. He perceives his relationship with Jill Banford as a life-or-death struggle, and he mutters to her, when she is safely out of earshot, "You are a nasty little thing. I hope you will be paid back for all the harm you have done me for nothing. . . . You will, if wishes are anything" (*F*, 152–53). Erik Erikson might be analyzing Grenfel's impulses when he refers to anal conflicts and the relevance of these conflicts to an individual's sense of law and order: "There is a limit to a child's and an adult's endurance in the face of demands to consider himself, his body, and his wishes as evil and dirty, and to his belief in the infallibility of those who pass such judgment. He may be apt to turn things around, and to consider as evil only the fact that they exist; his chance will come when they are gone, or when he will go from them."[24] The "greatest smack in the eye" advocated in *Education of the People* against these mothers (see chapter two) is delivered resoundingly by Grenfel in *The Fox*, when he cuts the tree that crushes his adversary's face. By 1921 Lawrence had realized that the ending of the 1918 version of the story, with Banford's complete if unwilling capitulation to Grenfel, was simplistic, and that the force of both women's resistance was underdrawn; thus Grenfel in the novella has to take these drastic measures to assert himself as master. The measures are so drastic that some readers have been led to confuse audacity with brilliance. Eugene Goodheart, for example, terms the murder of Banford a moment of self-realization for Grenfel, and Julian Moynahan lauds it as "an inspired and creative deed, . . . an image of the triumph of life over death."[25] The murder of Banford has drawn praise because Lawrence would have it represent the necessary passing away of an entire mode of living. In 1921 Lawrence had grand designs for his story: in the 1918–19 versions Bailey Farm is a setting for the action; in the final version, Bailey Farm is a microcosm of England. Grenfel, hunting the fox, feels trapped by all the farmhouses representing England "little and tight" (*F*, 146). Bailey Farm epitomizes English sterility, and Jill Banford, owner of the farm, personifies that quality.

Yet there is certainly no triumph in *The Fox*. In fact, in 1921 Lawrence changed words like *triumph* to *excitement* in order to qualify Grenfel's success (*F*, 129). Moreover, Lawrence did not end the story with Banford's death; if he had, it would have remained as clearly a fantasy as the 1918 version. Instead the story continues with two or three pages of direct authorial commentary that have confused and perplexed many readers. In a sense, the spirit of Jill Banford lives on in March's continued resistance to Grenfel, for, as Lawrence says in *Sea and Sardinia*, the "old, ghastly woman-spirit" is not to be vanquished. Put in psychological terms, Grenfel's "equivalent of matricide"[26] cannot bring him the freedom that he craves. But in another, equally important sense, Henry Grenfel's attempt to absorb Ellen March while he protects her is the very trick of the "devouring mother," as life-denying as Banford's attempt to treat him like a crude inferior. One might say, with Erikson, that the "necessary ego groundwork" for mutuality in an adult love relationship was never established in the earliest developmental stages, and that therefore "the situation falls apart into a variety of attempts at controlling by duress or fantasy rather than by reciprocity."[27] The ambiguity of Lawrence's attitude toward Grenfel, who fights his creator's battle, is one reason for the differing interpretations of the story.

Attention to the prototypes for the characters in *The Fox* helps to account for the turn toward violence that the story makes in its final version. This appeal to real life has special value when, like *The Fox*, the work under study has been revised over a period of years and its characters have changed markedly from one version to the next. Indeed, the changing patterns of Lawrence's relationships with others between 1918 and 1921 help to account for the alterations that the characters in *The Fox* undergo from their inception in a twenty-page short story to their final manifestation in a seventy-page novella.

When the Lawrences were evicted from Cornwall in October 1917, for alleged communications with German spies, D. H. Lawrence found himself in the uncomfortable—if not unusual—position of relying on others for shelter and support. Arriving in London on 15 October, the Lawrences stayed for a short time with Dollie Radford, and then borrowed a room in Mecklenburgh Square belonging to the Richard Aldingtons. In December, when the Aldingtons requested the return of their flat, the Lawrences moved on to Hermitage in Berkshire, "for a fortnight or so" (*CL*, I, 534), where they leased a cottage belonging to the Radfords' daughter Margaret. Here they stayed until April 1919, making frequent visits to London and also to Derbyshire, where Lawrence's sister Ada lived.

In April, when the Radfords needed their Chapel Farm Cottage at Hermitage, Ada Lawrence Clarke took a year's lease on a furnished cottage in Derbyshire for her brother and his wife, entirely at her own expense. The move to the Midlands, Lawrence's boyhood home, stirred up his feelings of being out of his proper place, and he yearned for Cornwall. After two forays to London, the Lawrences returned to Derbyshire in the middle of November after a short rest stop at Hermitage. By the beginning of December, Lawrence had written the first version of *The Fox*. At the end of April the Lawrences returned to Chapel Farm Cottage, where in July Lawrence revised the story at Pinker's request. The Radfords' need for their cottage occasioned another move in August, to the neighboring Grimsbury Farm where the Lawrences stayed for a couple of weeks. They returned to Chapel Farm Cottage for over a month, although they were briefly squeezed out by the Radfords and took rooms in Hermitage Village. In autumn the Lawrences left England: Frieda went to Germany in October to visit her mother, and Lawrence arrived in Italy in November.

Lawrence's on-again, off-again sojourn in the Berkshire area provided the setting, the characters, and the circumstances for several stories, among them *The Fox*. The cottage at Hermitage was actually semi-detached, the right half being occupied by a Mr. and Mrs. Brown and their seven- or eight-year-old daughter Hilda. English soldiers were billeted in the village then, and three of them moved in with the Browns (Hilda "billeted" with the Lawrences next door). Undoubtedly Lawrence drew on this situation for Henry Grenfel's stay at Bailey Farm. But Bailey Farm was inspired less by Chapel Farm Cottage than by Grimsbury Farm, located about nine miles from the Radfords' cottage and run by two cousins, Cecily Lambert and Violet Monk. The Lawrences occasionally moved to Grimsbury Farm when the Radfords needed their cottage, and Lawrence put the inconvenience to good use by modelling March and Banford on Monk and Lambert.

Lawrence stuck to certain facts about his experiences at Grimsbury Farm when he wrote "The Fox" in December 1918, at Mountain Farm Cottage in Derbyshire. But he adapted and interpreted these facts as he saw fit. According to Cecily Lambert, in a 1955 reminiscence, she and her cousin were very poor farmers indeed: "bad premises and not enough knowledge or strength" (*CB*, I, 505). In Lawrence's story, of course, the women's lack of skill at farming results from their fear of the life force. Grimsbury Farm was technically Lambert's (she and her cousin, like their fictional counterparts, were addressed by their surnames, a not uncommon practice at the time[28]), having belonged to a recently deceased grandfather who gains mention in the final version of Lawrence's story. The first meeting between the Lawrences and the farm girls occurred one autumn evening when Lawrence and Frieda simply arrived unannounced at the girls' doorstep, to their hostesses' chagrin, much as

4. Sanctions from the Animal World   59

Henry Grenfel intrudes on March and Banford's seclusion one dark November evening. The cousins were never sure of the reason for this unsolicited visit until years later, when, as Cecily Lambert bitterly explains, they decided that Lawrence had initiated this visit, and others, only in order to obtain copy (*CB*, I, 564).

It would be interesting to know Violet Monk's reaction to this first visit by the Lawrences, as well as to the succeeding events; unfortunately, it is only through her cousin's eyes that one can approach these prototypes for *The Fox*. According to Cecily Lambert, Monk "was not at all socially inclined and tended to be belligerent, resenting the intrusion of strangers and having to more or less entertain them when we were exhausted, hungry, and messy" (*CB*, I, 463). If these memories are accurate, Lawrence adapted them to his own purposes when he transformed Monk into March: the actively antisocial nature of the actual woman becomes the passive shyness and reserve of her fictional counterpart. Lawrence appropriated Monk's dark hair and eyes for his portrait of March, as well as her "flat boyish figure" (*CB*, I, 466), although in the 1921 version, Grenfel is fascinated by the "soft, white breasts" hidden beneath her tunic (*F*, 155). Monk attended to the "mannish jobs" on Grimsbury Farm, dressed in masculine clothing; but, like Ellen March, she enjoyed lace crocheting and occasionally dressed in a frock of "greeny blue curtainmaterial." Her personality, as Lambert describes it, was "a strange mixture of overwhelming conceit and arrogance allied to a kind of meekness and unsureness in direct contradiction," which Lambert attributes to her indulgence and domination by a "possessive mother" (*CB*, I, 466). Lawrence may or may not have known of Monk's "possessive mother," but Lambert's remark is especially interesting in light of Edmund Bergler's analysis of the story in terms of a pre-oedipal mother fixation. On the level of conscious intention, however, Lawrence uses Monk's contradictory personality traits to manifest his character's ambivalence toward the fox and later toward Henry Grenfel. Combined with her assumption of masculine duties on the farm and her aversion to breeding animals, March's personality traits reveal her overall ambivalence toward the female role. This attitude may reflect Lawrence's conclusion about Violet Monk herself.

Interestingly, Cecily Lambert fleshes out Monk's portrait with details that, in terms of *The Fox*, seem to apply more accurately to Lambert than to Monk. Violet Monk had apparently suffered a nervous breakdown because of a broken love affair and had joined her cousin on the farm in order to recuperate; Lambert describes her as being a very nervous person during the period when Lawrence knew her. Moreover, Lambert recalls that "towards me she was possessive and jealous which caused friction, since I loved life, people, and excitement of all kinds and enjoyed having visitors" (*CB*, I, 467). In *The Fox*, although Banford shares Lambert's gregariousness, it is Banford rather than March who is nervous, possessive, and jealous. In fact, Cecily Lambert's jealousy of her cousin obviously was stimulated in 1955 by the act of reminiscing about events that had occurred thirty-five years earlier, and her attribution of jealousy to Violet Monk may be a case of simple projection: for example, when she tells how she threw away her glasses (Banford, of course, is also nearsighted) and "eventually married a very attractive man and still am married," she cannot resist adding, "my cousin married, and the marriage lasted four years" (*CB*, I, 506). Thus, whatever the actual "facts" of the relationship between Monk and Lambert, D. H. Lawrence extracted from it the essential quality of hostility that he must have seen continually in operation.

Cecily Lambert's brother Nip was staying at Grimsbury Farm during his convalescent leave from the war, and Lawrence no doubt had the siblings' relationship in mind when he wrote that "Banford was as pleased and thoughtful as if she had her own younger brother home from France" ("F," 41). Grenfel was certainly modeled on Nip Lambert, for whom Lawrence felt such affection that he spoke in 1920 of following him to Zululand, where he had emigrated (*CL*, I, 608). Cecily Lambert recalls that her brother actively disliked Violent Monk, "and moreover was years younger" (*CB*, I, 466). The matter of Nip's age is of interest to a reader of *The Fox*. Nip may not have been too many years younger, since Lambert states that in 1918 and 1919 she herself was just out of her teens; the picture of the cousins at Grimsbury Farm, reproduced in volume one of Edward Nehls's *Composite Biography*, suggests that both girls were indeed young, quite possibly in their very early twenties. Yet Lawrence ages them ten years or more in the first version of *The Fox*. Lambert's assumption that her brother could not have been attracted to their cousin because she was years older than he is refuted by the story, where the great appeal provided by the age difference (Grenfel is twenty) is underscored by Grenfel's repetition of the nonimportance of that difference. Lawrence may have imposed his own conceptions, or obsessions, upon a young boy's visit with two older women. But another possibility is that he sensed something in the relationship between Nip Lambert and Violet Monk that Cecily Lambert overlooked or ignored: in 1920 Lawrence wrote cryptically to Cecily Lambert, "I hope [Monk's] girding her loins for the Veldt, or whatever it is in Zululand" (*CL*, I, 608); and in 1921, possibly with Monk and Nip Lambert in mind, he had Hannele accompany Captain Hepburn to Africa at the close of *The Captain's Doll*.

There was another important guest at Grimsbury Farm during the Lawrences' first Hermitage period in 1918: Cecily Lambert's father stayed with the girls while he was waiting for a new flat to be redecorated. According to Lambert, her father and Lawrence were continually at odds over the frequency of Lawrence's visits and the scurrilousness of Lawrence's character (which the father deduced from Lawrence's novels). As she recalled in 1955 the sequence of events in 1918, the two men argued and her father ordered Lawrence out of the house. Obviously bitter about being used for "copy," Lambert complains that "the attitude of D. H. Lawrence towards my father was understandable, but it was execrable taste to belittle me for no fault of my own while accepting my hospitality" (*CB*, I, 466). Actually Banford's father, who was left out entirely from the first version of *The Fox*, is treated rather noncommittally in the 1921 version of the story, where his worst quality is a tendency toward mockery. In fact, Lawrence may have felt well-disposed—at least not hostile—toward Mr. Lambert, for a January 1920 letter to Violet Monk says, "I'm glad Mr. and Mrs. Lambert have a house," and closes with "my kindest regards to Mr. and Mrs. Lambert" (*CL*, I, 612). That Lawrence certainly felt kindly toward Cecily Lambert is revealed in the affectionate letters he wrote her from Italy in 1919–20; indeed, the amicable relationship between them, at Grimsbury Farm and after, accounts for Lambert's feeling of betrayal by the final version of the story. She failed to understand not that life and art are two different things—although, of course, to a greater or lesser degree they are—but that the hospitality that she offered to Lawrence, and that he required, was in some ways offensive to him.

Perhaps this hospitality offended Lawrence because it contained a large element of what Lawrence considered to be patronage. He does not even hint at Banford's snobbish condescension in the 1918 "Fox," but the final version contains numerous references to Banford's resentment of the intrusive presence of such an uncouth, inferior boy. The picture of the sitting room (*F*, 135), with its fashionable tiles and latest dance music on the piano (Cecily Lambert played the piano for dancing lessons), is meticulously drawn; Grenfel's mere presence gives the room "the look of a lumber-camp." Catherine Carswell has written instructively about Lawrence's sensitivity to what she calls his upper class friends' "subtle patronage":

> It was naturally a shock when, out of what had seemed a pleasant friendship, there should spring such prodigies as *England, My En-*

gland! or the figures of Hermione and Sir Joshua in *Women in Love* [references to the Meynell family, Lady Ottoline Morrell, and Bertrand Russell]. True, he did this with any or all of us. But one cannot escape from the touch of malice in certain instances, nor from the belief that it is here as a make-weight for the special sensibility of a man whose genius has lifted him out of his class.[29]

Cecily Lambert was certainly not upper class, and neither is Jill Banford. The emphasis on class consciousness in the final version of *The Fox* may be due to the fact that Lawrence had another real-life person in mind when, in 1921, he elaborated on the character of Jill Banford: Margaret Radford, whose cottage at Hermitage was often lent or rented to the Lawrences. Margaret Radford was not only upper class, she was also a creative writer, a minor poet, and one would do well to keep in mind what Lord David Cecil writes about Lawrence's earlier break with Ottoline Morrell: "The relation between patron and artist is always a difficult one, especially in a case like hers when the patron was a kind of artist herself . . . and had all the temperament that goes along with the artist. Possibly Lawrence found her too dominating and disliked being under an obligation anyway."[30]

As described by Richard Aldington, Margaret Radford was "a strange, fragile, over-sensitive creature, shrinking from realities and drifting about . . . like a wisp of unhappy thistledown."[31] Thus she shared physical and emotional characteristics with Jill Banford, who is "a thin, frail little thing" ("F," 41), afraid of prowlers and suffering from a general nervousness. Lawrence's attitude toward Margaret Radford apparently underwent a change, for in his letters to Dollie Radford during the years 1915–17 he continually inquired about the daughter's health and sent his love to her (*CL*, I, 335–420 passim). Of course, Lawrence was not above a bit of hypocrisy in his dealings with people, especially those people whose favor he curried; but J. M. Murry has set on record the good relationship that Lawrence had with Margaret Radford and her mother.[32] However, in December 1917 Lawrence moved into Chapel Farm Cottage, where, as Frieda reports, his invisible wounds began to heal.[33] From this point on he must have greatly resented being at the mercy of the Radfords' benevolence, always liable to be exiled from the only domestic security and happiness he now possessed. As he wrote to Cecil Gray, in April 1918, "I feel unsettled here now, as if we must move soon. And we *must* move—the Radfords want to come here in May" (*CL*, I, 549). Dependent on others for shelter, he felt like a caged wild cat and yearned "for some sort of free, lawless life" (*CL*, I, 548).

4. Sanctions from the Animal World   63

By December 1918, when Lawrence wrote the first version of *The Fox*, his attitude toward Margaret Radford as revealed in his letters was exasperated but not necessarily hostile. Several months later, for instance, he referred to her rather mildly as "the impossible Margaret" (*CL*, I, 548). In the 1918 story, Lawrence vicariously succeeded in appropriating Chapel Farm Cottage and foiling Margaret Radford: Henry Grenfel marries Ellen March precisely in order to get a home for himself, and by implication he gains the farm as the story ends, with Banford-Radford unable to stop him. In fact, Lawrence may have chosen the name *Henry* for his character because the name comes from the Teutonic meaning "ruler of an enclosure, or private property." Harry T. Moore pointed out long ago the connection between Lawrence's real-life desire for Margaret Radford's cottage and the situation portrayed in *The Fox*;[34] but Moore's statement that in the story Margaret Radford (in the character of Jill Banford) fails to drive Lawrence (as Grenfel) away from Hermitage applies only to the first version of the story.

One may look to the events of the months following December 1918 for a partial explanation of why Jill Banford's power over Grenfel is so much more pronounced in the final version of *The Fox*, and why his reaction to her is so hostile. When Lawrence was at Mountain Cottage in Derbyshire he longed for the beauty and peace of Chapel Farm Cottage in Berkshire; but when he was at Chapel Farm Cottage, his privacy was liable to be interrupted at any moment by the insufferable Margaret Radford. The situation apparently grew worse as the months advanced. From Derbyshire, in March 1919, Lawrence wrote to Koteliansky (Kot) that he had received "a letter from Margaret Radford;—how happy, dear Lawrence, she is that she can be at Hermitage to receive us and stay ten days with us. 'Love rules the camp, the court, the grove!'" (*CL*, I, 584). Bewailing his position as Margaret Radford's underling—as he had bewailed his military assignment as an underservant six months earlier—Lawrence forgot that from his own position of relative security in Cornwall he had written just such a gushing letter to Margaret's mother: "Come, dear nice Dollie, we can lend you a little cottage . . . it will be primitive but nice! So you will come on the 14th.—Much love" (*CL*, I, 457). Now, as his sense of rootlessness deepened, Lawrence found that the Radfords' hold over him rankled more and more. Margaret Radford's effusive personality especially annoyed him, so that he must have felt like a fly caught in a spider's web, entrapped by the woman's venomous sweetness; he was given a home but paralyzed at the same time. The turnabout role of spider that Grenfel plays in the 1918 version of *The Fox*, in which Banford is "enmeshed in fine, electric cobwebs" ("F," 47) spun by the crafty visitor no longer suffices by the time Lawrence revised the story in 1921.

A letter that Lawrence wrote to Kot, when he was ensconced again at Chapel Farm Cottage in April 1919, uses the insect image and foreshadows the climax of the Taormina version of *The Fox*:

> The weather is not nice: Margaret Radford is here: under the circumstances I'd rather be at Mountain Cottage. . . . I would come and see you at once, but I've got a sort of obstinate sulky stupidity which prevents my doing anything. Partly it derives from the sweetly-loving Margaret. I wish one could exterminate all her sort under a heap of Keating's powder. I feel utterly 'off' the soulful or clever or witty type of female—in fact, the self-important female of any sort.[35]

In 1916—in another letter to Kot—Lawrence spoke in similar terms of intrusions on his precious isolation at Higher Tregerthen, Cornwall: "But they creep in, the obstructions, the people, like bugs, they creep insidiously in, and they are too many to crush. . . . Oh, if one could but have a great box of insect powder, and shake it over them, in the heavens, and exterminate them. Only to clear and cleanse and purify the beautiful earth, and give room for some truth and pure living."[36] And in "The Reality of Peace," written toward the end of 1917, Lawrence exhorted Death to "smash, beautiful, destructive death, smash the complete will of the hosts of man, the will of the self-absorbed bug" ("RP," 686). George Ford discusses Lawrence's rage against humankind as expressed by the insect image, noting its important role in *Women in Love* (Ford counts eighteen references to beetles and insects in Lawrence's letters written in 1915 and 1916[37]). Like Conrad, Lawrence recognized his own heart of darkness that caused him to say, with Kurtz, "exterminate all the brutes!" But Lawrence trusted, rather than feared, his urge to destroy.

From April to June 1918 Lawrence immersed himself in Edward Gibbon's *Decline and Fall of the Roman Empire*, living vicariously through the exploits of "indiscriminately bad" emperors who "just did as they liked, and *vogue la galère*, till they were strangled" (*CL*, I, 551, 550); in "a historical mood," he announced at that time that the mass of men should be viewed with contempt and that a few superior individuals ought to rule (*CL*, I, 561). Then, in June 1919, Lawrence wrote a preface to his play *Touch and Go*, speaking of death as the climax of a creative activity "in the progression towards new being" (*TG*, 293). Undoubtedly, the image of Margaret Radford as a buglike human who must be exterminated for the good of humankind lies behind the death of Jill Banford in the final version of *The Fox*. As Henry Grenfel watches Banford cross the meadow, when he first realizes the extent of his hatred for her, he thinks of her as a "creeping, dark little object": "'You're a nasty little thing, you are,' he was saying softly across the distance. 'You're a nasty little thing. I hope you'll be paid back for all the harm you've done me for nothing. I hope you will—you nasty little thing. I hope you'll have to pay for it. You will, if wishes are anything. You nasty little creature that you are'" (*F*, 152–53). The phrase "if wishes are anything" reminds one of the letter about Margaret Radford, quoted above, in which Lawrence confesses, "I wish one could exterminate all her sort under a heap of Keating's powder." In *The Fox*, Banford's death is arranged purely by Grenfel's wish that she should die. Earlier in the story, in a section added to the 1918 version when Lawrence revised it in 1921, Grenfel muses that "it is your own *will* which carries the bullet into the heart of your quarry. The bullet's flight home is a sheer projection of your own fate into the fate of the deer. *It happens like a supreme wish, a supreme act of volition, not as a dodge of cleverness*" (*F*, 131, emphasis mine). The tree's falling on target is accomplished by Grenfel's "terrible pure will" (p. 173), and he knows in advance of the fact that the tree must have killed Banford because "the inner necessity of his life was fulfilling itself, it was he who was to live" (pp. 173–74).

Grenfel's wish-fulfillment gains elucidation from Lawrence's hatred of his dependence on Margaret Radford and her family. By the end of June 1919, Lawrence was fed up with the "sweetly-loving" people who would turn against him—or so it seemed—at a moment's notice.[38] He wrote to Kot of the Radfords' "stinking impudence" at asking him to leave in a month, for then he should have to scrounge for another place to stay (*CL*, I, 588). And although he was asked back again in August, he remarked bitterly to Catherine Carswell that "the wretched Margaret is at the cottage now—she turned us out" (*CL*, I, 590). Even after the Lawrences left for Italy in the autumn of 1919, their relations with the Radfords severed, Lawrence took up the cudgel for Dorothy Yorke and her mother, who were homeless in England. He wrote to ask Cecily Lambert if she knew of any furnished cottage the Yorkes might use, since Margaret Radford had let them down "so nastily" about hers (*CL*, I, 599). Two months later he wrote again to Lambert and mentioned the outcome of the Radford-Yorke fiasco: "Margaret and her mother wrote so *sweetly* [one assumes in apology, explanation, or invitation]: but too late" (*CL*, I, 608). In the final version of *The Fox*, the Margaret Radford figure succeeds in running Lawrence off her property, for even after the death of the intransigent Banford, Henry Grenfel is foiled by March's unwillingness to stay on the farm.

The relationship between *The Fox* and Lawrence's life becomes even more complex when one considers a third element of the Banford character. Lawrence's typical method of character portrayal was to combine aspects of several real people in one fictional portrait. He modeled Banford not only on Cecily Lambert and Margaret Radford but also on Frieda Lawrence, another upper class woman, whom the author termed a "devouring mother" in the 1918 letter that first mentions "The Fox." The spirit of Frieda, though not her physical characteristics, figures importantly in Lawrence's 1921 elaboration of Jill Banford's personality. This fact might have offered Cecily Lambert refuge from her resentment at being used as "copy," for other women had consoled themselves with the thought that they were only a part of Lawrence's characters.[39]

In November 1918, Lawrence came down with what he thought was just a bad cold, and for the next four months he was ill, at times desperately so. Actually he was suffering from the great influenza epidemic of 1918–19 known as the "Spanish Lady," an epidemic mentioned in *The Fox* as the reason for Grenfel's having to stay at Bailey Farm. Lawrence's utter dependency on his wife at this time repeated the pattern initiated by his mother during his sickly childhood. A comparison with Lydia Beardsall Lawrence seems appropriate because, like Gertrude Morel in *Sons and Lovers,* Jill Banford is frail in physique but indomitable in spirit. Clara Dawes's reaction to Mrs. Morel in the novel parallels Henry Grenfel's realization about Jill Banford in *The Fox*: Clara "was surprised to find this little interested woman chatting with such readiness; and then she felt . . . she would not care to stand in Mrs. Morel's way" (*SL*, 322).

In the first version of *The Fox*, Grenfel completely dominates Banford and appropriates both her companion and her farm. In the final version more drastic measures are required: the murder of the birdlike Banford signifies that the devourer of chickens has figuratively swallowed the woman who has tried, in her own way, to swallow him. In Lawrence's conception of physiology, outlined in his two treatises on psychology, the growth and health of the teeth depend on the stimulation of the lumbar ganglion, the center of proud recoil into singleness. Banford clings to March in an unnatural dependency and resists any inclination toward separation; but Grenfel, put in the familiar Lawrentian situation of dependency himself, figuratively bares his fangs. "Where in us are the sharp and vivid teeth of the wolf, keen to defend and devour," Lawrence asks in *Fantasia*. "If we had them more, we should be happier" (*FU*, 99). In

Lawrence's novella, the slinking fox has pointed teeth "to thrust forward and bite with, deep, deep, deep into the living prey, to bite and bite the blood" (*F*, 149). Henry Grenfel, Banford's nemesis, can be seen by reference to *Fantasia* to function mainly from the lower center located at the back of the body:

> From the great voluntary ganglion of the lower plane, the child is self-willed, independent, and masterful. In the activity of this centre a boy refuses to be kissed and pawed about, maintaining his proud independence like a little wild animal. From this centre he likes to command and receive obedience. From this centre likewise he may be destructive and defiant and reckless, determined to have his own way at any cost. (*FU*, 83)

The continued power of Banford over Grenfel, however—evidenced by March's disinclination to stay on the farm after her death—suggests that the battle against the "devouring mother" may never be concluded decisively; for Banford represents that side of Frieda Lawrence that prompted her husband to term her, according to Mabel Dodge, "the enemy of life—his life—the hateful, destroying female."[40]

Mabel Dodge's accounts being notably one-sided, one would do well to consider the other aspect of Frieda Lawrence's mothering, her life-encouraging nurturance. Grenfel's attraction to March's breasts, and his desire for her support, indicate that Ellen March is also a Frieda figure—what Martin Green, in his own one-sided view of Mrs. Lawrence, terms a "Demetrian source of order as well as life."[41] In the 1918 version, Henry Grenfel swallows March as completely as he does Banford, but in 1921 Lawrence wrote into *The Fox* a greater respect for his wife's individuality. Frieda Lawrence's unwillingness to be swallowed by her husband received real-life expression at Grimsbury Farm, where, as Cecily Lambert reports, she did not share a bedroom with her husband because she did not wish to be "too much married" (*CB*, I, 503). Henry Grenfel's attempts to swallow March—that is, to submerge her personality in his (*F*, 178–79)—do not succeed, and the ambiguity of tone in the coda of the story suggests that Lawrence was sympathetic to Frieda's desire for separateness even as he wished to be her lord and master.

Yet Lawrence's sympathies lie ultimately with Grenfel more than with March; in fact, the author's primary intention in creating the fox and the man-fox was undoubtedly to draw a self-portrait, and his attraction to Nip Lambert suggests that he saw common elements in their personalities. By 1918, Lawrence had grown the reddish beard that was to earn him the sobriquet Red Fox by the Indians in Taos in 1923.[42] As early as 1904 Lawrence gave the appearance of this animal, not because of his looks so much as his manner. Ford Madox Ford has described his first impression of Lawrence: engrossed in manuscripts, Ford looked up and saw "a fox. A fox going to make a raid on the hen-roost before him." Ford was shocked by

> the fox-coloured hair and mustache and the deep, wary sardonic glance . . . as if [Lawrence] might be going to devour me—or something that I possessed. . . . He had come, like the fox, with his overflood of energy—his abounding vitality of passionate determination that seemed always too big for his frail body—to get something—the hypnotic two thousand a year; from somewhere.

Many years after their first meeting, Ford's first impression of Lawrence was reinforced when he read *The Fox*: "I really jumped when I came to his description of the fox looking over its shoulder at the farm girl. Because it was evident that Lawrence identified himself with the russet-haired human fox who was to carry off the as-it-were hen-girl of the story."[43]

Hilda Doolittle has put on record her own sexual attraction to Lawrence and subsequent attempt (rebuffed by Lawrence) to initiate an affair. Her third-person memoirs speak of Lawrence in 1918 in terms reminiscent of Ellen March's first dream of the fox:

> Julia [H.D.] was suddenly repelled by the mask he seemed suddenly to clap on his face; . . . It was the Rubens red of his beard, or Titian. The mouth . . . made him Satyr. There, suddenly in a second, he was stamped on her mind, the flame of the red beard, aggressive, horn-symbol, horn of plenty. The mouth showed the teeth, not remarkable in any way for symmetry or lack of symmetry, but teeth to tear, to devour.[44]

Lawrence's letters show that he too saw himself in terms of a fox. In 1917 (to quote but one example) he wrote to Catherine Carswell, "I feel myself awfully like a fox that is cornered by a pack of hounds and boors who don't perhaps know he's there, but are closing in unconsciously. It seems to me to be a crucial situation now: whether we are hobbled by the old vile world, and destroyed, or whether we manage, with the help of the unseen, to make good our escape" (*CL*, I, 497). The images in this letter seem to foreshadow the final version of *The Fox*:

> As Grenfel stood under the oaks of the wood-edge he heard the dogs from the neighboring cottage up the hill yelling suddenly and startlingly. and the wakened dogs from the farms around barking answer. And suddenly it seemed to him England was little and tight, he felt the landscape was constricted even in the dark, and that there were too many dogs in the night, making a noise like a fence of sound, like the network of English hedges netting the view. He felt the fox didn't have a chance. (*F*, 146)

As already noted, the final version of the story more clearly characterizes Grenfel as a fox, by major changes as well as by such simple word substitutions as "yap of laughter" (*F*, 124) for "clap of laughter" ("F," 40); Grenfel is foxlike from the outset, rather than—as in the first version—a man merely seen as a fox by a sexually repressed female. Perhaps Lawrence felt more like a fox himself as the years went on, in the sense of both a reckless, instinctual creature and a pariah to society: his life after 1919 was markedly rootless, for his travels took him to various places around the world in search of the better society. *The Fox*, revised and lengthened at the start of these world journeys, gains a more complete conceptualization of Henry Grenfel as a result of the author's self-image at the time.

During his leadership period, Lawrence went over the border from the human world into the animal kingdom. His special interest in animals in these years is evidenced by the proliferation of animal titles in his canon after 1916: *Goats and Compasses* and *The Flying Fish*, both unpublished, the one a philosophy treatise[45] and the other a novel fragment; *The Ladybird* and *The Fox*, novellas; *Birds, Beasts and Flowers* and *Tortoises*, poetry; *Reflections on the Death of a Porcupine*, essays; *Kangaroo* and *The Plumed Serpent*, novels. The novella *St. Mawr*, bearing as its title the proper name of the horse in the story, provides the most striking example of Lawrence's tendency to elevate animals into heroes.

Reading up on European history for his contracted textbook, Lawrence found an enviable strength and wildness and insouciance (one of Lawrence's favorite words) in leaders of the past—among them emperors of Rome, Luther, and Napoleon (see chapter ten); but he was unable to find real leaders or heroes in the human kingdom, at least not in his own times. Birkin is Lawrence's spokesman in *Women in Love* when he wishes that the entire human race could be exterminated, leaving only the plants and animals to populate the universe (*WL*, 116). To Lawrence, wild animals not only act from instinct (in his term, "blood-consciousness"), they also have a strong, innate sense of inviolable space: instead of suffocating their children, they force their children's independence. During his leadership period Lawrence admired even more the damage that wild animals are capable of wreaking on their enemies. He wrote in 1921, "But I don't *want* the tiger superseded. . . . Leave me my tigers, leave me spangled leopards, leave me bright cobra snakes, and I wish I had poison fangs and talons as good. I *believe* in wrath and gnashing of teeth and crunching of cowards' bones" (*CL*, II, 651). The fact that, shortly afterward, Lawrence referred to his novella *The Fox* as if it were itself a fox ("Now he careers with a strange and fiery brush") indicates that by this medium Lawrence felt empowered to gnash his teeth and take revenge on those in real life whose oppression he found both intolerable and insurmountable.

5. Over the Border: *The Ladybird* and *England, My England*

In the autumn of 1921, while living in Sicily, Lawrence made preparations for leaving Europe, which he considered "dead of a love disease like syphilis" (*CL*, II, 673). He had in his possession certain manuscripts, among them "The Thimble," published in 1917 in the American magazine *Seven Arts*; "The Mortal Coil," published the same year in the same magazine; "The Fox," published in 1920 in *Hutchinson's Story Magazine*; and several other stories. Lawrence got his literary affairs in order by expanding the first three stories into novellas called *The Ladybird*, *The Captain's Doll*, and *The Fox*, which he intended for publication together, and by collecting several of the tales for a volume to be called *England, My England*. These works, especially the novellas, are radical statements on leading the good life; indeed, *The Ladybird* contains Lawrence's first elaboration in fiction of the ideal of leadership that he had tentatively articulated in *Women in Love*.

The Ladybird originated in a 1915 story about the necessity for starting life over after the holocaust of World War I. Entitled "The Thimble," this short piece centers on a jewel-encrusted thimble (sans ladybird) symbolizing the old England, heavy and moribund with the weight of false and outdated ideals. The only two characters are the Hepburns: he returning home, disfigured by the war; she awaiting him, disillusioned by the war. Together they come through to a new kind of life. By throwing away the thimble, they hope to take control over their destinies and grow into a real marriage.

When Lawrence wrote the story he too was disillusioned by war and very eager to emigrate to America. He wrote to his friend Lady Cynthia Asquith (daughter-in-law of the prime minister), whose help he enlisted in procuring passports, "What is the whole empire, and kingdom, save the thimble in my story? If we could but bring our souls through, to life" (*CL*, I, 373). Mrs. Hepburn herself is modeled quite frankly on Lady Cynthia, who visited Lawrence often in 1915, at the Greatham home of the Meynells: Lawrence had already boasted to her that he had "done a rather good word-sketch of you: in a story" (*CL*, I, 372). Shortly afterward, in November 1915, he urged his friend to reserve for herself the choice of leaving for America; his letter strongly implies that Lady Cynthia's husband is a defeated man who has cast his lot with England, and that therefore the wife must leave him and join the Lawrences in America (*CL*, I, 382).

Lady Cynthia is one of the few women of wealth and prestige whose assistance to him Lawrence seems not to have resented, at least not overtly. He did not complain about her to others in his letters, as was his wont, and his letters to her, while suggesting that her criticisms of his notions were rather frequent and intense ("Believe me, my feet are more sure upon the earth than you will allow" [*CL*, I, 377]), show that he valued her opinion and even enjoyed their sparring ("I very much want you to tell me what you think. . . ." [*CL*, I, 376]). There was one subject, however, on which Lawrence felt Lady Cynthia had no business expounding: this was the care and raising of children. Lawrence always had strong opinions on this subject himself, especially since Frieda kept it constantly at the fore of their life together. Thus, in November 1916 Lawrence wrote to Lady Cynthia that "Frieda went to London and saw her children: and began to realise, I believe, that the mother-child relation is not so all-important; indeed, not profoundly important at all, touching the quick of being. It is, in real truth, one of the temporal, almost accidental connections, the connection between parents and children. But I suppose you will not agree to this at all" (*CL*, I, 483). A few months earlier he had expressed similar sentiments to Catherine Carswell:

> You should be glad you have no children: they are a stumbling-block now. There are plenty of children, and no hope. . . . Meanwhile even the mice increase—they cannot help it. What is this highest, this procreation? . . . It is a tracing back, when there is no going forward, a throwing life onto the bonfire of death and oblivion, an autumnal act, a consuming down. This is a winter. Children and childbearing do not make spring. It is not in children, the future lies. (*CL*, I, 468)

Other writings indicate that, to the contrary, Lawrence felt the mother-child relation to be of utmost importance, since children betoken the future; this is the message of his poem "War Baby," written to celebrate the birth of Catherine Carswell's baby in the spring of 1918. And his story "The Thimble" continually refers to the main characters as newborn babies, about to begin their lives ("T," 60, 61).

On several occasions, Lawrence advised Lady Cynthia on the raising of her own son John, who gave evidence of psychological problems from a very early age (today he might be classified as autistic[1]). Whether Lawrence felt that Lady Cynthia was ruining John by placing too much emphasis on an unimportant connection, or that she was ruining him by mishandling a relationship that was very important indeed, Lawrence felt free (for he was sometimes invited) to enter her private, domestic sphere. In 1915 he had criticized her for trying to make her son love and obey her in order to overcome her own sense of insufficiency (*CL*, I, 342)—a common flaw in the personalities of Lawrence's fictional female characters like Hermione Roddice in *Women in Love*. Almost three years later he was still offering to be the boy's "proper psychic influence" (*CL*, I, 537). Given this attitude toward Cynthia Asquith, it is not surprising that Lawrence dreamed of her "so hard a few days ago, so must write" during a visit with his sisters in the Midlands in 1918; his letter complains of the strange, psychic connection between mother and child that he observed among his relatives and that he believed to represent the phenomenon of modern motherhood in general (*CL*, I, 554).

Lady Cynthia did not take Lawrence's strong hints about her maternal inadequacies, and she soon became pregnant again. In March 1919 Lawrence wrote to Catherine Carswell that "Cynthia Asquith is going to have another baby—and feels doomed. Oh Lord!" (*CL*, I, 580). The birth of this baby, her third, seems to have caught Lawrence in a particularly irritable mood, for he wrote of the blessed event in a decidedly petulant manner: "I suppose we shall have to see you Madonnaing in the penny pictorials for a while. . . . Are you preparing to sally forth into the *monde* as a sort of young matron? Pfui! Ah, bad! What is the new line? You'll have to have a new line. *Mère de trois*. It's a bit of a quandary. Capitoline Juno? Ox-eyed Hera? Many-breasted Artemis?" (*CL*, I, 592). This attitude toward Cynthia Asquith in her role as mother is perfectly consistent with Lawrence's attitude toward the other women in his life, and it figures in the new direction that Lawrence gave "The Thimble" when he turned it into *The Ladybird* in early winter 1921.[2]

The husband and wife surnamed Hepburn in "The Thimble" are here rechristened Apsley, a name much closer to that of the real-life Asquiths. While children are used only metaphorically in "The Thimble," to betoken the renewal of life, several real children figure in *The Ladybird*: Lady Daphne has suffered a stillbirth; her two brothers, sons of Countess Beveridge, who plays a prominent part in this version of the story, have been killed in war. Most importantly, the central character in *The Ladybird*, a German prisoner of war, is continually referred to as a child. Lawrence first presents Count Johann Dionys Psanek in the following terms: "He was a small man, small as a boy, and his face too was rather small. But all the lines were fine, as if they had been fired with a keen male energy" (*L*, 45). Lady Beveridge, who has visited Count Dionys in the hospital, describes him to her daughter as "so small," with "[s]omething of the terrible farawayness of a child that is very ill and can't tell you what hurts it" (p. 50). The Count himself apologizes to Lady Daphne that he had a head "like a child's windmill," talking nonsense (p. 53).

Indeed, the small stature of the Count is mentioned on and off throughout the story. When he is very ill, he is quite conscious of his size in relation to that of Lady Daphne. When he first meets her, as he lies in bed and she stands next to him, she looms so tall that her presence frightens him and he can barely look at her. Their first conversation centers on this disparity in size:

> "You are so tall," he said, still frightened.
> "I was always tall" she replied. . . .
> "And I, small," he said. (*L*. 52)

After this cryptic repartee he asks his visitor to sit down so that they may become equals. As he begins to recover from his war wounds, the Count begins to express his inmost, radical ideas to Lady Daphne and to insist that these ideas, far from being childish notions, have great validity. Yet even this insistence contains physical referents: "I am a man, even if I am little. . . . Give me room for my anger" (p. 63). Count Dionys's assertion of his manhood, independence, and pride provokes in Lady Daphne a (to Lawrence) characteristically female attempt to keep this little man in his place: feeling herself being seduced by him, she focuses on his small stature and uses it almost like a charm to ward off an evil spell: "She disliked the thought of the Count. An impudent little fellow. An impertinent little fellow. A little madman, really. A little outsider. No, No. She would think of her husband: an adorable, tall, well-bred Englishman . . ." (p. 69).

Lady Daphne's husband, Basil, is diametrically opposed to Count Dionys. His name derives from the Greek for royal, and he is the cream of England's crop.³ He also worships his wife as "moon-mother of the world" (*L*, 77), and literally throws himself at her feet to shower kisses upon her shoes and stockings. Thus he contributes to the pattern of movement in the story, with males and females bobbing up and down in a strange sort of mating dance. Basil's kneeling before his wife reveals his positioning of her above him in the pantheon; he is Major but she is a goddess: "She really felt she could glow white and fill the universe like the moon, like Astarte, like Isis, like Venus. The grandeur of her own pale power" (p. 79). Basil would gladly make himself a sacrifice to her, an offering on her altar (p. 81). One recalls in this context that Lady Daphne's prototype was named Cynthia; to L. P. Hartley, "she had a mysterious, a moonlit, leprechaun quality that was not quite of this world. She was not called Cynthia for nothing, and she had at least as much in common with the regent of the night as with us ordinary mortals."⁴

In contrast to Basil, the Count has sought and found "the God who pulls things down: especially the things that men have put up" (*L*, 73), like churches and factories. Not coincidentally, his God is a man's God, as he repeats for emphasis to Lady Daphne (p. 74). And a man's God, apparently, does not worship Woman but rather pulls her down as well. In a section of *The Ladybird* apparently missing for fifty years and never published with the text even today, Count Dionys contemptuously spits out words to Lady Daphne that are poetic in form, vitriolic in content: "But beat on her, little heart, my heart. Beat on her and destroy her, then. It is time she fell to dust."⁵ Ironically, the Count's crest bears a ladybird, which, he notes to Basil, is "a Mary-beetle. The beetle of Our Lady" (p. 96). Lawrence must have been fascinated by the link between an insect and the Virgin Mary, and uses the beetle as part of his symbology of inversion in this story. The underworld, darkness, snakes, decomposition and destruction, love of self, power—all are elevated to the highest principles. The Virgin Mary is in essence pulled down from her pedestal and "her" beetle put in her place.

This ladybird gives the story its title and appears on the thimble that encompasses Lady Daphne's finger as she dutifully sews shirts for the Count. Symbolically, this thimble is, of course, a wedding ring. The earlier version of the story, "The Thimble," makes the connection clear by noting that the object deep within the recesses of the sofa has "a thin rim, like a ring"; the movements of Mrs. Hepburn's hands into the sofa even parallel (or parody) sexual activity—"Her long white fingers pressed into the fissure, pressed and entered rhythmically, pressed and pressed further and further into the tight depths of the fissure...." ("T," 59)—

although the story, without the Count, concerns desire and frustration rather than desire and fulfillment. *The Ladybird* converts the symbolic masturbation of the early tale into sexual intercourse with a Dionysian figure who, like the fox in Lawrence's novella of that name, comes to rescue a female from a sterile marriage to a false spiritual mate. The thimble, with its gold snake at the bottom, marks and seals their union.

The prominent and favorable role of snakes in this version of the story points to a rewriting and revising of the Book of Genesis. Critics have pointed out that the name Psanek is an anagram of *snake*[6]; and the Count, hissing that he hates the world, enjoins his heart to strike (*L*, 74). The novella arises from the same impulse that prompted the poem "Snake," also created in Sicily during the same period, in which Lawrence lauds the snake as hero, "a king in exile, uncrowned in the underworld, / Now due to be crowned again" (*CP*, II, 80).[7] In Lawrence's idiosyncratic version of Genesis, Eve is more properly the bride of Satan than of Adam.

Indeed, references to the Adam and Eve story increase dramatically in Lawrence's writings after 1917, during his leadership period, when he cried out for a strong and passionate hero to save society. Like Walt Whitman, whose "Children of Adam" poems he now read and admired, Lawrence became a "chanter of Adamic songs," praising the sensuous life and "singing the phallus" in work after work. In an introduction to his own phallus-centered paintings, Lawrence declares that ever since the Fall humankind has worked hard to spiritualize matter or, in other terms, to intellectualize emotion. But Cezanne's insistence on painting the appleness of an apple points to a new Fall: "The fall not only of Jesuits and the Christian idealists altogether, but . . . the collapse of our whole way of consciousness, and the substitution of another way" ("IP," 578). Lawrence uncovers this "substitution of another way" in many works of literature that ostensibly tell a different story. His definition of the hero emerges clearly from his trust in the instincts as, in Romantic fashion, he ascribes to John Milton the belief that "the true hero of *Paradise Lost* must be Satan," who signifies the passions that humans are wont to repress ("IP," 559).

Prime examples of similar Lawrentian interpretations of literature are found in his discussions of various American works (later revised and collected as *Studies in Classic American Literature* [see chapter nine]). In the May 1919 issue of *The English Review*, for example, Lawrence maintains that in *The Scarlet Letter* Nathaniel Hawthorne seems to worship the madonnalike Hester Prynne who piously attends to the needs of the community, yet he actually admires the sensual Hester who has followed her instincts in her liaison with Arthur Dimmesdale. The novel, Lawrence says, records the challenge to Dimmesdale's spirituality posed first by Hester and then by Roger Chillingworth: "*The Scarlet Letter* is, in truth, a legendary myth. It contains the abstract of the fall of the white race. It is the inverse of the Eve myth, in the Book of Genesis. It contains a passional or primary account of the collapse of the human psyche in the white race" (*SM*, 139). Lawrence's discussion of *The Scarlet Letter* as an inverted Eve myth occupies only half a page in the first version of the study; in the third version, written in America in 1922, the discussion is lengthened to four pages, although Lawrence replaces Adam and Eve with Americans, who by that time had become an important target for his spleen. In the second version, written in 1920 but never published during Lawrence's lifetime, Lawrence adds an important comment about Hawthorne's novel: "In this myth of the second Fall, it is the serpent who marries Eve, it is the spiritual Adam who is brought down to prostitution" (*SM*, 166).

The snake occupies as central a position in the Lawrence canon as in the Book of Genesis or *Paradise Lost*, but Lawrence's intention for it is diametrically opposed to that of the Scriptures or John Milton. William York Tindall first explained Lawrence's use of the dragon or serpent in terms of the Eastern system of yoga.[8] A central concept of yoga is that of Kundalini, "the serpent power lying coiled and dormant at the base of the spine." The yogi, through exercise and meditation, sends the divine dragon upward thorugh seven centers or chakras, the last being the Third Eye of the head. Lawrence came across this concept in the theosophical writing of James Pryse, disciple of Mme. Blavatsky, but in characteristic fashion he ignored any chakra above the neck. He acknowledges his debt to yoga in the foreword to *Fantasia of the Unconscious*. The power of the serpent reaches its apotheosis in *The Plumed Serpent*, the crowning achievement and end point of Lawrence's leadership period; but it plays its part in numerous other works: in *The Ladybird*, as already noted, Count Dionys' thimble has a snake coiled at its base; Egbert, in "England, My England," longs for "old gods, old, lost passions," signified by the "presence of unseen snakes" (*CSS*, II, 323–24); Somers in *Kangaroo* is continually compared to a serpent; and, in *The Man Who Died*, Jesus announces after his sexual encounter with Isis that "the gold and flowing serpent is coiling up again to sleep at the root of my tree" (*MD*, 47). In these ways Lawrence recrowned the snake that his childhood training—epitomized by the Christian temperance song, "There's a Serpent in the Glass"—had dethroned.

In *The Fox*, Lawrence in effect stands the moralism of *Paradise Lost* on its head by investing in the snakelike fox the instinctual, spontaneous life that is so needed at Bailey Farm. The chaste and frustrated Ellen March is initially thrilled by the fox, but in essence the animal is merely a disguise for her own repressed heterosexuality. Henry Grenfel, in his fox guise, woos March by his resemblance to the animal and then gradually replaces it in her consciousness. Union with Grenfel is not complete, however; it merely foreshadows the marriage to "dark gods" that other works (culminating in *The Plumed Serpent*) explore more fully. *The Fox* records only the fall of the white psyche and must not be read as Lawrence's *Paradise Regained*.

Milton's *Paradise Lost* hints at his *Paradise Regained* when Adam moves from despair to faith after recalling Christ's promise that Adam and Eve's "seed shall bruise / The Serpent's head" (10.1031–32). Their embrace will eventually produce the savior of humankind who, taking upon Himself the sins of others, will offer His life to combat Satan, sin, and death. To Lawrence, as to William Blake, this notion of godhead was anathema. As early as *The Rainbow* (1915) his characters speak for a god "not mild and gentle, neither Lamb nor Dove. He was the lion and the eagle. . . . They were not passive subjects of some shepherd, or pets of some loving Woman, or sacrifices to some priest" (*R*, 341). As critic John Stoll notes, here, in its incipient stages, is "the power doctrine upon which the later Lawrence hero rests his claim for psychic and social renewal."[9] This power doctrine receives its fullest expression in the leadership period, when animals are controlling symbols in Lawrence's work and human power struggles gain sanctions from the wild state, in which animals kill—but do not murder. The lust for blood that the protagonist controls in Lawrence's early story "The Old Adam" is uncaged during the author's middle writing phase. The plumed serpent of the novel by that name is both eagle and snake and thus poses a double-barrelled threat to Christianity.

Lawrence's first version of *Paradise Regained* is to be found in *The Ladybird*, which Lawrence in 1923 said had "more the quick of a new thing" in it than *The Fox*, which belonged more to the old world (*CL*, II, 743). In *The Ladybird*, the snakelike Count Dionys steals an Eve from her old, fallen Adam and, by achieving with her a marriage based on blood-consciousness, becomes the new Adam himself. Count Dionys creates of Daphne a new Eve because he has convinced her of his pioneering manhood: he has crossed the border between the old world and the new. The concept of *Grenzleute*, or borderline people, fascinated Lawrence, who personally crossed numerous literal borders in his search after a new

Eden. In a letter written in the autumn of 1921 he remarked that "the *Grenzleute* are those who are on the verge of human understanding, and who widen the frontiers of human knowledge all the time—and the frontiers of life" (*CL*, II, 663). Daphne yearns "to cross the border" and be gone from her upper consciousness and her daytime world (*L*, 100); under Count Dionys's tutelage she succeeds in doing so without ever leaving her home. Alvina Houghton makes that journey in *The Lost Girl* when, through marriage to Ciccio and removal to Italy, she goes "out of the world, over the border, into some place of mystery" (*LG*, 306). Alexander Hepburn in *The Captain's Doll*, with his views on male supremacy, exists in another country from Countess Hannele, "beyond some borderline" (*CD*, 250). *The Boy in the Bush*, in a scene added by Lawrence in 1923 to Molly Skinner's manuscript, ends with the hero—on his stallion named Adam—crossing the border between civilization and wilderness, about to set up a patriarchal colony in the outback. In "The Border-Line", the power of the body can circumvent even death, for a very corporeal ghost manages to rescue his woman from a false marriage. *Lady Chatterley's Lover*, written when Lawrence was sexually impotent and dying from tuberculosis, is almost literally a last-gasp attempt by this author to return to the Garden after the fall from white consciousness. The story is another Lawrentian inversion of the Eve myth, with its savior snake (Mellors) seducing a desperate Eve (Connie) away from her insipid Adam (Clifford).

In *The Ladybird*, as in many of Lawrence's other works, there is a character who not only speaks clearly for his creator but who also acts out his creator's wildest fantasies concerning women. In works from the leadership period these fantasies are often of revenge and murder, but in this case the wish-fulfillment is sexual. In his room at the Apsley home, Count Dionys sings a song that mysteriously lures Lady Daphne first to his door and then to his couch. The song concerns a swan-turned-woman, mismatched to a husband and three children, who abandons her family in favor of a more appropriate union with the king of the swans.[10] Once seated beside the Count, Lady Daphne slides down until her face lies against his feet, worshiping him as if he were an Egyptian king-god (*L*, 103), submitting to him as she had once accepted the worship and submission of her husband. The Count in effect takes her as his queen, but not as his mother: he is to be "Master of the life to come. Father of the soul that would come after" (p. 104); she is to be his consort rather than a mother-goddess, the Lord's bird ("Wenn ich ein Voglein war' . . . Flog ich zu dir—"), rather than he the Lady's.

By 1921, when Lawrence wrote *The Ladybird*, Lady Cynthia Asquith was married and the mother of three children. She has said publicly that she thought Lawrence's word-sketch of her in "The Thimble" was very good,[11] but what she thought of her portrait in the novella is not known. In biographical terms, *The Ladybird* suggests Lawrence's desire to take Lady Cynthia as a wife, or at least as a lover,[12] although she herself would have denied this impulse; a diary entry of 1916, written when the Lawrences were staying with the Meynells at Greatham, states that a friend had almost asked Viola Meynell to dinner with Lady Cynthia, "but hearing her young man (D. H. Lawrence) was passionately in love with me she had thought better of it. What enormous leaps to conclusions people do take!"[13] There is something disingenuous in Lady Cynthia's exclamation when it is added to the several other diary entries pooh-poohing the notion of Lawrence's sexual attraction to his friend.

Obviously Lawrence's attraction to Lady Cynthia was not untinged by the need to dominate (motivated by the fear of domination) that marred his relationships with other, less desirable women. In *The Ladybird*, the Count articulates his ideal of leadership in a conversation with Major Apsley that ranges from the political sphere to the domestic. Count Dionys considers himself to be a natural aristocrat "whose soul is born single, able to be alone, to choose and to command" (*L*, 89). Such a man deserves the unquestioning allegiance of the masses, he believes, and the uncritical support of his wife. Lady Daphne's response is typical of Lawrence's fictional women: "Little men have always wanted power," she says (p. 91). By continually harping on his size, especially when she tries to fight him, Lady Daphne attempts to make the Count feel small psychologically as well as physically, and hence insignificant; this is the trick of the "devouring mother," who thwarts her child's attempts at independence. Count Dionys' rejoinder—"I have been told before . . . little men are always bossy"—reminds one again of Herbert Howarth's assessment of Lawrence's leadership ideal: that one who has been dominated by his mother may grow to advocate the rule of men.[14] Shortly after the Count's discussion of leadership, Lady Daphne falls under his spell and in effect moves backward in time to worship of the Egyptian sun-king-god, whose emblem, the ladybird, stretches likewise back in time, past its role as domestic pet or mascot of the mother goddess and back to the Egyptian scarabeus associated with defecation and decomposition (pp. 96–97).

Major elements of *The Ladybird*—the struggle to escape the domination of women and their love ideal; the search for a father (or a father-god)—figure also in several short stories of the period. Like *The Ladybird*, these stories, included in *England, My England*, lend themselves to interpretation in the light of Lawrence's hostility toward the Magna Mater. One such story is "You Touched Me," which Lawrence created in the summer of 1919 when he was revising the first version of *The Fox* for magazine publication. These two stories have much in common. The two sisters of "You Touched Me" are probably modeled on the cousins who served as prototypes for March and Banford: here Violet Monk "becomes" Matilda Rockley, the spinster wooed in a strange way by a younger man; Cecily Lambert "becomes" the innocuous sister Emmie, who joins with Matilda in a futile attempt to ward off the intruder. The barren farm of "The Fox," run by land girls in the wartime absence of men, is transposed into a shutdown pottery works and drab pottery house, bereft of leadership because of the father's kidney disease. The inheritance of the house and property is at issue in both stories. In "The Fox," Henry Grenfel returns on leave to the farm of his dead father (who becomes his grandfather in the final, expanded version), unaware that it has been sold but soon determined to regain it; in "You Touched Me," Hadrian Rockley, adopted emotionally if not legally by the elder Rockley, also returns on leave to a home that is not really his and succeeds in appropriating it.

Hadrian and Henry are both motivated by the desire for the security of a home. As already mentioned (see chapter four), Lawrence may have chosen the name Henry for his character because of its derivation from the Teutonic word meaning ruler of an enclosure or property. Undoubtedly he chose the name Hadrian because of its association with the leader of the Roman Empire: in *Movements in European History*, Lawrence's history textbook revised only months before the creation of "Hadrian" (for so the story was then called), Lawrence declares Hadrian to be a "great and noble ruler" of ancient times (*MEH*, 6). Seemingly there is nothing great or noble about Lawrence's fictional Hadrian, who begins as "just an ordinary boy from a Charity Home, with ordinary brownish hair and ordinary bluish eyes and of ordinary rather Cockney speech" (*CSS*, II, 395), and grows up to be a small, rather ratlike young man. But Hadrian has had a sojourn in Canada, always for Lawrence a symbolic geography of wildness,[15] and he returns with great self-confidence, "vigorous enough in his smallness" (p. 397). Indeed, Matilda and Emmie are nervous about his arrival—"*What* a little man!" they exclaim (p. 398)—and they soon learn that Hadrian is an "indomitable, dangerous charity boy" (p. 407). As such he has much in common not only with Henry

Grenfel but also with their creator, who expressed his resentment about receiving patronage in a February 1920 letter to Amy Lowell: "I am a sort of charity-boy of literature, apparently. One is denied one's just rights, and then insulted with charity. Pfui! to them all" (*CL*, I, 622).

Hadrian is twenty-one to Matilda's thirty-two, an age difference approximating that between Grenfel and March in the first version of *The Fox*. Matilda, like March, repulses the young man's pursuit by pointing out, "I am old enough to be your mother"; unlike March, Matilda has, in a way, even *been* Hadrian's mother (*CSS*, II, 409). In a way, too, Frieda was Lawrence's mother; he seems to have sought out those many women in his life (some older than he, some not) who would take on the maternal role in their relationship. In much of his fiction, especially in the leadership period, marriage to such a woman is motivated by the double desire of need for nurturance and wish to exert control. In "You Touched Me," Lawrence splits himself between the small but vigorous charity boy, desirous of taking revenge on those women who have nurtured and "civilized" him, and the sickly father, cared for by his daughters. At Hadrian's suggestion, Mr. Rockley decides that Matilda must marry the boy or lose her inheritance, a decision that prompts a revealing authorial side: "[h]e seemed to have a strange desire, quite unreasonable, for revenge upon the women who had surrounded him for so long, and served him so carefully" (*CSS*, II, 407). Although Mr. Rockley lies immobile in his sick bed, so that Matilda looks "down on him both literally and figuratively," still he triumphs over her by exerting his will and controlling the purse strings (p. 409). By creating this situation—and the similar situation in *The Ladybird*, where Count Dionys languishes helplessly in his sickbed at first but later rises to dominate the women who tend him—Lawrence takes his revenge upon his own upper class wife, whose nursing of him throughout his near-fatal bout with influenza in 1918 and 1919 had put him most dramatically in a hateful position of dependency.

"You Touched Me" may appear to be an oedipal fantasy, with the child marrying the mother and replacing (killing) the father. Its title may suggest a bonding together of male and female through physical embrace, as in "The Horse-Dealer's Daughter," to name another story of the period. Yet it may also be read as a ritual succession of kings. The dying Mr. Rockley seals his relationship with his "son" by having Matilda kiss them both; "I'm glad you're mine," he sighs to Hadrian (*CSS*, II, 410). The important relationship, then, is between the two men, rather than between the man and the woman. The lack of physical contact between the "lovers" suggests that noli me tangere rather than "you touched me" is the motto of the story, and that revenge upon Matilda for her mothering of him and a desire for control over the homeplace motivate Hadrian's proposal of marriage.

Similar pre-oedipal concerns are to be found in "The Blind Man," written in the autumn of 1918, published in *The English Review* in July 1920, and selected for the *England, My England* volume in 1921. The letter that Lawrence wrote to Katherine Mansfield in 1918 about Jung and the truth of the mother-incest idea includes the notation that Lawrence had completed "The Blind Man"; like "The Fox," finished shortly afterward, this story turns on the "devouring mother," an interest of Lawrence's throughout his life and a preoccupation during his leadership period.

The maternalism of the title character's wife provides the subtle underpinnings of the story. Isabel Pervin is expecting the couple's second baby—their first died when Maurice Pervin went off to war—and her pregnancy is noted throughout: she longs "to luxuriate in a rich, physical satisfaction of maternity" (*CSS*, II, 348); she has "a warm, maternal look" and a "transfigured Madonna face" (p. 351), and she seems "rich with her approaching maternity" (p. 361); her cousin Bertie, visiting at the farm, remarks on her obvious wish to be delivered of the child and prompts a conversation on the subject (p. 359). More importantly, in terms of the symbolic import of the story, she is already a kind of mother to her own husband, whose blindness is not only the objective correlative of his blood-consciousness—his noncerebral way of life—but also the mark of his isolation from the outer world and his reliance upon Isabel: "With his wife he had a whole world, rich and real and invisible" (p. 374). As Richard Wheeler points out, the "unconscious logic" of the story dictates that the first infant had to die to enable Isabel to mother her wounded husband. He notes further that there is a relationship between Maurice Pervin's blood-consciousness and his infantile connection with Isabel, for the images of rocking, flooding, and lapping tides (p. 355) used by Lawrence to characterize this kind of consciousness "suggest that this 'new way' of knowing is modeled on an old way, the first way, of knowing in human life," when the child in the womb experiences what Freud termed the "oceanic" state of oneness with the mother.[16]

Isabel has ambivalent feelings toward her husband's dependency on her. On the one hand she longs "to possess her husband utterly; it gave her inordinate joy to have him entirely to herself" (*CSS*, II, 348). On the other hand, she feels the care of Maurice as a "terrible burden" and worries that she will be unable to provide enough love and attention to both her husband-baby and her child-baby. For his part, Maurice Pervin often feels that all is not perfect in his womblike existence with Isabel. The merging of his self into hers arouses in Maurice a fear of his lack of control over his own life, and a rage to "*compel* the whole universe to submit to him" (p. 356). When Cousin Bertie arrives, and captures Isabel's attention for the while, Lawrence describes Maurice's feelings of exclusion in terms of the nursery:

> A childish sense of desolation came over him. . . . He seemed shut out, like a child that is left out. . . . He fumbled nervously as he dressed himself, in a state almost of childishness. . . . He was fretful and beside himself like a child, he had almost a childish nostalgia to be included in the life circle. And at the same time he was a man, dark and powerful and infuriated by his own weakness. By some fatal flaw, he could not be by himself, he had to depend on the support of another. And this very dependence enraged him. (*CSS*, II, 357)

The impetus for "The Blind Man" came from a holiday in the Forest of Dean that the Lawrences took with their friends the Carswells in August 1918. Catherine Carswell—like Isabel Pervin a reviewer for a Scottish newspaper—busied herself with the care of her three-month-old son John, thus providing Lawrence with further opportunities to observe at close quarters the mother-child relationship that always fascinated and distressed him. Catherine's relations with her husband Donald may also have provided Lawrence with material, for the evidence suggests that Lawrence tended to view his friends' marriages through the same pre-oedipal lens through which he viewed his own. A letter to Catherine written the previous year addresses itself to some difficulties that Donald was experiencing in his law practice and to the resultant tensions in the Carswell household; it offers advice couched in familiar Lawrentian terms:

> *You* canot bear him again out of *your* womb. He must be born of himself out of his own unknown. And your sheltering of him would only *frustrate* his death and re-birth. Your cherishing of him in sleep would only *deny* him his right to real existence. Your desire to foster him and shelter him is *too strong*. It is an enclosing him in an old womb, like the woman who grips her child inside her and won't let it be born. (*CL*, I, 504)

Lawrence reiterates these remarks in another context in the 1918 letter to Katherine Mansfield announcing the completion of "The Blind Man" and referring to the "kind of incest" committed by Middleton Murry and by himself (*CL*, 565).

Indeed, it is likely that several real-life family constellations find their way into "The Blind Man." Paul Delany sees Lady Cynthia Asquith and her husband, along with author James Barrie (for whom Lady Cynthia became a secretary in 1918), as the "principal models" for the characters in this story.[17] More probably the Carswells, the Murrys, and the Lawrences themselves figure in it. If Bertie Reid draws his life from Donald Carswell—both are Scotsmen and barristers—then Lawrence breaks up the Carswell marriage, as he breaks up the Asquith marriage in *The Ladybird*, by pairing off the woman with a male figure bearing a distinct psychological resemblance to himself. The connection with Middleton Murry probably enters into the story as well, with Murry transposed into Bertie Reid: "Bertie's literary criticism, Oxford degree, short stature, and ambiguous station in the Pervin household all nicely fit the character of John Middleton Murry," one analyst of this story remarks.[18] Maurice's failed attempt to form a friendship with Bertie by the laying on of hands recapitulates Lawrence's abortive effort to swear Murry into a Blutbrüderschaft when the Murrys set up housekeeping near the Lawrences in Cornwall in 1916. The author stands apart from Maurice, and by suggesting how figuratively shortsighted this character is, in his faith in male friendship achieved, Lawrence simultaneously admonishes himself for a similar faith. But he reserves his condemnation and scorn for Bertie Reid, who is incapable of forming the kind of friendship sought by Maurice. It is Bertie whom Lawrence had in mind when he wrote to Katherine Mansfield, "I've done 'The Blind Man' the end queer and ironical. I realize *how* many people are just rotten at the quick" (*CL*, I, 566). One reason that Lawrence adopted the noli me tangere stance was that he felt his touch had been repudiated so often, by Murry and others. When Lawrence laments to Miss Mansfield that he has not met or formed the friendship that he desires he adds, "Excuse this sudden burst into dogma. Please give the letter to Jack. I say it to him particularly" (*CL*, I, 566).

Elements of the Lawrences' own marriage are also visible in the story. Frieda's constant hungering after her children and Lawrence's need for her nurturance as admitted in the "devouring mother" letter of the period suggest that Isabel and Maurice are based in part upon Frieda and Lawrence. With its focus on regression to a pre-oedipal, oceanic state, the story also conjures up images of Lawrence's early childhood. He names one of his characters Bertie, his own boyhood nickname, and Isabel relates to Bertie in the same way that she relates to Maurice: with solicitude mixed with contempt. Both men are child-men, returning at the end of the story to the Magna Mater, who sees the foolish and mistaken idealism of the one and the weakness and the fear of the other. She literally and figuratively has the last word. In another sense, Maurice is Lawrence's coalmining father, associated with darkness and the underground. In the stable, the disparity in size between Maurice and Bertie—one seems to grow and the other to shrink—implies a meeting between father and son; but theirs is a failed rapprochement, for the intellectual Bertie, like the man who created him, is incapable of accepting Maurice on his own terms. According to W. S. Marks, "the stable's Christian connotation suggests the Son's return to his lowly birthplace, where he must humbly acknowledge the all-too-human parent he has denied in favor of an ideal or heavenly one."[19] The search for a father does in fact motivate Lawrence's writing during his leadership period, but it leads to no acknowledgement of the human parent. Instead, the lack of an adequate father figure is compensated for by the creation of fictional fathers of mythic and heroic proportions, most notably Count Dionys in *The Ladybird* and Don Ramón in *The Plumed Serpent*.

Lawrence did not revise "The Blind Man" when he selected it for *England, My England* in 1921; the story appeared in book form as originally published in *The English Review* in July 1920. But the title story of that volume underwent a significant metamorphosis. Lawrence first wrote "England, My England" in 1915, after observing the relations among members of the Meynell family at Greatham, and published it in *The English Review* of October 1915. Over half the story concerns Evelyn Daughtry's war experiences and his destructive urges that find fulfillment in war. Marital discord figures importantly in this version, but the parent-child relationship is not its cause except as Evelyn's father-in-law maintains his hold over Evelyn's wife, Winifred.

When Lawrence revised the story in 1921, three years after the armistice, he was no longer so deeply concerned with war's destruction; instead, he concentrated on the necessity for male leadership to keep women within bounds. Harry T. Moore's statement that "the Egbert of the story was really a victim of the ostensibly benevolent paternalism that dominated the colony" of his father-in-law[20] actually applies not to Egbert but to his predecessor, Evelyn Daughtry, in the 1915 version. In the 1921 revision, Winifred's father embodies the patriarchal principle that

Lawrence had come to espouse. That the subject passionately engaged Lawrence is indicated by the space given in this story to the father's leadership: he devotes three paragraphs to a description of "the old, almost magic prestige of paternity" wielded by Godfrey Marshall, whose "smoky torch of paternal godhead" burns so brightly that the children must submit to his authority. Lawrence interrupts the flow of the story to denigrate any psychoanalytic interpretation of this father-child relationship—"Let the psycho-analysts talk about father complex. It is just a word invented."—and asserts the natural power of father over child until such time as the girls find another man to rule over them and the boys grow into their own male mystery (*CSS*, II, 314–15).

Winifred Marshall does not find a man like her father, however; unlike Godfrey Marshall, Egbert abnegates his own responsibility as a man and as a father and causes his wife first to flounder and then to overvalue her maternalism. In this story, as in "The Blind Man," the main character is a lost boy dependent on his mother-wife, and his feeling of isolation is exacerbated by the fact that there are other, "real" children demanding her attention. Egbert's relations with his wife are satisfactory, even idyllic, until Winifred bears these children; afterward, lacking direction from him, she becomes child-centered and he is gradually "excluded from the circle" (*CSS*, II, 310). Further, after her daughter's crippling accident Winifred becomes "purely the *Mater Dolorata*. To the man she was closed as a tomb" (p. 322). In fact, she and her father treat Egbert like another child rather than a husband, so that he goes for the doctor "like a boy sent on an errand" (p. 320). When the family moves to London, Egbert is homeless. He cannot even stay for long with his own mother because of what he feels to be her overbearing manner, so much like Winifred's "heavy, unleavened solicitude and care" (p. 324). Finally, "annulling the whole convention of the domestic home" (p. 325), Egbert accepts his drift toward death and goes forth in war to meet a German bullet.

The wartime setting appears again in "Monkey Nuts," a short story written at about the same time as the first version of *The Fox* and collected in 1921 for the *England, My England* volume. Like *The Fox* the story is set in Berkshire, and Harry T. Moore surmises that its female protagonist also is based on Violet Monk.[21] Joe, a young soldier, is afraid of Miss Stokes, and with justification, for she is a "devouring mother" type whose attentions threaten his life. When they go out for a walk he feels helpless against her force and driven almost to insanity by her domination. The pressure of her arm about him makes "all his bones rotten"

(*CSS*, II, 373), and the more he sees her the thinner he gets, as if she were gradually devouring him. Lawrence further suggests Miss Stokes's rapacity by the terms he chooses to describe her attraction to Joe: "She glanced him over—save for his slender succulent tenderness she would have despised him" (p. 370).

Joe's ambivalence toward Miss Stokes is both the hallmark of their relationship and the main feature of the story. He begins to meet her regularly, but rather ashamedly, as though he cannot help himself; moreover, he becomes increasingly despondent, until he finally blurts out, "There'll be murder done one of these days. . . . I don't want her" (p. 375). The ambiguity of the remark—who is to murder whom?—suggests the complex tensions at work. In a sense, of course, Joe does want her, and she in fact almost succeeds in regaining him: only Alfred's hand on his shoulder, reestablishing their male comradeship, prevents it. Alfred is forty to Joe's twenty-three, a fatherly type. Under Alfred's tutelage, Joe succeeds in vanquishing Miss Stokes, the enemy, and he feels more relief at her disappearance "even than he had felt when he heard the firing cease, after the news had come that the Armistice was signed" (p. 378).

The emphasis in these short stories on the battle against the "devouring mother" supports the impression one gains from all of Lawrence's works of the period, fiction and nonfiction alike: male leadership must be encouraged as a necessary corrective to female domination. The stories veer back and forth from a risk-taking intimacy and a commitment to separation and repudiation. Quite often the physical contact that would-be lovers or friends make with one another is as painful as a slap and felt as a degradation: the hand that Willy Nankervis insinuates between his wife's breasts in "Samson and Delilah," as he returns after sixteen years to appropriate the house; Hadrian's kiss; Maurice's tracing of Bertie's face; and, most dramatically, the tram girls' touches on John Thomas's back in "Tickets, Please!" that soon become outright blows. Even "The Horse-Dealer's Daughter," which portrays the deathly lure held by the mother-waters for a lost girl, and her fairy-tale rescue by a young doctor, ends on a note of fear for the viability of this new union. In a novella of the period, *The Captain's Doll*, the narrator explains that once people are able to be alone they must choose not to be alone: "[t]hat people should all be stuck up apart, like so many telegraph-poles is nonsense" (*CD*, 225). Yet the new relationship that Alexander Hepburn chooses with Hannele is very different from the one he experienced with his mother-wife (who was eight years older than he); it demands her honor and obedience and refuses her possessiveness.

The evidence suggests that in his own life Lawrence fought against his dependency on others, particularly on women, by trying to dominate them completely: Helen Corke speaks of Lawrence's "impossible demand" for "the absorption of my being in his,"[22] and a letter by Frieda relates an instance when her husband had "worked himself up and his hands were on my throat and he was pressing me against the wall and ground out: 'I am the master, I am the master.'" The frustration that Lawrence must have felt when his efforts at mastery were rebuffed—for Frieda's anecdote continues, "I said: 'Is that all? You can be master as much as you like, I don't care.' His hands dropped away, he looked at me in astonishment and was all right"[23]—are humorously revealed by a third anecdote, this one from yet another Magna Mater, Mabel Dodge (who once cried out to Lawrence about his wife that "she has mothered your books long enough. You need a new mother!"). As Mabel tells the story, she and Frieda were sitting in an orchard with apples piled about them, feeling "gay, indomitable, and fruitful like orchards. We were united for a moment . . . in a mutual assurance of self-sufficiency," when Lawrence dropped out of a tree, saw the women sitting there, moaned, "O *implacable* Aphrodite," and climbed back into his tree-haven.[24] Although the anecdotist's reliability is uncertain, her story takes its place among numerous others in memoirs and Lawrence's own fictional canon, all pointing toward the conclusion that "whoever has been mother-overwhelmed may grow to advocate the male ascendancy." Frieda Lawrence deserves the final word on the subject, as her husband's muse over the better part of his writing career and the woman he called a "devouring mother": "In his heart of hearts I think he always dreaded women, felt that they were in the end more powerful than men. Woman is so absolute and undeniable. Man moves, his spirit flies here and there, but you can't go beyond a woman. From her man is born and to her he returns for his ultimate need of body and soul. She is like earth and death to which all return."[25]

6. "The Italian Brutal Way": *Aaron's Rod*

Lawrence's fiction is characterized by a specialized vocabulary comprised of such words as *swoon, blood, flame, demon,* and *dark* used repetitively and incantationally. *Aaron's Rod*, written and revised in Lawrence's leadership period, pivots on a word not found to such a degree in any work before that period: this word is *alone*. The key note is struck early on, when Aaron Sisson explains to Josephine Ford why he has left his wife and children: "I want to be left alone. . . . I only want to be left alone" (*AR*, 63). The need for singleness that initiates Aaron's truancy also keeps him moving from place to place, as he seeks to break free from the entanglements that he invariably stumbles into. The same psychological dynamics are shown by the novel's other protagonist, Rawdon Lilly, who, more philosophical than Aaron, verbalizes the need that drives them both.

Each protagonist is single for most of the book, Aaron on the lam from his family, Lilly apart from his wife as she visits her people in Norway. The men feel that they must keep themselves at a distance from their women. Lawrence saw this distance as the sine qua non of the good marriage. Lilly articulates Lawrence's belief that married people who are "two in one—stuck together like two jujube lozenges" are hateful, and that "everybody ought to stand by themselves, in the first place—men and women as well. They can come together in the second place, if they like. But nothing is any good unless each stands alone, intrinsically" (*AR*, 85). These sentiments are familiar to readers of *Women in Love*: in effect, Lilly rephrases Birkin's star polarity dictum when he speaks of being "together and apart at the same time, and free of each other, and eternally inseparable. . . . You learn to be quite alone and possess your own soul in isolation—and at the same time to be perfectly *with* someone else"

(p. 99). Typical of Lawrence's novels is that no married couple in *Aaron's Rod* actually exemplifies this ideal. The Lillys come closest, but their acerbic remarks to and about each other suggest that all is not well at home, although Tanny's absence for most of the book deprives the reader of the real proof of the pudding. In Aaron Sisson's case, it is not clear whether his aloofness from his wife Lottie has stimulated her frenzied attempts to dominate him or whether he has developed this central isolation in order to protect himself from her domination. Whatever the sequence, Aaron's mental disengagement from his wife leads to a complete break between them and to the formulation of his important resolution: "Henceforth, life single" (p. 123). As Aaron's mind dissociates in his relationship with his wife—"a soul outside himself" (p. 122), "some central part of him stood apart from her, aside, looking on" (p. 156)—so he disassociates himself from life in general, in this period of recoil from attachments: at the Frankses' home, for example, he looks on at "the whole scene from the outside, as it were, from beyond a fence" (p. 137).

The psychological apartness felt by Aaron and Lilly is mirrored and reinforced by the actual physical, spatial positions that Lawrence has them assume throughout the novel. He presents Rawdon Lilly first in a box at the opera,[1] looking down at the audience and referring scornfully to public opinion about moral issues: Lilly is in his element, superior in two senses (*AR*, 44). Aaron Sisson, taken into the box by acquaintances, meets up with his soon-to-be blood brother and admires the view that the box affords (p. 50). The long and high view is taken by both men time and again: Lilly from his balcony over Covent Garden in London (p. 81); Aaron from a hillside overlooking Novara, Italy (p. 146); Aaron from his balcony in Milan (p. 176); Aaron and Lilly from Argyle's balcony in Florence (p. 232). And over and above all the characters, taking the longest and highest view, is Lawrence himself.

Escaping the frenetic atmosphere of wartime London, Lawrence fled in 1916 to primitive, otherworldly Cornwall, where, he wrote to Koteliansky, "it is almost as if one lived on a star."[2] But the real world infringed on Lawrence in the form of those military authorities who, suspecting him of spying for the Germans, threw him out and, in a sense, down. After 1917 Lawrence increasingly adopted a hands-off position toward others. In *Aaron's Rod* he draws attention to his own superior position as creator, picks fights with his reader, and thereby succeeds in keeping the reader at a distance: "If I, as a word-user, must translate [Aaron's] deep conscious vibrations into finite words, that is my own business. . . . These words are my own affair. . . . Don't grumble at me then, gentle reader, and swear at me that this damned fellow wasn't half clever enough to think all these smart things. . . . You are quite right . . . yet it all resolved itself in him as I say, and it is for you to prove that it didn't" (pp. 160–61).

Lawrence's attitude toward the reader is reflected in his protagonists' attitudes toward the other characters in the novel: offhand, uncaring, even rude. When Lilly is punched in the stomach by Jim Bricknell, after giving Jim good advice, he holds himself aloof, becomes noncommittal, and breaks off their relationship. When Lilly doesn't want a person around he says so straight out, whether that someone is Jim (p. 73) or Aaron (pp. 105–106). Similarly, Lawrence in his leadership period adopted a defensive and flippant tone, the implication being that the general public would only misunderstand him and figuratively punch him in the stomach—as it had upon reading and banning *The Rainbow* in 1915. So the novelist thumbs his nose at the reader, composing his book cavalierly and carelessly, almost defiantly so. He tells the reader in one sentence that Jim Bricknell is both "a tall big fellow" and "thin, though not too thin" (p. 23); in another, that Aaron "plunged away . . . walking slowly" (p. 21). His diction is clumsy at times—*subduedly* (pp. 65, 95), *friendlily* (p. 188), *shutupedness* (p. 220); his witty repartee decidedly unwitty (p. 189); at least one comparison—of Aaron to Miriam, Moses's sister (p. 265)—confusing (because he is Aaron, Moses' brother). Above all the novel shows little of Lawrence's characteristic power of description or feel for incident. As a result, *The Dial*, which considered serializing the entire book, eventually published only chapter fourteen, a fast-paced and exciting section.[3]

The reason for Lawrence's lack of care may be found in the novel itself: When Aaron writes a letter to Sir William Franks, detailing his repudiation of love, Lawrence remarks that "when a man writes a letter to himself, it is a pity to post it. Perhaps the same is true of a book" (*AR*, 256). Although Aaron does post his letter, and Lawrence his book, the fact remains that *Aaron's Rod* is the fictional highwater mark of the author's recoil from connection into isolation—from getting in touch to noli me tangere. The picaresque form of this novel is anticipated by Birkin's question in *Women in Love*, when he is alienated from both Hermione and Ursula: "Why strive for a coherent, satisfied life? Why not drift on in a series of accidents—like a picaresque novel? Why not? Why bother about human relationships?" (*WL*, 286). Lawrence considered *Aaron's Rod* to be "the end of the Rainbow, Women in Love line. . . . I am tired of Europe—it is somehow finished for me—finished with *Aaron's Rod*."[4] The picaresque quality of the novel exactly captures the chaos of Europe and the disintegration of human relationships.

The connections from which Lawrence fled in the early years of his leadership period were the ties to his motherland and his mother-wife. Like Aaron Sisson, Lawrence left England shortly after World War I and moved to Italy; like Rawdon Lilly, he lived apart from his wife for a time as she traveled to see her people. The desire for freedom from domestic entanglements is not exclusively masculine: Lawrence recognizes in *Aaron's Rod*, as in other works, that women too may feel tied down; here Lottie feels that Aaron has "an unfair advantage—he was free to go off. While she must stay at home with the children" (*AR*, 10). But Lawrence's imaginative sympathy goes out to the man, whose proper realm, so he believes, is society at large. Aaron explains to Josephine Ford that he left Lottie "in order to have a bit of free room round me—to loose myself" and twice states his desire for "fresh air" (p. 61). By implication, he feels smothered by his family. His travels to Italy take him in search of a new homeland and, on a more intimate scale, for a new home—both to be accepted on his own terms.

The picaresque quality of the novel ensures that Aaron will try out a variety of homes, most of which turn out to be unsatisfactory (Lawrence himself never owned a home until 1924[5]). At the Frankses' splendid and gracious home in Novara, Aaron feels the sting of their charitable hospitality (p. 129), as his creator was wont to do when presented with patronage of any sort; he escapes into their garden "like a bird dashing out of a trap where it has been caught: that warm and luxurious house" (p. 145). Moving on to Florence, Aaron rents a cold, dark room and thinks of "the cozy brightness of a real home—it has stifled him till he felt his lungs would burst. The horrors of real domesticity. No, the Italian brutal way was better" (p. 205). But even Florence, whose naked statues proclaim it the "town of men" (p. 208), is actually a town of women yearning to encage and domesticate the male. Capitulating to his sexual desire, Aaron forms a liaison with a *marchesa*, with whom he spends the night: predictably, the next morning he has trouble letting himself out of her house, with its "various locks and latches of the massive doors," and begins "to feel he was a prisoner, that he was locked in" (p. 265). He escapes one woman but falls prey to another, this time his *padrona*—a familiar bugbear in Lawrence's life as well as his art: safely back in his rented lodgings, he soon finds that he can't get out because of his landlady's locking and bolting of the doors, and once again he feels as if "the doors of Florence were trying to prevent his egress" (p. 266).[6]

One feels no necessity to look to Freud for an explanation of houses as female space, since Lawrence spells out the connection himself. An unpublished foreword to *Sons and Lovers*, written only seven months after

Lawrence had run away with Frieda, records his early feelings of gratitude toward the woman who had restored him to health and warns other men against taking Woman for granted:

> But if the man does not come home to a woman, leaving her to take account of him, but is a stranger to her; if when he enters her house, he does not become simply her man of flesh, entered into her house as if it were her greater body, to be warmed, and restored, and nourished, from the store the day has given her, then she shall expel him from her house, as a drone. It is as inevitable as the working of bees, as that a stick shall go down stream.[7]

Lady Ottoline Morrell puts another light on the subject when she notes that when Lawrence was frustrated at not being taken seriously as a propagandist he would turn "with drooping tail and [seek] refuge in Frieda, his 'dark abode.'"[8] And, as we have seen, Lawrence himself, during his leadership period, wrote of casting himself into Frieda's womb and then struggling to get out (*CL*, I, 565).

Lawrence's admission of a childish dependency upon Frieda suggests that in *Aaron's Rod* Lawrence not only divides aspects of himself between Aaron Sisson and Rawdon Lilly but that he also parcels out an important personality trait to Jim Bricknell. Jim brings into the novel the all-important motif of eating that on a basic psychological level signifies the search for nourishment that only a mother can provide. His oral needs are shown by his constant swilling of drink and stuffing of food, in a conscious effort to get fat, and by his repeated lament, "I'm not satisfied," when asked what is wrong with his friends' love for him. Lilly is disgusted by Jim's moaning for a woman's love and finds him singularly immature: "What gives you such a bellyache for love, Jim? . . . Why are you such a baby? . . . Would you like to be wrapped in swaddling bands and laid at the breast?" (*AR*, 53, 48). Josephine Ford, Bricknell's fiancée, understandably breaks off their engagement—later she will complain that most men seek women because they are afraid of being alone—and Jim, who always feels on the verge of "going to pieces," feels broken himself. Needing another mother substitute, he immediately attaches himself to Clariss Browning, a married mother of two, and at her mention of a good cook in her house pleads to be invited to dinner! (p. 56). Love brings Jim Bricknell an influx of energy that he feels in the pit of his stomach; without this kind of love transfusion he feels that he is dying (*AR*, 58). His needs are explainable in terms of the "sympathetic" mode of love that Lawrence describes in his two treatises on psychology, written at the same time as *Aaron's Rod*. We recall that according to Lawrence's theories, the very first center of preconsciousness that comes into being after birth is located in the solar plexus of the infant, beneath the navel:

> From this centre, the child is drawn to the mother again, crying, to heal the new wound, to re-establish the old oneness. This centre directs the little mouth which . . . seeks the breast. . . . In a measure, this taking of the breast reinstates the old connection with the parent body. It is a strange sinking back to the old unison, the old organic continuum—a recovery of the prenatal state." (*PU*, 21)

The child is dependent upon the mother for food and hence for life, yet every taking of nourishment is a kind of return to the womb of undifferentiated existence. Jim, with his overactive solar plexus, has needs that are not only insatiable but self-defeating. Yet he is aware only that he has this compulsion to keep his stomach "full and solid" (*AR*, 71) so that he feels "restored at the middle" (p. 74). In the words of *Psychoanalysis and the Unconscious*, he feels only "the aching abdomen of the severed child" (*PU*, 21).

In response to Jim's prattling about his solar plexus—for Jim does use that anatomic term—Rawdon Lilly gives him a lecture straight out of Lawrence's psychology books:

> Then you should stiffen your backbone. It's your backbone that matters. You shouldn't want to abandon yourself. You shouldn't want to fling yourself all loose into a woman's lap. You should stand by yourself and learn to be by yourself. Why don't you be more like the Japanese you talk about? . . . They keep themselves taut in their own selves there at the bottom of the spine—the devil's own power they've got there. . . . Why can't you gather yourself there?" (*AR*, 75)

"At the tail," Jim asks incredulously, and Lilly answers, "Yes. Hold yourself firm there." Jim thinks these remarks humorous, and Lawrence knows well how they must sound to the uninitiated. Nonetheless, in terms of Lawrence's theories on psychology, Jim Bricknell's psyche is unbalanced; for, as already noted, Lawrence believed that soon after the solar plexus begins to operate in the child, a second, complementary center comes awake, this one located in the lumbar ganglion at the back of the body. In contrast to the infant's cries for nourishment are its first harsh screams of defiance, which stimulate an electric charge from the lumbar ganglion; in contrast to the infant's molding or cleaving to the mother, this charge causes the child to kick and become rigid, thereby asserting its separation from the mother: "[i]t stiffens its spine in the strength of its own private and separate, inviolable existence. It will admit now of no trespass" (*PU*, 24). A primary circuit is now established between the two centers of consciousness, one at the front of the body and one at the back. With proper mothering, the circuit meets a polarized response from the caretaker so that, like finely tuned engine parts, the two family members hum along in exquisite sensitivity to each other. But if for some reason a circuit of consciousness is never fully established, the child will show "a certain deficiency in development, a psychic inadequacy" (*PU*, 44).

Jim Bricknell's behavior shows that he has been fixated at the oral stage of development (to use Freudian terminology), with its emphasis on assimilation—"the great intake of love and of milk, of psychic and physical nourishment" (*FU*, 76). Consequently, his lumbar ganglion has never awakened—or, perhaps, he has lost control of it—and, the common parlance being precisely accurate, he shows no backbone. Without an active lumbar ganglion and a stiffened spine, he cannot walk properly; in fact, Lawrence has Bricknell stagger about "like a man with locomoter ataxy: as if he had no power in his lower limbs" (*AR*, 76). Much has been said of anal intercourse in the Lawrence canon, but little of the desire for independence from the mother that comes to a head in the so-called anal period of psychic development.[9] As important as genital potency was to Lawrence, and as often as he writes about tumescence, what was perhaps more important to him was the stiffening at the other side of the body, at the bottom of the spine or the "tail"—that is, "getting one's back up." The "Italian way" of love in which Birkin and Ursula (and Mellors and Connie Chatterly) presumably engage is not only buggery per se but also a generalized, pregenital rejection of the mother's enveloping love: in *Aaron's Rod*, as mentioned above, Aaron tries to catapult himself from the cozy but smothering domesticity of his English home into the "Italian brutal way" of living apart from women, self-reliantly. In an unpublished version of the love scene between Aaron and the Marchesa, which Lawrence said was "impossible" for him to alter (though someone did alter it), Aaron engages in something suspiciously like anal sex after feeling "the approach of [the Marchesa's] power": "his desire had an element of cruelty in it: something rather brutal. He took *his* way with her now, and she had no chance now of the curious opposition, because of the way he took her" (the Marchesa's "shyness or shame of what had been" is a good clue in a Lawrence work to the nature of the sexual act).[10]

The difference between Jim and Aaron is shown in the motif of communication that figures importantly in the novel. Lilly tells Aaron about an old regulation decreeing that if a husband leaves his family, as Aaron has his, the wife and children are immediately dispatched to him "like a forwarded letter"; but Aaron defiantly states that in that case he would just keep moving on (*AR*, 96). In contrast, Jim's behavior at the Lillys' Hampshire cottage elicits Lilly's contemptuous remark that "you haven't been here a day, but you must telegraph for some female to be ready to hold your hand the moment you go away. And before she lets go, you'll be wiring for another. *You want to be loved*, you want to be loved—a man of your years. It's disgusting" (p. 76).[11] By implication, a man of Bricknell's years should long ago have outgrown the need to hold a woman's hand and should now be proudly walking alone. Lawrence's connection between the ability to walk and the desire for independence from the mother, and his relating of this desire to the power "at the tail," are in strict accord with Freudian and neoFreudian thought.

Lawrence's theories about the delicate and necessary balance between the "sympathetic" action of the solar plexus and the "voluntary" action of the lumbar ganglion explain Aaron Sisson's puzzling illness in *Aaron's Rod*. In flight from his wife because she is smothering him—Eliseo Vivas is wrong to say that Lawrence fails "to elucidate an important point in which the reader is legitimately interested, the grounds on which Aaron leaves his wife and children"[12]—Aaron reluctantly gives in to the sexual enticements of Josephine Ford, Jim Bricknell's ex-fiancée, and as a result develops a vague, debilitating malady. His rather cryptic explanation to Rawdon Lilly—"If I had kept myself back, my liver wouldn't have broken inside me" (*AR*, 84)—does little to illuminate the exact nature of this malady, but Lawrence's theories make the diagnosis clear: overactivity of the psychic centers at the front of the body. According to *Fantasia of the Unconscious*, "[a]ny excess in the sympathetic dynamism tends to accelerate the action of the liver, to cause fever and constipation" (*FU*, 96). Presumably, Aaron's liver has "accelerated" to the point of breakdown; in fact, what worries Aaron most about his illness is that his bowels no longer work! (*AR*, 90). As the solar plexus controls assimilation and tends toward merger with the mother, so the lumbar ganglion controls excretion and tends toward rejection of and independence from the mother. Aaron's constipation signals the breakdown of his electrical circuits' polarized duality as a result of what he considers to be a kind of "jujube" relationship with Josephine. But clearly Aaron is a sick man even before the flare-up that almost causes his death: for he is always "withheld" and "retracting" (p. 89), like England herself, in which "everybody seems held tight and gripped, nothing is left free" (p. 195). Lawrence's frequent images of "anal retention" or constipation suggest that humankind's service to the love ideal has caused sickness to be endemic in this modern age.

Thus it can be seen that the emphasis on aloneness in *Aaron's Rod* is a reaction to the male's overreliance on the female for nourishment and support, life and health. Rawdon Lilly's disdainful comments about Jim Bricknell's childish need for mothering are turned against him by his wife's rejoinder—which he does not refute—that he himself has a woman to hold his hand (*AR*, 76). So Frieda must have railed at Lawrence, when he criticized Murry and others. Although Tanny is off the scene for most of the novel, her implied assumption of superiority obviously rankles her husband, stimulating his attempts at asserting his independence. These attempts take a curious form. When Aaron Sisson becomes so sick, Lilly takes him into his home and nurses him back to health: the rub-down that has occasioned so much commentary, much of it focusing on a homosexual relationship between the two men,[13] indicates that Lilly takes on maternal qualities, massaging Aaron "as mothers do their babies whose bowels don't work" (p. 90). Indeed, the entire chapter showcases Lilly's skills at the traditionally feminine arts of cooking, darning, and washing and reveals that by combining the "masculine" and the "feminine," Lilly feels himself to be "independent of outside aid" (p. 93). The chapter takes on special significance when one recalls Lawrence's near-fatal bout with influenza in the early months of 1919. Totally dependent upon Frieda's nursing—her "tender mercies," as he called them (*CL*, I, 581)—Lawrence fumed and fussed at and about his wife and threatened to split from her for good. Instead he split himself: into Aaron Sisson, deathly ill with influenza, and Rawdon Lilly, who nurses Aaron back to health. In this way, Lawrence—who excelled at the domestic arts but could not quite act as his own mother-nurse—did, in fantasy at least, become "independent of outside aid."

As Aaron recuperates, he and Lilly hold a discussion that will bond them together not "two in one—like jujube lozenges" but rather "together and apart at the same time." This discussion centers on woman in her maternal role. The vitriolic nature of their comments and the space devoted to the topic in this chapter (entitled "Low-Water Mark") and in the central chapter of the novel ("Wie Es Ihnen Gefällt," a summary in the narrator's voice) indicate the importance of the issue in Lawrence's life and art. Asked the innocuous question of whether he has children (he doesn't), Lilly launches into a tirade against the privileged position that women assume simply because they are able to have babies. Aaron, who does have children, resents the secondary role played by the husband: "When a woman's got her children, by God, she's a bitch in the manger. You can starve while she sits in the hay. It's useful to keep her pups warm" (p. 95). The two men in reaction to each other's complaints create sparks that cause a veritable explosion of their resentment. The resentment is undoubtedly Lawrence's own, since he was working on *Aaron's Rod* in April 1918 when Frieda went off to London, over her husband's objections, to visit her children—three in number, like Aaron's. Lawrence's jealousy toward Frieda's maternal attachments finds expression in Lilly's call for assertive manliness and a new relationship between men—reminiscent of Birkin's Blutbrüderschaft—to supplement marriage:

"Men have got to stand up to the fact that manhood is more than childhood—and then force women to admit it," said Lilly. "But the rotten whiners, they're all grovelling before a baby's napkin and a woman's petticoat. . . .

"And if they think you try to stand on your legs and walk with the feet of manhood, why, there isn't a blooming father and lover among them but will do his best to get you down and suffocate you—either with a baby's napkin or a woman's petticoat."

Lilly's lips were curling, he was dark and bitter.

"Ay, it is like that," said Aaron, rather subduedly.

"The man's spirit has gone out of the world. Men can't move an inch unless they can grovel humbly at the end of the journey."

"No," said Aaron, watching with keen, half-amused eyes.

"That's why marriage wants readjusting—or extending—to get men on their own legs once more, and to give them the adventure again. But men won't stick together and fight for it. Because once a woman has climbed up with her children, she will find plenty of grovellers ready to support her and suffocate any defiant spirit. Any woman will sacrifice eleven men, father, husbands, brothers and lovers, for one baby—or for her own female self-conceit."

"She will do that," said Aaron.

"And can you find two men to stick together without feeling criminal, and without cringing, and without betraying another? You can't.

One is sure to go fawning round some female, then they both enjoy giving each other away, and doing a new grovel before a woman again."

"Ay," said Aaron.

After which Lilly was silent. (*AR*, 95–96)

But Aaron is not ready to answer the call to discipleship in Lilly's remarks and cannot refrain from deflating Lilly, as Jim Bricknell had done when he literally knocked the wind out of the man. Although, thanks to Lilly, Aaron's lower spine is working again and he has gotten back on his own legs, he is irritated by the implied superiority and self-sufficiency in everything that Lilly does, and snarls to him that he's "the idol on the mountain-top, worshipping [him] self" (*AR*, 100). Since Tanny makes similar remarks to him, Lilly understandably retorts that "you talk to me like a woman, Aaron" (pp. 100, 104). With characteristic restraint, Lilly waits for Aaron to recognize and accept the bond: preparing to leave England, he tells Aaron, "I'll write to you an address that will always find me. And when you write I will answer you" (p. 103). One best gauges the significance of these promises by setting them in the context of Lawrence's continual traveling after 1919, when he was "out of touch" with England a good portion of the time.

Aaron does write and Lilly does answer: they are the only true communicants in the book. But in order to commit himself fully to the principle of lordship that Lilly articulates, Aaron must first see that the problems with women that he and Lilly share are particular neither to their unique personalities nor to their marital situations but rather are symptomatic of a widespread, even international sickness in society. His travel between England and Italy and his conversations with people of different class, station, and sexual proclivity show him the universality of maternal domination and destruction. Lady Franks, for example—like her appropriately named she-dog Queenie, who "apparently fattened on the secret detestation of the male human species" (*AR*, 149)—feels secure in her role as ruler of society; her attempt to convince Aaron to go back with his wife is an attempt at "the restoring of woman to her natural throne" (p. 143). Meanwhile she keeps the fiery male-spark in her own husband safely contained, or caged. She tells Aaron that Sir William needs calm and rest, chiding him by implication for overstimulating her husband the night before with provocative conversation about Lilly. When she leaves the room, Aaron looks in the fire and muses, "Behind these iron gates of curly iron the logs burned and flickered like leopards slumbering and lifting their heads within their cage. Aaron wondered who was the keeper of the savage element, who it was that would open the iron grille and throw on another log, like meat to the lions" (pp. 149–50).

The "savage element" is also "kept" by women in the middle classes: the Marchese complains that in the bourgeoisie the husband is the horse and the wife the driver. The husband loves the direction she affords, and the abdication of his responsibility for his own life: "he feels so good, like a good little boy at her breast. And then there are the nice little children. And so they keep the world going" (pp. 236–37). Always the connection is made between the domination of the mother in the family group and the sad state of society at large. The two chapters in which Aaron returns to his home with Lottie are entitled "The Pillar of Salt" and "More Pillar of Salt." These titles refer to the disintegration of Aaron's family life and connect it, via the biblical reference, to the disintegration of society, the need to flee that society, and the danger (for Lottie's husband rather than Lot's wife) of looking back rather than ahead. Set just after the first world war, *Aaron's Rod* takes constant note of the conditions that have changed because of the war: the food no longer available, for instance. But the war marked the end of less tangible things as well—the old kinds of relationships between people. Maternal protectiveness was shown up by World War I as a completely inadequate means of salvation for the soldier on the front (so Lawrence states in his essay, "The Risen Lord"). Therefore, family groups can only play at keeping the world going; they are actually a dead horse. Likewise Sir William Franks and the kind of life he represents—philanthropic and genteel—are old and "breaking up" (p. 140); like the Beveridges in *The Ladybird*, he lives by an outdated creed.

Lawrence draws the connection between Sir William's love-for-mankind ideal and his need for mothering when Sir William gets a medal for his humane war efforts pinned over his middle. "Almost directly over the pit of my stomach.... I hope that it is not a decoration for my greedy *appetite*," he jokes (p. 136); but the joke is not funny to Lawrence, who suggests by the incident that Sir William's largesse is the result of a desire to be loved as great as Jim Bricknell's. There is little actual nourishment in any of the love relationships shown in this novel. Sir William's philanthropy is not always well received: "even the honey of lavish charity had turned to gall in the Italian mouth" (p. 152). Lottie's continual opposition to Aaron nauseates him (p. 154), and woman, in turn, sickens of her diet of man, "driven mad by the endless meal of the marriage sacrament" (p. 163). The devouring nature of loving and being loved is perhaps most clearly expressed by the Marchese, who complains that there is something in the relationship between him and his wife "which bites us, which eats us within . . . drives us, and eats away the life—and yet we love each other, and we must not be separate" (p. 235).

The land of milk and honey was sought long ago by Moses and Aaron, but the promised land they found has become a Sodom and Gomorrah. Lawrence's Aaron, with Lilly as brother-guide, seeks a new world to replace and improve upon the one breaking apart in war. As noted earlier, Lawrence was especially rankled by the wartime use of women in traditionally male jobs, a practice that he relegated to Sodom.[14] But the old Judeo-Christian world also asserted the centrality of woman, "particularly as mother" (*AR*, 154); and to Lawrence the assuming of the *female* activities by the female also resulted in the devouring of her young. The new world that Lawrence seeks in his leadership novels is in two senses outside the pale of modern civilization, in the unfenced and primitive societies of swarthy Indians.[15] "I can't do with folk who teem by the billions," Lilly thinks when caring for Aaron in his illness. "Only vermin teem by the millions. Higher types breed slower. I would have loved the Aztecs and the Red Indians. I *know* they hold the element in life which I am looking for—they had living pride" (p. 92). Breeding mothers and the overvaluation of children create the teeming masses—vermin—that Lilly (and Lawrence) excoriates. "Higher types" breed slower because they value singleness rather than massness, and it is this emphasis on proud singleness in any relationship that Lawrence finds particularly nourishing.

During the time when Lawrence lived in Italy, the Fascist order had not yet been established, but as *Aaron's Rod* shows it was well on the way, with constant street fights as heralds. In a letter of January 1921, Lawrence wrote, "If I knew how to, I'd really join myself to the revolutionary socialists now. I think the time has come for a real struggle. That's the only thing I call for: the death struggle. I don't care for politics" (*CL*, II, 639). In his novel, Lawrence through Lilly articulates an ideal of leadership that is divorced from politics and connected to a hatred of women. Through Lilly's brother-disciple, Aaron, Lawrence indicates the appeal of this ideal to the common man. Aaron muses that if he has to give in to something "then it should be to no woman, and to no social ideal, and to no special institution. No!—if he had to yield his wilful independence and give himself, then he would rather give himself to the little, individual *man* than to any of the rest. For to tell the truth, in the man was something incomprehensible, which had dominion over him, if he chose to allow it." Then Aaron lies "pondering this over, escaping from the *cul de sac* in which he had been running for so long, by yielding to one of his pursuers: yielding to the peculiar mastery of one man's nature rather than to the quicksands of woman or the stinking bog of society" (p. 280). It cannot escape notice that woman is mentioned first as the entrapper, the false shelter, and that submission to a male leader is considered only as a way out from woman, and then only reluctantly. The message of *Aaron's Rod*, in essence, is stay single and alone, advice which Lawrence believed to be a bad-tasting but restorative medicine: "That *Rod*, I'm afraid it is gentian root or worm-wood stem. But they've got to swallow it sooner or later: miserable tonicless lot" (*CL*, II, 687). As he finished the novel, Lawrence prepared to leave for America, where, so Mabel Dodge had indicated, the "Red Indians" formed a viable and thriving community.

7. A Lesson in Disillusion: *Kangaroo*

About to travel westward, toward the "Red Indians" and Mabel Dodge, Lawrence got last-minute cold feet and decided to head in the opposite direction: no doubt he was frightened off by the indomitable nature of Mabel herself, which she made extremely clear in her importunate letters. At any rate, Lawrence decided to enter America by the backdoor, heading east until he eventually arrived in San Francisco. This change in travel plans afforded him a brief sojourn in Australia that resulted in two novels: *Kangaroo*, written in an uncharacteristically short period of time in 1922, and *The Boy in the Bush*, a collaboration with an Australian nurse, Lawrence's contribution being a reworking of the manuscript that she sent him in 1923, when he was living in North America.

Kangaroo is undoubtedly the worst of Lawrence's novels: "nobody's choice for Lawrence's masterpiece," as Frank Kermode politely phrases it.[1] While *Aaron's Rod* can always be justified as a "picaresque novel," should justification be deemed necessary, *Kangaroo* must be called something other than a novel; Harry T. Moore writes that it is "no more a novel than *Also Sprach Zarathustra* and *Sartor Resartus* are novels."[2] Lawrence himself provides the descriptive term for his work when, in a five-page declamation to the reader, he insists that a novel should be first and foremost a "thought-adventure" (*K*, 285). A "thought-adventure" *Kangaroo* surely is, but a good story it is not. Lawrence tries to have his cake and eat it too, for he does believe that whatever else he is doing, he is writing a novel; but it is a "gramophone of a novel" (p. 286), as he admits, an amplification of the author's ideas on leadership. If the reader has other expectations for this book he or she will be sadly disappointed and soundly insulted. In the midst of a long "thought-adventure," during which Richard Somers speaks only to himself, the author sneers, "I hope, dear reader, you like plenty of *conversation* in a novel: it makes it so much lighter and brisker" (p. 288). The next chapter begins, "Chapter follows chapter, and nothing doing" (p. 289). Lawrence is impatient with us for expecting novelistic conventions and explains that since we *know* things must be happening in the external lives of his characters, we don't have to be told who is brushing her hair or who is out fishing. Besides—and here Lawrence's thumb is at his nose—"if you don't like the novel, don't read it" (p. 290). This flippant attitude marks *Aaron's Rod* and *Fantasia of the Unconscious* as well.

Readers of this novel, whether or not they like it, will find in it the same issue of independence from the mother that informs Lawrence's other works, especially those of his leadership period. All during the war Lawrence had tried to leave England, but he had had to rest content with cutting his attachment through words, in letters and literature. In *Women in Love*, Birkin says that love for England is "a damnably uncomfortable love: like a love for an aged parent who suffers horribly from a complication of diseases for which there is no hope" (*WL*, 376); Gerald responds, "Isn't he angry with his mother country!" (*WL*, 377). Paul Delany accurately states of Lawrence that "if in [*Sons and Lovers*] he had fought free of his devouring mother, in *Women in Love* he was similarly casting off the incubus of a devouring mother country."³ One might add, too, the mother continent, for in a letter of October 1921 from Sicily, Lawrence refers to Europe itself as a dying mother (*CL*, II, 665). But the feeling for the "aged parent," as Birkin perceptively notes—drawing, of course, on Lawrence's feelings as his mother lay dying of cancer in 1910—is not unmixed. Thus as Richard Lovat Somers cuts free from his homeland in its death throes, and sets off for the new country of Australia, "he [feels] a long navel string fastening him to Europe, and he want[s] to go back, to go home" (*K*, 15).

Once Somers puts some distance between himself and Europe he begins to revel in his new-found freedom from the past. As in *Aaron's Rod*, the motif of letter-writing expresses this freedom: "he wished that every mail-boat would go down that was bringing any letter to him" (*K*, 153). Similarly Lawrence wrote to Koteliansky from Australia, "We don't know one single soul. . . . I could live like that forever: and drop writing even a letter: sort of come undone from everything" (*CL*, II, 712). The Lawrences did indeed lead solitary lives during their stay in Australia, but Lawrence recognized that even a "thought-adventure" of a novel cannot go far with only two people; so he invented neighbors and friends for

Somers and thereby provided opportunities for "plenty of *conversation.*" These conversations sometimes turn on the matter of Australia in its relationship to England, with England as the motherland and Australia, its colony, as the child. When a friend, William James, asks Somers his opinion of Australian independence from the British empire, Somers replies in terms of escape from the "devouring mother": "[i]t might do her good if she were thrown entirely on her own resources. You've got to have something to keep you steady. England has really kept the world steady so far. . . . Now she's not keeping it very steady. And the world's sick of being bossed, anyhow. Seems to me you may as well sink or swim on your own resources" (*K*, 58). These sentiments apply as well to Lawrence's male characters in their relationships with women as they do to Lawrence himself in his lifelong attempt to be kept steady on the one hand and to fight free from domination on the other.

Though *Kangaroo* is ostensibly about politics, neither Somers nor his creator really cares much for the subject (*K*, 59). Lawrence did observe firsthand the opposition of the Returned Servicemen's League to the Australian Communist party. However, the important conflict in the novel is not between the Diggers and the Socialists, rival political factions, but rather between Richard Lovat Somers and his wife. Discussion of politics with William James and his brother-in-law Jack Calcott is especially meaningful to Somers because it signals his escape into a realm of activity outside Harriet Somers's bailiwick. To Harriet, in turn, Somers's interest in politics is only "a bit of little boy's silly showing off" (*K*, 93), and the more she chafes at his independent, exclusionary activity the more he is determined to keep it "out of her sphere." Somers recognizes that his wife sees his forays into politics as a betrayal of her love rather than as a supplement to it, and in dreams he identifies Harriet with his dead mother, his sister, and all the other "devouring mothers" he has known, who cannot allow their man a separate existence. Yet he needs to be "kept steady" just as he resents "being bossed," to use his own phrases concerning Australia's relations with England:

> He had an ingrained instinct or habit of thought which made him feel that he could never take the move into activity unless Harriet and his dead mother believed in him. . . . In the individual man he was, and the son of man, they believed with all the intensity of undivided love. But in the impersonal man, the man that would go beyond them, with his back to them, away from them into an activity that excluded them, in this man they did not find it so each to believe. (*K*, 95)

7. A Lesson in Disillusion   107

The continuation of this particularly Lawrentian conflict in *Kangaroo* shows that, Delany's comment notwithstanding, Lawrence had not fought free of his "devouring mother" with *Sons and Lovers*.

Harriet Somers's comments to her husband are surely taken right out of Frieda's mouth; certainly after Tanny Lilly's expostulations to her husband in *Aaron's Rod* they have a familiar as well as authentic ring to them. Harriet expresses her resentment of Somers's secretiveness about his conversations with William James by denigrating his worth and inflating her own: "You're not big enough, not grateful enough to do anything real. I give you my energy and my life, and you want to put me aside as if I was a charwoman. Acknowledge *me* first, before you can be any good" (*K*, 163). The narrator insists here that Harriet is right to feel this way—that her loving attentions to her spouse should get some credit for contributing to his success. Somers has broken the vital connection between husband and wife that is at the root of all purposive activity (a position Lawrence elaborates in *Fantasia of the Unconscious*). The author-narrator's understanding of a wife's feelings is overlooked by critics of Lawrence who would paint a one-sided picture of him as a confirmed woman-hater. Nevertheless, that Lawrence's sympathies lie more with Richard than with Harriet is made clear by her continual references to her husband as a child, references that put her in the shrewish company of women like Hermione Roddice in *Women in Love*. Somers in conference with Jack stimulates her remark that "men are like impish children—you daren't leave them together for a minute" (*K*, 298). Spoken to so often in this manner—made to feel "small"—it is no wonder that Somers calls himself "a detestable little brat" (p. 288) when he disagrees with people.

The central chapter in the novel, like that in *Aaron's Rod*, explains the nature of the conflict between a particular husband and a particular wife who also typify men and women in general. In "Harriet and Lovat at Sea in Marriage," Harriet Somers is Aphrodite the sea-mother, who suckles her husband though he thinks he is in command (*K*, 172). To Somers, Harriet is the nest or cup—that is, a comfortable haven to which he returns for sustenance. All of Lawrence's heroes—whether they are self-aware and articulate like Somers or instinctual and taciturn like Henry Grenfel, Ciccio, and Aaron Sisson—yearn for such a home. And many of Lawrence's heroines, even as they delight in their earth-motherly power over men, chafe at the burden of providing that home. Harriet, who rebels at Somers's independent activity, also cries, "I've done enough containing and sustaining of you. . . . It's almost time you left off wanting so much mothering. You can't love [live?] a moment without me"

(p. 173). Lawrence fully understands the difficulty that a strong woman like Harriet or Frieda has in crediting her husband with "the mystery and the lordship of the forward-seeking male" (p. 176) when he is master of no one and nothing and has antisocial tendencies to boot. Lawrence's and Frieda's isolation in Australia provides the basis for Harriet's analysis of Somers that "[h]e has nothing but her, absolutely. And that was why, presumably, he wanted to establish this ascendancy over her" (p. 177).

Ascendancy over the mother-wife is associated in all of Lawrence's leadership fiction with dark and violent gods. In order to convince Harriet of his masterliness in their relationship, Somers must first "break open his doors to this fearful god who is Master, and enters us from below, the lower doors" (p. 178). While the white gods of Christianity call the supplicant to an eucharistic love feast, the dark gods sound the call to blood sacrifice (*K*, 273, 289). That the call is first made in a chapter called "'Revenge!' Timotheus Cries" indicates that blood sacrifice is for Lawrence not only a ritualistic means of reinstituting the life flow or ensuring its continuance but also a way of getting back at oppressors. Somers himself is seething with violent emotions. He muses that "somebody will have to water Australia with their [*sic*] blood before it is a real man's country" (p. 75), the grammatical error (to which Lawrence was prone) allowing Lawrence to keep the sex of the sacrificial victim unspecified. Somers justifies his own exploding feelings by stating that "[s]ome men have to be bombs, to explode and make breeches in the walls that shut life in" (pp. 166–67); and the article that he reads in the Sydney newspaper about erupting volcanoes—which, some critics complain, shows that Lawrence's imaginative powers in this novel were slight, since he apparently copied an actual news article—gives Somers sanctions from the natural world for his destructive urges: later, Somers's anger at World War I is compared to "frenzied lava quiescent in his soul" (p. 265), the metaphor blurring the distinction between amoral nature and the human realm in which people have the responsibility to control their dangerous emotions. Lying beneath the surface are Somers's hostile feelings toward Harriet's domination, which he expresses in the violent image that their marriage knot "can never be untied; it can only, like a navel strig, be broken or cut" (p. 94). It is Harriet who is associated with "the walls that shut life in," through her desire to enclose a war memorial (pp. 193–94) and to make Australian homes over from shacks and bungalows, in which one can feel free, into suffocatingly domestic manor houses, each "a snug, cosy box to be secured inside" (p. 147). In a real sense it is Harriet whom Somers would like to bomb. However, perhaps because this novel is so nakedly a story of Lawrence and Frieda, Lawrence does not fell a tree on Harriet, as he does on Banford in *The Fox*, nor have her fall out of a window, like Mrs. Hepburn in *The Captain's Doll*, nor thrust a knife into her heart, a fate presumably suffered by the Woman Who Rode Away; instead he reserves the actual outpouring of killing violence for a stand-in figure, and a surprising one at that.

The nickname of the leader of the political group known as the Diggers gives the novel its title: Kangaroo, otherwise known as Ben Cooley. Like Rawdon Lilly, Ben Cooley mouths sentiments that are clearly Lawrence's own: about education being useless for most people, for example (*K*, 109). He too rails out against dominating women and goes a step further than Lilly in declaring that the true leader of humankind "would be a patriarch, or a pope: representing as near as possible the wise, subtle spirit of life. . . . Man again needs a father—not a friend or a brother sufferer, a suffering Saviour. Man needs a quiet, gentle father who uses his authority in the name of living life" (pp. 109–10). Declaring himself a son of man rather than of woman, Cooley offers Somers a spark of true leadership that promises to become a blaze. Harriet, though she is somewhat taken by Cooley, recognizes the danger that he poses to her and responds to him in a deceptively jocular fashion that leagues her with Lady Franks in *Aaron's Rod*, keeper of the male "savage element": "But I shall make myself into a Fire Brigade, because I am sure you will be kindling fires all over everywhere. . . . and I, poor domestic wretch, shall have to be rushing to put them out. . . . I really don't feel safe with fires anywhere except in fire-places and in grates with hearths" (p. 123).

Jack Calcott is attracted to the Digger movement because Kangaroo would be "a boss like a father who gets up first in the morning and locks up at night before you go to bed" (pp. 189–90). What he and Somers seek is patriarchal authority. Throughout *Kangaroo*, and especially in the chapter "Nightmare," Lawrence portrays society's post–World War I feelings of disintegration; his characters are motivated by the need to attach themselves to a figure who seems to care deeply about the welfare of others, and who can restore a sense of passion and quest to life. Writer James B. Reston, Jr., who has thoroughly researched the phenomenon of Jim Jones and the Peoples Temple, has been struck by the great similarities between Lawrence's depiction of the Diggers Movement and the real-life attraction of the Peoples Temple.[4] He notes that American society's confusion during the Vietnam era pushed many in search of commitment and identity: a good number of Jones's followers were from fatherless families, and willingly bowed to the authority of "Dad" Jones (for so he liked to be called). Jim Jones's recruitment process was similar to Kangaroo's: the questioner asked the potential recruit what he cared about, and whether he would like to see the breakup of society as currently constituted; touch was used to bind the two together (the importance of touch to Lawrence's thinking, as to healing and a feeling of well being in general, is well documented;[5] Jim Jones carried touch to the extreme of overt sexual acts with his followers); after the leap into commitment was made, the hierarchy reinforced obedience to authority by playing on the fear of anarchy. Reston was so impressed by these similarities that he added a section from *Kangaroo* as a frontispiece to his book on the People's Temple, its title—*Our Father Who Art in Hell*—indicating the patriarchal ideal of leadership espoused by Jones.

In *Kangaroo*, Somers finds the patriarchal ideal conspicuously absent in Australia. Here, for the first time in his travels, Lawrence saw a truly democratic way of life, and he didn't like it (*CL*, II, 707). The easy familiarity among people, the assumed equality, the casual touching—all this, for Somers, marks a return to the spirit of his childhood and severely depresses him (p. 31). Australia discourages one-upmanship even in its architecture: Sydney is built to sprawl because Australians want "none of your stair-climbing shams and upstairs importance" (*K*, 107). To Somers, as to Lawrence, democracy is allied with the ascendancy of woman, for its popularity signifies that the sympathetic mode of consciousness dominates: "When the flow [of psychic energy] is sympathetic, or love, then the weak, the woman, the masses, assume the positivity" (p. 309). When in the "Nightmare" chapter Somers blames the horrors of the war on English liberalism, which "proved a slobbery affair, all sad sympathy with everybody, and no iron backbone" (p. 230), he means literally that the failure lay in the activity of the lumbar ganglion at the lower back of the body. Somers's desire for his dark god to enter him by "the lower doors" can only refer to the anal portals that, so Lawrence's psychology books tell us, come under the child's control when the lumbar ganglion comes awake, sparking independence from the mother. Seen in this light, Somers's "quiescent lava" is an image of anal retention similar to Aaron's deathly constipation, got in service to the love ideal.

Lawrence seeks in politics what he seeks in all of life's activities: a balance of forces. The true leader would emit two great vibrations to his followers: "power, causing trust, fear and obedience" and "protective love, causing productivity and a sense of safety" (*K*, 306). This combination is what Jack describes when he speaks of a boss like a father who keeps strange bedfellows out of the house and locks up securely at night. Significantly the implicit assumption is that a woman is not able to provide both vibrations, while a man can; Rawdon Lilly, though not a political leader, shows evidence of this capacity to be both "fatherly" and "motherly" in *Aaron's Rod*. Willie Struthers, head of the Socialist party in Australia, is an unacceptable leader in *Kangaroo* because his political creed takes the "flaws" of democracy to their logical extreme. Like a mother who loves all her children, no matter how different they are, socialism preaches fellow-feeling among working men of all nationalities and colors:[6] These are the "niggers and dagoes" (for this is Lawrence's most bigoted, vitriolic, even hysterical novel) that Jack Calcott would keep out of his bed. Somers is momentarily tempted by Struthers's Whitmanesque extolling of comrades and thinks of comradeship—Gerald and Birkin call it Blutbrüderschaft—as a "new sacral social bond, beyond the family" (p. 200). But he ultimately looks elsewhere for his sacred community—what Ferdinand Tönnies in his classic (1887) distinction between types of societies termed a *Gemeinschaft* as opposed to a *Gesellschaft*[7]—since "[h]uman love, human trust, are always perilous, because they break down . . . ; because of the inevitable necessity of each individual to react away from any other individual, at certain times, human love is truly a relative thing, not an absolute" (*K*, 201). The breakdown of Lawrence's trust in human beings can be charted in the evolution of his views on Whitman from his second essay on the poet, written in 1920, where he praises Whitman's love of comrades (*SM*, 263), to his third essay, published in *Studies in Classic American Literature* (1923), where he takes him to task for his merging (*SCAL*, 169–70 [see chapter nine]).

The fascistic political leader in *Kangaroo*, Ben Cooley, seems to emit two vibrations: he mouths the appropriate Lawrentian sentiments about the need for an authoritative patriarch and shows maternal protectiveness as well because "[h]is presence was so warm. You felt you were cuddled cosily, like a child, on his breast, in the soft glow of his heart and that your feet were nestling on his ample, beautiful 'tummy'" (*K*, 117). He seems to be the most highly evolved of humans. Yet before long Kangaroo gives evidence that he has too much self-willed love for humankind—that, in fact, he is just a "devouring mother" in men's clothing. When Somers tells Cooley of his visit with Willie Struthers, Cooley is infuriated by this seeming betrayal of his love and calls Somers "a perverse child" (p. 210). Somers argues that Kangaroo ought to encourage the Socialists to foment the revolution so that the Diggers can step in and establish "benevolent fatherly authocracy" (p. 211), and again Cooley calls him "a wayward child! Like a wayward child!" Then Cooley grabs Somers to his breast and squeezes him to the point of near-suffocation, an action that allies him with all the smothering mothers in the Lawrence canon and that elicits from the man-child a typical Lawrentian response: "He ought to die!" (p. 212).

Like Banford in *The Fox*, Miss Frost in *The Lost Girl*, Carlota in *The Plumed Serpent*, and other witches, Kangaroo does die—must die, Lawrence would have it, for the good of society—killed seemingly by the mere wish that he should die. After being struck by an assassin's bullet, Kangaroo withers away because Somers has refused him a love-transfusion in the form of a commitment to him and his creed. Kangaroo cannot see that for Somers he offers no real alternative to the "treacly democratic Australia" (p. 62) that catches people like flies in oozy ointment, till they suffocate in "unctuous sympathy" (p. 285). Somers had tried to explain to Kangaroo that his love was a loathsome syrup, and that he was wrong to want "to carry mankind in his belly-pouch, cosy," instead of letting people stand "hard" and "separate" (p. 213). "Taking the lumbar stance," as Frank Kermode so aptly puts it, Somers "won't give in to the solar plexus."[8] Kangaroo's failure to heed Somers, and his cold dismissal of him, turn him into a repulsive and frightening piece of inhumanity whose belly-pouch has, as it were, changed in a flash from a cozy nest to a suffocating coffin. Lawrence expresses Somers's fear of Kangaroo in his feeling that he is trapped in Kangaroo's house: "it seemed like a dream, as if it were miles to the outer door, as if his heart would burst before he got there, as if he would never again be able to undo the fastening of the door" (p. 215). The reference to a dream stirs up in the reader archetypal fears of entrapment familiar to all dreamers; and the reference to the house—especially in its relationship to a belly-pouch—reminds one of Aaron Sisson's fear of entrapment by women in their houses; in fact, Richard Somers—who in a sense is only Aaron a few leagues over the sea—dreams he is in a European city, "staying in a big palazzo of a house [which describes both the Frankses' home in Novarra and the Marchesa's in Florence]—and he struggled to get out" (p. 353).

Like Edgar Allan Poe, about whom he wrote essays, Lawrence had a great fear of suffocation or premature burial (undoubtedly caused in part by the physiology of tuberculosis, with its choking phlegm). He refers to Poe in *Kangaroo*, when Somers recalls that during the war he had felt like the man in "The Pit and the Pendulum," where "the walls come in, in, in, till the prisoner is almost squeezed" (p. 263). Surely Lawrence's fear of suffocation and his stress on it in his fiction are related to the problems that he saw in Poe's own psyche: a tendency toward incestuous merger with a woman that leads to tuberculosis and death (see chapter nine).[9] The "kind of incest" that Lawrence wrote of in 1918, in which man seeks entry into and then struggles out of his "devouring mother's" womb, is relevant to Somers's ultimate rejection of Ben Cooley in *Kangaroo*. However, as George Ford notes, "Lawrence does not talk about symbols; he creates the experience."[10]

Richard Somers strikes out for newer, more promising territory as the novel ends. With Jim Jones's followers it was a different story. As Jones's charisma diminished in the late 1970s, a dilemma was posed for several Peoples Temple members: once commitment becomes moot and turns to dissonance, what does one do about the situation? The inhabitants of Jonestown did not have an easy exit from the armed camp in its hostile jungle setting. Besides, Jones's manipulation of potential and actual defectors, playing on their guilt for wishing to leave him, was apparently very effective.[11] Ultimately more than nine hundred people, including Jones himself, committed murder and/or suicide at their leader's bidding, gestures of allegiance but perhaps also of despair. In these acts, Jim Jones's desire for domination reached its perverse fulfillment.

Somers, in contrast, recognizes that Cooley's love ideal of leadership is a menacing octopus, a many-armed monster lying in wait beneath the womb-waters to strangle the unwary (there are seven references to octopi [on pp. 270–71, 335].) By repudiating Cooley, "for the moment [Somers cuts] himself clear. . . . If no other ghastly arm of the octopus should flash out and encircle him" (p. 271). Somers succeeds, then, in cutting the navel-string with Kangaroo, since he cannot simply untie it; the marriage knot with Harriet remains firm. (In real life, of course, Lawrence separated from Frieda on several occasions, but like the octopus she seemed always to have another arm.) The connection with Somers's motherland is about to be severed at the novel's close, as Lawrence's was already severed, since he wrote this last chapter in New Mexico and revised the rest of the novel extensively.[12] The novel began with Somers's yearning for Europe, and his feeling that a navel-string fastened him there; it ends with his departure for America that signals, he realizes, a break with his past: as the ship pulls out and he holds onto the umbilical streamers, he feels "another heart-string going to break like the streamers, . . . leaving his own British connection" (p. 365). At the time, Lawrence did not know that with Mollie Skinner's manuscript he would have yet another chance to find in Australia and his "British connection" the fulfillment of his leadership ideal. All he knew was that his travels outside of England had so far brought him no closer to his ideal society: he wrote to Mary Canaan from the R.M.S. *Tahiti*, sailing to San Francisco, "Travel seems to me a splendid lesson in disillusion—chiefly that" (*CL*, II, 713).

8. The Outlaw Hero: *The Boy in the Bush*

Lawrence must have been delighted to read in September 1923 the manuscript sent to him by Mollie Skinner, a nurse he had met in Australia. Here, ready-made and at his suggestion, was a rollicking adventure story, based on the life of Mollie's brother, which possessed in raw form all the elements of a good Lawrentian exposition on heroes and hero-worship while freeing Lawrence from a task that, judging from *Aaron's Rod* and *Kangaroo*, was becoming onerous to him: the creation and sustaining of plausible and interesting plots, characters, and dialogue. Lawrence reworked the manuscript, called by Miss Skinner *The House of Ellis*, and had it published as a collaboration between them under the title *The Boy in the Bush*. The novel has not been widely read, probably because of its collaborative nature. It deserves to be well known, not only because it is an exciting and colorful book in itself but also because its Lawrentian elements—obvious to any serious reader of Lawrence, without reference to original manuscripts and typescripts[1]—show it to embody an important stage in the evolution of Lawrence's ideas on leadership.

The novel should actually be called *The Man in the Bush*, thematically if not euphoniously, for the point of it is that Jack Grant, the protagonist, matures from boyhood to manhood by going through the crucible of experience in the outback. Indeed, one of Lawrence's major changes in Mollie Skinner's manuscript, so he wrote to her in November 1923, was "to make a rather daring development, psychologically. You may disapprove." Miss Skinner disapproved to the point of tears (*CB*, II, 272). What Lawrence had done was to make her book his, by defining manhood as independence from the "devouring mother" and by finding in the natural world sanctions for revenge against that figure.

Unlike Lawrence, Jack Grant is very young and in excellent health, but he comes to Australia from England much as Lawrence himself did, as a pariah to society. And the problems that Jack has with women, problems that are adumbrated early in the novel, are similar to Lawrence's. Only a reader who has read much of Lawrence, in fact, is prepared for the martial perspective from which Jack views his relationship to the three young women whom he meets soon after landing in Freemantle. These women, fluttering around Jack and teasing him, are so frightening to him that they seem to take on maenadic qualities rather like the tram girls in the 1918 story "Tickets, Please!" (reportedly based on an incident from Lawrence's youth[2]): "With girls and women he felt exposed to some sort of danger—as if some were going to seize him by the neck, from behind" (*BB*, 27). A confrontation over a necktie becomes a life-or-death struggle. The three girls, nieces of Jack's Australian contact, barge in on Jack when he is dressing in preparation for an evening concert, and, along with their Aunt Matilda—obviously the "heavy" in this story, in two senses—try to take over the tying of his tie. As Mary Ellis pushes herself on Jack, his knees "[feel] weak and his throat strangled" (p. 28). She finishes the job "just as he [is] on the point of suffocation" (p. 29). Then at the concert the women press against him again, arousing in him not sexual desire but rather "a smouldering desire for revenge" (p. 31). Back in his room, which cannot be locked, Jack barricades the door with a heavy chair lest he be smotheringly assaulted yet another time; then he muses how "[h]e hated women. He hated the kind of nausea he felt after they crowded on him." Clearly this world of women is hostile territory so far as Jack Grant is concerned.

The next day Jack heads for Wandoo, the outback home of the Ellises, where he is to live and work. For Lawrence the living is more important than the working: as George Ford notes, Lawrence often skimps on showing us his protagonists at their jobs; instead, "home, with its loves and hates, is the setting of most of Lawrence's novels."[3] At Wandoo Jack feels instantly relieved to see that the cubbyhole where he is to sleep isn't "stuffy" but is, rather, "rough and remote" (p. 46). If it has the disadvantage of being in a household filled with women, including those Ellis girls, then Jack can always get rougher and more remote by heading farther out into the bush to clear some land with Tom, the Ellis boy who quickly becomes his comrade. Indeed, it is only when he is off in camp with Tom that Jack feels totally at ease (pp. 93–94), in scenes reminiscent of Cyril and George's idyll in *The White Peacock*. After the death of Dad Ellis, a rather ineffectual patriarch at Wandoo, Jack and Tom ride away into the colony for a whole year, glad "to be men out alone in the world, away from the women and the dead stone of trouble" (p. 205), and "beyond all fences" (p. 239). Here, on the road together, they can occupy the transient cabins built in what Aaron Sisson would call "the Italian brutal way," with none of the overly upholstered domesticity that Lawrence detested. As shown time and again in his work, Lawrence, like Jack Grant,[4] had "a dread of solid houses of brick and stone and permanence. There was always horror somewhere inside them" (p. 206).

In the course of his friendship with Tom, Jack comes to see that they are not in fact equals: that Tom is fit only to be a follower, while Jack is not only "one of the few that are masters" (*BB*, 219) but also "something of a hero" (p. 332). One reason for this disparity is that Tom is fixated on his mother. Tom is a Heathcliffe-like figure who as a child was brought back to Wandoo by the long-wandering Dad Ellis, wrapped in a blanket, his maternity a mystery. Tom is obsessed by this mystery, an obsession disparaged by Jack: "It was queer the way he hankered after his own real mother. Jack, for his part, didn't care a straw who was his mother's relation and who wasn't. But you would have thought Tom lived under a Matriarchy, and derived everything from a lost mother" (p. 235). For his part, Jack does everything in his power to sever the cord between himself and his own mother, who, from the way she is described—"And she was like a wild sweet animal. Always the sense of space and lack of restrictions, and it didn't matter *what* you did, so long as you were good inside yourself" (p. 6)—must qualify as one of the best parents, by Lawrentian standards, in all of his fiction. The letters from home fill Jack with the "nausea" that readers of Lawrence's leadership fiction have come to expect, and much is made of Jack's indifference to England, his feeling of being cut off from everything there, and his writing to his mother only out of a sense of duty (pp. 96–97). One notes that he has no trouble in writing to his male friends back home.

Jack's relationship with his father is key to an understanding of his subsequent growth into manhood and leadership. In a sense he is as obsessed with his father, who is "lost" to him, as Tom is with his mother:

> This had been a thorn in his consciousness since he was a child. Best get it out now. Because the fear of *not* loving his father had almost made him hate him. If he ought to love him, and he didn't love him, then there was nothing to do but hate him, because of the hopeless obligation. But if he *needn't* love him, then he needn't hate him, and they could both be in peace. He would leave it to his Lord. (p. 175)

This Lord is quite as mysterious to Jack (and to the reader) as Tom's mother is to Tom and occupies a more central position in the novel both literally (Jack first ruminates upon him midway through his adventures) and figuratively. The Lord that Jack trusts issues dark commands antithetical to those his aunts, following Jesus, had issued, "to be a good, loving little boy" (p. 174). When Jack agonizes over his uncivilized, antisocial desires to kill Easu, one of the Ellis cousins, or to repudiate his father, one is reminded of Lawrence's early remark to Jessie Chambers that "[t]he chapel system of morality is all based upon 'Thou shalt not.' We want one based upon 'Thou shalt.'"[5] Jack's trust in his dark god establishes a relation with a new father, wilder than the old (who is a pallid gentleman), beyond good and evil. His search for a paternal birthright is conveniently suggested by elements probably in the original text: the biblical allusions to Jacob and Esau, with Jack (Jacob) continually fighting with Easu (whose real name, rather unsubtly, *is* Esau), and by the "lost legacy" motif of romance that helps to establish Jack as a man to be reckoned with.

There are always smother-mothers to spare in Lawrence's works, as there seem to have been in his life; what Lawrence greatly lacked was a male authority figure. Early in his childhood his own father had been dispossessed by his mother and was rarely to be found in the house. That the Lawrence children neither respected nor loved him was a "thorn in his consciousness" for D. H. Lawrence as the similar situation is, in *The Boy in the Bush*, for Jack Grant. John Arthur Lawrence is rarely mentioned in Lawrence's letters, although the man lived until 1924; from the lack of attention accorded him, one would think him unimportant to his son. In fact, Lawrence once said to Jessie Chambers, "in a tone of deep chagrin, 'I've never really had a father.'"[6] Having been failed by his real father, Lawrence was forever in search of an ideal father who would not disappoint him. Paul Delany points out that the male friends with whom Lawrence either had homoerotic experiences or fantasized them were older than he—such friends as Jessie Chambers's brother Alan and the Cornish farmer William Henry Hocking. To Delany, these fantasies of "being held and soothed by a strong, usually older man . . . might have more to do with his need for security and affection than with any active homosexuality."[7] Certainly in his adult years Lawrence sought relationships with men he could look up to, but one by one he discarded them after finding faults in their personalities. Actual political leaders and bureaucrats in England, especially during the war, seemed namby-pamby or rigid. In his leadership fiction, Lawrence drew ever closer to picturing his ideal father, a figure who draws his power from Lawrence's antisocial tendencies.

From the early years of the war Lawrence felt himself to be an "outlaw" and a "desperado"—these self-descriptive terms, and variations thereof, are used often in his letters. In the manuscript provided by Mollie Skinner, Lawrence found the perfect setting for his feelings: the Australian bush of the 1880s, which signified for him what the sea signified for Melville and the western frontier for Cooper, an untamed territory over the border from stultifying civilization. The outback satisfied the emotional need expressed by Lawrence to Mountsier in early 1917: "I have *finally* decided that it is only possible to live out of this world—make a sort of Garden of Eden of blameless and fulfilled souls, in some sufficiently remote spot—the Marquesas Islands, Nukuheva. Let us do that."[8] With his killing of Easu (in "self-defense"), Jack in a sense removes the "thorn" from his consciousness as Grenfel removes his when the tree strikes Banford: both are "blameless but fulfilled souls." The dark god, with his "dark feelings" (p. 300), so possesses Jack in this act of blood sacrifice that Jack becomes himself a Lord of Death: the outlaw Cain, "with the dark unction between his brows" (p. 308). But how unlike Gerald Crich, another Cain, who has killed his actual brother and carried the burden of that death around with him until his own self-obliteration in the frozen wastes! Jack's battle with his rival nearly kills him, but, unlike the orderly in "The Prussian Officer," Jack comes back from death, restored by his "black, deep, male volition" to live and to assume authority and superiority. He emerges from the ordeal of this battle as a man, no longer anyone's "dear boy" (p. 311).

Lawrence in his leadership period brought to fruition his romantic attachment to what has come to be known as the Byronic hero. Against the Christian ideal of saintliness Jack Grant poses "the old heroic goodness of untamed men" (p. 338). Lawrence expressed through Jack his own admiration for the "indiscriminately bad" Roman emperors that he had read about in Gibbon, who "just did as they liked" (*CL*, I, 551, 550). After a long section of Australian dialogue that is undoubtedly pure Skinner, Jack thinks a thought, about the hoi polloi in the outback, that is pure Lawrence: "He wouldn't care if some tyrant would up and extirpate the breed" (p. 255). Sanctions for such behavior came for Lawrence from the animal world, since he could not find them in the modern human realm. Indeed, there are references throughout this novel to wolves and foxes, starting as early as Mr. George's suspicion that Jack himself might be a "wolf in sheep's clothing" (pp. 20, 21) and continuing until the end (as on p. 324). The notion of wildness cloaked in respectability, ready to jump out and attack—expressed in the familiar wolf-and-sheep image—appears in another familiar lupine figure, in reference to the character known as Gran: that figure is Red Ridinghood's grandmother. Lawrence mentions the Red Ridinghood folk tale in the education essays that he revised in 1920, where he states that the children's stories taught in school should not be all sweetness and light but should actually contain violent messages that the child can recognize instinctually—messages like the one conveyed in "Little Red Ridinghood," that a grandmother may have sharp teeth (*EP*, 626–27). In *The Boy in the Bush*, there is something "uncanny" about the Ellises' Gran (the adjective twice describes her [*BB* 75, 147]) as she sits on her bed behind a curtain, in a kind of sanctum sanctorum, "like Red Ridinghood's grandmother" (p. 71). In many Lawrence works, like *The Virgin and the Gipsy*, the Gran in sheep's clothing is a "devouring mother": as in fairy tales, the grandmothers (and stepmothers and landladies and witches and evil queens) are actually mothers at a remove, distanced by psychological processes that would defend the child against the fear of recognizing its hostility toward the mother while at the same time allowing the expression of that fear and hostility.[9] But in *The Boy in the Bush*, Gran comes to be seen by Jack as a wise woman who, in her admonition that one should be true to one's self, sticks up for "the sins that are necessary to life" (p. 335).

Jack Grant grows to be a Lawrentian hero because he comes to trust the streak of wildness in him that marks his self-sufficiency. Lawrence's explanation of why Jack does not like to dance goes far beyond dancing; it allies Jack with the animal world by explaining him in terms of that world:

> he always kept a certain unpassable space around him, a definite *noli me tangere* distance which gave the limit to all approach. It would have been difficult to define this reserve, Jack seemed absolutely the most open and accessible individual in the world, a perfect child. He seemed to lay himself far too open to anybody's approach. But those who knew him better, like Mrs. Ellis or his mother, knew the cold inward reserve, the savage unwillingness to be touched, which was central in him, as in a wolf-cub. There was something reserved, fierce and untouched at the very centre of him. (p. 258)

In *Education of the People*, Lawrence comments on the she-wolf legend, noting the difference between the mother animal and the mother human: the latter envelops her child in a kind of smothering love, but the former has an acute sense of the separation between mother wolf and

8. The Outlaw Hero 121

wolf-cub. Lawrence himself wishes that he had been suckled by a she-wolf—"It might have made a man of me"—and adds that "Romulus and Remus had all the luck. We see now why they bred a great, great race: because they had no mother: a race of men. . . . Alas, there isn't a wild she-wolf in the length and breadth of Britain" (*EP*, 623–24, 632–33). Lawrence saw "Little Red Ridinghood" as revealing the necessary repudiation, even cruelty, of mother toward child in order to allow the child to learn self-reliance and self-containment.

The Boy in the Bush, replete with wolf and fox images, also relies heavily for its animal symbolism on the horse, an animal used in "The Blind Man" (1920) to symbolize dark and powerful sexuality but not achieving its culmination until *St. Mawr* (1924), written after Lawrence had been horseback riding in New Mexico for many months. In terms reminiscent of Rawdon Lilly's expostulations to Jim Bricknell about standing on his own two feet and keeping taut "at the tail" (*AR*, 75), Jack astride a horse makes an important resolution:

> "Whatever I do, I'll never go despicable and humiliated about the legs and seat," said Jack to himself [thinking of Dad Ellis], as he pressed the stirrups with his toes and felt the powerful elasticity of his thighs, holding the live body of the horse between his muscles in permanent grip. And it seemed as if the powerful animal life of the horse entered into him, through his legs and seat, and made him strong." (*BB*, 236)

Jack Grant astride his horse is no Gerald Crich, keeping a steed under control to show the mastery of his mechanical human will over the animal's instinct. On the contrary, Jack learns from his horse how to be "a good animal" (to use Annable's phrase in *The White Peacock*); its powerful animality entering him through his "seat" is nothing other than Richard Somers's wished-for dark god entering through the "lower doors" of his body. Jack's resolve never to go "despicable and humiliated about the legs and seat" gains poignancy from Mollie Skinner's comment that her brother Jack, on whom this character is based, passed by Lawrence (they never spoke until the day Lawrence left) "broken by the war, his handsome legs dragging" (*CB*, II, 138). So too Lawrence restored potency to Cecily Lambert's brother Nip, home on convalescent leave from the war zone in East Africa, by transforming him into Grenfel the fox. One may even surmise that by attributing to the "seat" the source of wild, destructive power Lawrence helped to restore to himself some of the dignity that he lost during his callous rectal examination by the military authorities in England—a type of examination remembered by Somers with horror, rage, and the desire for revenge in the "Nightmare" chapter of *Kangaroo*.

Ultimately, Jack Grant's "horsiness" is directed against the women who suffocate him. His success in riding the wild stallion Stampede may be improbable by standards of realism, since he accomplishes it as a newcomer to Australia;[10] but it is symbolically appropriate, signifying to the onlooker Monica what Grenfel's killing of the fox signifies to March—that here is a man to be reckoned with. Astride Stampede, Jack shows

> a certain masterfulness that was more animal than human, like a centaur, as if he were one blood with the horse, and had a centaur's superlative horse-sense, its non-human power, and wisdom of hot blood-knowledge. [Monica] watched the boy, and her brow darkened and her face was fretted as if she were denied something. . . . The queer soft power of the boy was too much for her, she could not save herself. (p. 124)

As he gains confidence in himself, Jack brings down the women in his new life one by one, like ducks in a shooting gallery (or like hens; he muses about Aunt Matilda, "Great stout old hen, she had played cock-o'-the-walk long enough" [p. 333]). In the battle with Aunt Matilda for Mary's allegiance, his eyes are potent weapons: when he turns them on Mary, "something in her soul [falls] prostrate" (p. 267). Later, when Mary resists him, he fumes that she "ought to go down on her knees before the honour, if I want to take her" (p. 356). In this "one up, one down" writing period, as Herman Daleski so aptly calls it,[11] the woman's down is the man's up: Jack maintains that "he was not going down on his knees, not for half a second, not to any woman on earth, not to any man either. Enough of this kneeling flummery. . . . And fast and erect he would continue to stand." Indeed, at the simple thought of being brought down by women, Jack's muscles stiffen (p. 271). In reference to Monica he thinks, "It was not he who must bow the head. It was she" (p. 272). The either-or nature of this statement indicates that Birkin's star-polarity in *Women in Love* has become that satellite-disparity that Ursula feared.

The feistiness in Monica that in a sense attracts Jack to her, as it did Lawrence to Frieda, is the very quality that Jack seeks to subdue. And Monica, described at first as a panther, a wildcat, and a she-lion (pp. 24, 25, 27), relinquishes her female power and submits to Jack's will, accepting the fact that "she could never finally know him, and never entirely possess him. . . . *[S]he* would have to belong to *him*" (p. 318). Like other Lawrence heroines, Alvina Houghton and Kate Leslie among them, Monica feels saved by this relinquishing of her power to a "magical" man.

She differs from them in one respect. She actually fulfills the terms of ideal wifehood as Lawrence sets them down in *Fantasia of the Unconscious*: belief in the pioneering spirit of the husband; willingness to await his return to the home, and to follow where he leads; acceptance, as a reason for being, of the role of woman in relation to such a man (*FU*, 219). While other Lawrence novels are open-ended, with the wife in imperfect agreement with her husband (*Women in Love*, *The Plumed Serpent*, *Kangaroo*) or the couple separated (*Aaron's Rod*, *Lady Chatterley's Lover*) or about to be separated (*The Lost Girl*), only this novel ends by picturing the wife's 99 percent commitment (Monica has occasional lapses) to supporting the activities of her husband—activities that are decidedly outside her domestic realm. Monica has learned the lesson that Lawrence, through Jack, wished to teach in his leadership period: that women need men for completion; without men they are "only fragments" (p. 353).

In contrast to the woman, Lawrence believed, the man is truly a man only when he is apart from his mate. The biological explanation for the difference is provided in Lawrence's psychology treatises, where, as we have seen, he notes that women by nature are positively charged in the plexuses at the front of the body, urging them toward connection, while men act primarily from the ganglia at the back of the body, which impel them toward separation. *The Boy in the Bush* offers no such technical explanation or scientific jargon. Instead it develops the character of Jack Grant from boyhood to manhood by showing his gradual sloughing off of the need to be a child in a family, dependent upon others for his identity. When Jack first enters the Ellis household he feels he has "sunk into the family, merged his individuality" (p. 57). In a later section, known to have been added by Lawrence to the Skinner manuscript,[12] Jack expresses his love for the Ellises because they seem "to fill the whole of life for him" and he does "not want to be alone, save at moments" (p. 70). Jack wishes never to have children of his own, but rather to remain himself a child—an Ellis child. However, he is no Peter Pan. He does grow up, and his maturity hinges on the development of an isolate and untamed self.

The other males in the novel grow older but not necessarily wiser, their failures at becoming true "heroes" somehow connected with their losing control of their lives to women. Easu married to the curler-headed, Medusa-like Sarah Ann has lost his "flame of life" and is now "only ugly and defeated, common, and a little humiliated" (p. 292). Len's entanglements with the local schoolmarm turn him into a "collar horse" (like the middle class Italians in *Aaron's Rod*) and make "a chap sick of bein' a humin bein'. Wish I grew feathers, an' was an emu" (p. 289). Tom, in a lapse of sanity, has married a barmaid out in Honeysuckle and is able to escape her clutches only by running off with Jack. In contrast to all these ensnared or infinitely ensnarable men, Jack keeps free of smothering, taming domesticity by keeping alive his hatred and scorn for that prison:

> He still hated the nauseous one-couple-in-one-cottage domesticity. He hated domesticity altogether. He loathed the thought of being shut up with one woman and a bunch of kids in a house. Several women, several houses, several bunches of kids: it would then be like a perpetual travelling, a camp, not a home. He hated homes. He wanted a camp. . . . What was more ridiculous than men wheeling perambulators and living among a mass of furniture in a tight house? (p. 353)

Jack's solution to the "one-couple-in-one-cottage" routine constitutes the ending of the novel and the source of Mollie Skinner's tears: he will have "several women, several houses, several bunches of kids," like the nomadic patriarchs of the Old Testament (*BB*, p. 350). Untamed men are apparently able, by the sheer force of their charismatic personalities, to commit those "sins that are necessary to life," especially in the wild and woolly Australia of the 1880s, where a frontier geography (and mentality) allows marriage vows to be taken with a grain of salt if the "wrong" person is married—such as Tom's bride in Honeysuckle or Percy's wife and child back east. Lawrence objected to Mollie Skinner's original ending for her story, which had Jack divorcing Monica and marrying Mary. No, said Lawrence: that would be immoral. Even stronger: "Public, popular morality seems to me a pig's business."[13] To Lawrence, a mark of Jack's integrity in the altered text is that he sticks by his wife, even though she has become very unexciting in her preoccupation with her babies; but he does wish to supplement his marriage to Monica with another woman, which is quite all right—indeed, splendid. The problem for Jack as the novel ends is to find the right woman to join his harem.

Jack works toward the solution to this problem when he "throws a sort of lasso over" Mary Ellis and Hilda Blessington, the two women on the outskirts of his conversations with Aunt Matilda and Mr. George about taking another wife to supplement Monica (p. 337). Accompanying Jack's own need for wildness, it seems, is his need to subdue to his purposes the women around him. Given the fiery nature of Frieda Lawrence, Monica's capitulation at the end is the stuff of fable and wish-fulfillment. Lawrence received the Skinner manuscript shortly after Frieda left for Europe to visit her children, always a sore point with Lawrence and one that he had eased before with the balm of fiction-writing (see chapter six). The separation between husband and wife was preceded by "perhaps the very worst quarrel" of their lives together (according to Catherine Carswell);[14] its seriousness, at least from Lawrence's point of view, is revealed in a chilling letter to Frieda that speaks of making financial arrangements for her future, presumably without him: "I'm glad if you have a good time with your flat and your children. Don't bother about money—When I come we will make a regular arrangement for you to have an income if you wish. . . . The Australian novel [*The Boy in the Bush*] is very nearly done" (*CL*, II, 762). A letter written on the same day, to the Baroness von Richthofen, is more emotional: "Oh, mother-in-law, you are nice and old, and understand, as the first maiden understood, that a man must be more than nice and good, and that heroes are worth more than saints. Frieda doesn't understand that a man must be a hero these days and not only a husband. . . . I am no Jesus that lies on his mother's lap" (*CL*, II, 763). Obviously feeling very cut off from Frieda, Lawrence created in the tawny-eyed woman modeled to a degree on her a fantasy Frieda, bearing her husband lusty twin boys and calling him, without sarcasm, "General." In a novel replete with mystery births and lost legacies, this element is the most fabulous of them all.

Wish-fulfillment plays its part in the character portrayals of Mary and Hilda as well. Both these women owe something to the real-life figure of Dorothy Brett, Mary as the granddaughter of an English earl (Brett was the daughter of a viscount) and Hilda with her "slight deafness" (though Brett's was more than slight). Although the virginal Mary ultimately repudiates Jack, Hilda Blessington implicitly accepts his offer by stating that she would like to be some man's second or third wife, provided his first wife or wives were still living (pp. 367–68), and by promising to visit the Grants at Christmas. Biographical matters extraneous to his text add yet another dollop of irony to it. A decade earlier, Lawrence had tried to entice Jessie Chambers to visit him and Frieda in Italy, after they had run away together, but Jessie had considered the invitation to be insult added to injury and had ignored it.[15] Perhaps in the fall of 1923, Lawrence realized intuitively that he had a more willing acolyte in Dorothy Brett. In March 1924, three months after he added the last scene to the Skinner manuscript ("You may disapprove"), Brett did indeed join the Lawrences for an apparently chaste ménage à trois, one that would last until 1925, when Frieda, having finally had enough of Brett, kicked her out (although in some ways Brett had the last laugh, living on in Taos more than twenty years after Frieda's death and remaining close to Lawrence, buried there since 1930, until the end).

At the end of *The Boy in the Bush*, Jack has achieved the kind of Rananim with Monica, Hilda, Tom, and Len that Lawrence always craved for himself, in which all members are "faithful to the living spark" that is among them, and especially to that of the leader (pp. 333, 336). There are many references in this novel, as in all Lawrence novels, to sparks and flames, since fire is one of the most important Lawrentian images. In works from the leadership period, however, during which Lawrence crystalized his cosmology in *Fantasia of the Unconscious*, the source of that fire—the sun—becomes increasingly important, not only as a figure of speech but also as a ruling principle of life. Hilda, like Jack, is a free spirit with a grudge against society for its stress on conformity and uniformity; damaged psychologically by her civilized upbringing, she commits herself to Jack because only with him can she "kindle her spark of revenge into a natural sun" (p. 368). The natural sun of Australia is, in fact, the shining forth of Jack's mysterious Lord.

While in England "the sun had seemed to [Jack] to move with a domestic familiarity," in Australia it is a "wild, immense, fierce, untamed sun, fiercer than a glowing-eyed lion with a vast mane of fire . . . fierce and powerful beyond all human consideration" (p. 182). Although the Lord controls the moon as well, that orb is associated with the female principle and arouses in Jack, as in Rupert Birkin (in the "Moony" chapter of *Women in Love*), great fear because of its appearance "like some white demon that slowly and coldly tastes and devours its prey" (*BB*, 182). The sun, in contrast, arouses his admiration and respect. By the end of the novel Jack has exchanged his mare Lucy for the potent stallion Adam, named no doubt after what Lawrence elsewhere calls the "Old Adam" (at one point he calls the horse "old Adam" here, too [p. 362])—that is, "the dark, sensual centres in a man," the adjective *old* referring to Adam before the fall from blood-consciousness into a mental (white) consciousness (*SM*, 169). Jack's stallion is blazing, ruddy, and brilliant (*BB*, 364), "shining bright almost as fire" (p. 363), the very incarnation of the sun. Jack himself has become a creature half-man and half-horse, like a centaur; in fact, as in most cowboy stories, of which this is one, the hero establishes a closer relationship with his horse than with his woman (or women). In Lawrence's next published novel, *St. Mawr*, the horse itself becomes the hero. Other than Jack Grant, who was created at his suggestion but is not totally of his own making, Lawrence by 1924 had shown no fictional human being able to live by the ideal of leadership and to manifest the principle of lordship in any society larger than two. But the flowering of his leadership ideal was well under way, in the first draft of a Mexican novel known at that time as *Quetzalcoatl*.

9. The American Experience: *Studies in Classic American Literature*, "The Woman Who Rode Away," *St. Mawr*

"It was in 1915 the old world ended." So intones the narrator of *Kangaroo*. In that year, when "the genuine debasement began, the unspeakable baseness of the press and the public voice, the reign of that bloated ignominy, *John Bull*" (*K*, 220), Lawrence thought seriously of leaving the old world for the new. He booked passage for America and arranged for a passport in hopes of setting up his Rananim on the west coast of Florida, only to postpone the journey after deciding to stay and fight the ban against *The Rainbow*. The following month he prepared again for travel, and went so far as to sell his furniture; but this time he was forbidden to leave the country without a military examination. Rather than submit to the insult, Lawrence temporarily abandoned plans for his sunny utopia and left London for Cornwall, a move which he rationalized as "the first move to Florida" (*CL*, I, 405). From Cornwall he looked wistfully toward America as the land of opportunity, where publishers would not balk at his latest novel, *Women in Love*, and where the exigencies of war would not weigh upon him. The month after the United States entered the war, Lawrence would cry that "America is a stink-pot in my nostrils, after having been the land of the future" (*CL*, I, 512), but this feeling was short-lived.

Lawrence never gave up hope of getting to America eventually. In the meantime he satisfied his craving for that country by reading and re-reading its best known eighteenth- and nineteenth-century authors—Franklin, Cooper, Hawthorne, Poe, and Melville among them—and by composing essays on these authors in 1917 and 1918, most of which were published in *The English Review*. After the war, while living in Italy, Lawrence revised some of these essays and again made plans to visit the United States, wooed by Mabel Dodge in New Mexico; but finding that he was not yet ready to face America (or Mabel Dodge), he went east instead to Ceylon, Tahiti, Australia. Finally, in 1922, Lawrence arrived in Taos and, after one more revision, he published his *Studies in Classic American Literature* with Thomas Seltzer in New York in 1923.

A key concept in all of Lawrence's essays on classic American literature—the first versions, composed in England in 1917 and 1918; the reworkings in Sicily, in 1919 and 1920; and the final revisions in the United States, in 1922 and 1923—is separation from the "devouring mother." In this, they are of a piece with all the major works of Lawrence's leadership period. Imbued with the spirit of Cornwall, lapped by "the flicker of pre-Christian Celtic civilization" (*CL*, I, 410), Lawrence wrote "The Spirit of Place" as an introduction to the series (it was published in November 1918). The essay explains that the Celtic and Iberian peoples were driven to the new world during the Renaissance not by a desire for wealth or religious freedom but rather by a "mystic opposition, even hatred, of the civilising principle of the rest of Europe." The first principle of Celtic civilization was "individualistic, separatist, almost antisocial, a recoil of the individual into a mystic isolation, quite the contrary of the European religious principle, which was the fusing into a whole" (*SM*, 21–22). This one passage provides a lexicon of Lawrence's heavily favored vocabulary words of the leadership period: *individualistic, separatist, antisocial, recoil, isolation*—words of opposition to the principle of "fusing into a whole," which Lawrence associates with women in their maternal roles. This association is made clearer in *Twilight in Italy* (1916) and in the final version of "The Spirit of Place" (1923), both of which discuss the Renaissance in terms of female ascendancy and the loss of fatherhood (*TI*, 79; *SCAL*, 4); Lawrence notes that even in modern times, men emigrate to America in order to escape the rule of women and "to recover some dignity as men" (*TI*, 59). And, in the final essay on Benjamin Franklin, he compares the American immigrant to a son escaping from the domination of his parents (*SCAL*, 20).

Lawrence attributes to civilizations, then, the same psychological needs that motivate individuals: the desire for union, the recoil into separation. His first essays on American literature show Lawrence working through the theories that would later find expression in *Psychoanalysis and the Unconscious* and *Fantasia of the Unconscious*.[1] In the essay on Hector St. John de Crèvecoeur, published in January 1919, he speaks of the two plexuses, in the breast and bowels, that tend toward merger of self and other. Although Lawrence makes no mention of the corresponding ganglia, words like *recoil, isolation, separation,* and *otherness* reveal his preoccupation with the principle of opposition. Gradually the essays move toward an elaboration of this principle: the piece on Cooper, published in February, stresses the "splendid pride in singleness"; the May 1919 essay on Hawthorne speaks of ganglia as well as plexuses, although the two are lumped together as the spontaneous, instinctual consciousness opposed to the mental consciousness located in the brain; finally, in June 1919, "The Two Principles" examines in some detail the ganglia at the back of the body. By and large Lawrence eliminated most of the scientific jargon from the final versions of these essays, since the modes of consciousness had by then found their elaboration in his psychology treatises.

Throughout the early versions of the literature essays, Lawrence attributes to wild animals well-developed ganglia and a corresponding sense of separateness. He finds in the writings of Crèvecoeur a recognition by that author of the principle of otherness that animates the wild kingdom, a refusal to be "encompassed" (*SM*, 60). In other places, Lawrence couches this refusal in familiar terms from the New Testament (John 20:17): noli me tangere (do not touch me). In *Education of the People* Lawrence asserts that noli me tangere "is our motto as it is the motto of a wild wolf or deer. I want about me a clear, cool space across which nobody trespasses" (*EP*, 649). And in *The Boy in the Bush*, Jack Grant keeps "a certain unpassable space around him, a definite *noli me tangere* distance" that links him to the wolf (*BB*, 258). Lawrence carries a no trespassing sign in all the versions of his literature essays, as he does in the other works of the period. According to the first essay on Poe, the perfect human relationship follows the animal paradigm in that neither party desires "to transgress the bounds of being" (*SM*, 130); the final essay on Melville's *Typee* and *Omoo* repeats that in this perfect relationship, "each party leaves great tracts unknown in the other party" (*SCAL*, 143). Although Lawrence frequently dichotomizes the forms of consciousness as upper and lower, or mental and instinctual, or spiritual and sensual, the dichotomy that seems to arouse his greatest concern is that between the "sympathetic" centers at the front of the body and the "voluntary" centers at the back. Indeed, Lawrence's interpretation of *Moby-Dick* is usually interpreted in turn as an account of the sensual body hounded to death by "white" America. Yet Lawrence is especially intrigued by Melville's stress on the whale's enormous backbone, and by Melville's remark "that much of a man's character will be found betokened in his backbone. I would rather feel your spine than your skull" (*SM*, 245). Lawrence respects Melville's whale not merely as the sensual consciousness but, more specifically, as the "sacral consciousness" (*SM*, 235) originating at the base of the spine. Elsewhere he notes that the sacral ganglion is the power center for tigers and cats in the wild kingdom and for soldiers and fighters in the human realm ("The Two Principles" [*SM*, 189]).

Although Lawrence frequently states that one must have all one's plexuses and ganglia in balance in order to lead a healthy and fulfilled life, the effect of his constant harping on separation and otherness in these literature essays is to nullify that pronouncement. What ultimately comes across to the reader is Lawrence's great fear of the plexuses' tendency toward merging and his consequent recoil into isolation. This tendency toward merging—this "longing for identification"—is "at the base of the incest problem," according to Lawrence's first and final essays on Edgar Allan Poe (*SM*, 125; *SCAL*, 76). Lawrence regards Poe as a master at this subject and analyzes his tales in terms of it; indeed, he deems best those tales that do deal with this longing for identification, no doubt because in them Poe is writing most nakedly about himself (*SM*, 117). Of course, Lawrence believed that he, too, had an incest problem with his "devouring mother" wife. The "devouring mother" is, in fact, a formidable figure in the essays on American literature, though the term itself is never used. She appears, for instance, in the first essay on Nathaniel Hawthorne, in the character of Hester Prynne. Clearly Hawthorne intrigued Lawrence, provoking the longest of all the essays (the editor of *The English Review* cut it by eleven and one-half pages). Lawrence specifically compares Hester to the Madonna and lambastes her as a supreme representative of the Age of Woman, in which man "clings to woman like a child, and she becomes the responsible party. . . . With all her passion she cherishes and nourishes her man, and yet her cherishing and nourishing only destroys him more. . . . [Hester] kills [Dimmesdale] by her very possessive love itself" (*SM*, 144–45). Lawrence intuitively recognizes that Hester's love relationships contain large elements of hatred. He interprets Hawthorne's remarks about Hester's relations with the community—"The poor, whom she sought out to be the objects of her bounty, often reviled the hand that was stretched forth to succour them" —to mean that Hester's "succour was her helpless attempt to cover her implacable hate, and the poor responded intuitively" (p. 147). On her growing dread of the village children Lawrence remarks that "[t]he Astarte or Hecate principle has in it a necessary antagonism to life itself, the very issue of life: it contains the element of blood sacrifice of children, in its darker, destructive mood; just as it worships procreative child-birth, in its productive mood" (*SM*, 147). George Ford states that "Persephone becomes Circe" in Lawrence's fiction, the transformation occurring as Lawrence outgrew his Oedipus complex.² It would be more accurate to state that, in Lawrence's view, Persephone and Circe coexist; they are the Janus faces of the pre-oedipal mother. As for Hester's own perverse child, Pearl, Lawrence considered her so representative of modern children that he probably had her in mind when creating his only story with a child protagonist, "The Rocking-Horse Winner," in which a boy named Paul is destroyed trying to please his mother named Hester.³ It cannot escape notice that in this story Lawrence has changed Pearl into a boy and given him the name of the autobiographical hero of *Sons and Lovers*.

To Lawrence, *The Scarlet Letter* portrays the worship of the Magna Mater and the havoc that this worship wreaks on humankind. The dominance of Hester in her relationship with Dimmesdale rouses Lawrence's fury at the dominance of women in any sphere of life: "Whatever the outward profession and action may be, when woman is the leader or dominant in the sex relationship, and in the human progress, then the activity of mankind is an activity of disintegration and undoing" (*SM*, 143). With its diatribe against America, the third version of this essay on *The Scarlet Letter* blurs the obsession with the mother; yet Lawrence here becomes more specific about the "outward professions," and those that he excoriates most soundly are, not surprisingly, those that extend into the public realm qualities typically associated with maternalism—nurturing, healing, educating the young: these professions include nursing and teaching (*SCAL*, 92–93). Interestingly, Lawrence's discussion of Hawthorne's *The Blithedale Romance*, in the 1920 revision of that essay (*SM*, 170–71), shows a great attraction to the nurturing qualities of Hollingsworth, the penal reformer. Lawrence no doubt identified with the sensitive and frail narrator of the story, who falls sick and is tenderly nursed by the do-gooder Hollingsworth, only to be repulsed, ultimately, by Hollingsworth's attempts at domination, and to renounce what Lawrence (in the same situation with Frieda) termed the bullying qualities of the nurse's "tender mercies" (*CL*, I, 581). Only in *Aaron's Rod*, a work of Lawrence's own making, does a male nurse combine a woman's nurturance with a man's respect for otherness, healing the sick without smothering him with solicitude.

In the early years of his leadership period, Lawrence felt that he had lost control over his own affairs and longed to take action on his own behalf. "I *should* like my revenge on the world. Are we *really quite* impotent, all of us?" he asked a friend (*CL*, I, 561). In the autumn of 1918, after the infuriating indignity of a military medical examination, Lawrence felt that he was "out on a new track—let humanity go its own way—I go mine. But I *won't* be pawed and bullied by them—no" (*CL*, I, 564). To such a "brigand" and a "desperado" as Lawrence called himself (*CL*, I, 430, 563), only the uncivilized and untamed could offer hope of friendship, heroism, even salvation. A letter of the period rails against the "stink" of the love-thy-neighbor creed practiced by such people as John Middleton Murry and one of Murry's literary idols, Dostoevsky; it also praises James Fenimore Cooper's *Deerslayer* as an "exquisite" novel (*CL*, I, 492). Lawrence had read Cooper years ago with Jessie Chambers; now he surreptitiously found in Cooper's novels a model for his own behavior. Lawrence's first essay on Cooper's Leatherstocking novels pinpoints Natty Bumppo as Cooper's deepest, wildest, most passionate self and the best self of all Americans. Like a wild animal, Deerslayer refuses to be "pawed and bullied," especially by the greatest threat to his integrity, Judith Hutter. Clearly, Lawrence greatly admired Deerslayer's ability to resist the "devouring mother":

> He would melt like wax in the hot, possessive passion of Judith; she would absorb him, envelop him utterly. He would become an inclusive part of herself, flowing into her. . . . She would be fulfilled and suffused with him, and he would be gone, merged, consumed into the woman, having no being of his own apart from her. And she, possessing him utterly, as if he were enveloped in her own womb, would worship him.
>
> This Deerslayer will never have. He sticks to his own singleness. A race falls when men begin to worship the Great Mother, when they are enveloped within the woman, as a child in the womb. And Deerslayer represents the heroic spirit of his race passing into singleness and perfection beyond his own race, into the pure unknown of the future. For him there is no slipping back into the womb. (*SM*, 108–109)

Although the third version of this essay does not dwell at such length on the dangers posed by the Magna Mater, it does emphasize the relationship between Natty Bumppo and the Indian Chingachgook as the nucleus of a new society. It is likely that this relationship gave Lawrence the idea for the Ramón–Cipriano connection in *The Plumed Serpent*, the first draft of which was begun while Lawrence was correcting the proofs of *Studies in Classic American Literature*.[4]

Lawrence's visit to America in 1922 brought him in touch for the first time with "real" Indians, and therefore put him (so he thought) in a better position than Cooper to write of the uncivilized life.[5] Unfortunately, his guide and hostess was the indomitable Mabel Dodge, whose attitude toward Lawrence was made all too clear by her report of their first meeting at the train station in Lamy, New Mexico: "the womb in me roused to reach out to take him."[6] Already struggling to escape Frieda's own rapacious womb (as he saw it), Lawrence was certainly not about to fall into Mabel's, try as Mabel might to replace Frieda. Lawrence distrusted Mabel's motivations for associating with Indians, and her marriage to her Indian lover provoked these scornful remarks to Seltzer: "Did you hear Mabel Sterne has married Tony & is going to take a ranch to live a 'freer life'. . . . It gives me a sort of end-of-the-world feeling."[7] That his initial reception to Indian ceremonies was cool may be attributed to his distaste for this woman who provided him access. The final versions of the studies in American literature contain several oblique references to Mabel Dodge and her mistaken notions of living, including an attack on those "who glorify the savages in America" (*SCAL*, 137). Indeed, Lawrence's distaste for Mabel was one probable cause for the significant change in his attitude toward Melville's South Sea Island adventures between the first and final versions of his essay on *Typee* and *Omoo*. In the first version, probably written in 1920 but never published until 1961, Lawrence yearns for the Nukuheva that Melville discovers and scoffs at Melville for leaving. Lawrence had already written to his American agent in 1917, probably when reading Melville, that he wished to set up a Garden of Eden in a remote spot like Nukuheva;[8] another letter of the period refers to "the ultimate place" for settlement in America as "Typee or Rananim" (*CL*, I, 499). In the second version of this essay, however, Lawrence emphasizes the impassable gulf between the civilized and the primitive and argues that "one cannot go back" (*SCAL*, 136). And in the second version of his essay on Cooper's Anglo-American novels, Lawrence specifically notes the "race resistance" between an Indian man and his wealthy white mistress (*SCAL*, 37).

Yet in many ways Lawrence continued to glorify the primitive life himself, as he revealed in a letter to Mabel Dodge two months later: "People tell me you are divorcing Tony. . . . Probably it is not true. I hope it's not. . . . Tony always has my respect and affection. And when I say in my book: 'One cannot go back,' it is true, one cannot. But your marriage with Tony may even yet be the rounding of a great curve; since certainly he doesn't merely draw you back, but himself advances perhaps more than you advance, in the essential 'onwards.'" (*CL*, II, 757). Probably Lawrence had mixed feelings, then, toward Mabel's "freer life" lived Indian style: he both despised and envied it. These confused feelings received imaginative extension in his long story "The Woman Who Rode Away," written in 1924 after one of Lawrence's periodic escapes from "Mabeltown." Shortly before leaving on a trip to Mexico with a Danish friend, after Frieda had left for England, Lawrence wrote of Mabel, "I have *my* idea of what she owes me. As for a vendetta, I'm ready. To hell with her, anyhow. I'm through with her now."[9] That he was ready for a vendetta is clear from this story, based partly on his travels in Mexico and partly on Mabel's experiences in an ancient Indian ceremonial cave high on a mountainside.[10] Lawrence's version, about an unnamed American woman who seeks adventure with the Indians, is a curious mixture of a fable of regeneration, or a fertility myth, with a vehicle of revenge. The two aims are incompatible and many readers are horrified by the result. Mabel herself described the fable as "that story where Lorenzo thought he finished me up."[11]

"The Woman Who Rode Away" is a kind of sequel to a novel that Lawrence had begun earlier, using the facts of Mabel Dodge's life. Entitled "The Wilful Woman," the work depicts the journey to New Mexico from civilization of a strong-willed, thrice-married woman who tears her current husband to bits and puts him together again when so inclined.[12] "The Woman Who Rode Away" depicts the journey out; in it, an unhappily married woman is "overcome by a foolish romanticism" (*CSS*, III, 549) and rides away from home to encounter a primitive Indian tribe. She is not overcome with fear at their meeting because she has "confidence in her own female power" (p. 554), but her confidence is gradually undermined as the Indians render her totally helpless and will-less. Eventually the woman realizes she is to be a human sacrifice to the sun god: "[h]er kind of womanhood. . . . was to be obliterated again, and the great primeval symbols were to tower once more over the fallen individual independence of woman" (p. 569). This story is a direct transmutation into fictional form of the notions expressed in the essays on American literature, where Hester Prynne's "oriental characteristic" provides Lawrence with a glimmer of hope for a "new era, with a whole new submissiveness to the dark, phallic principle. . . . Generation after generation of nurses and political women and salvationists. And in the end, the dark erection of the images of sex-worship once more, and the newly submissive women. . . . And the women *choose* to experience again the great submission" (*SCAL*, 94). With the help of drugs, the woman who rides away acquiesces in her own death and is eventually led to slaughter so that the Indians' land will be fertile and the men regain their powers.

(The correlation between barrenness of the land and the ascendancy of woman is assumed in this story, as in *The Fox*, which also ends with the death of the dominating female.) Lawrence wrote to Mabel in November 1923, not long after finishing "The Woman Who Rode Away," "One day I will come to you and take your submission: when you are ready" (*CL*, II, 761). Since Mabel never indicated readiness, Lawrence accomplished in fiction what he could not accomplish in fact: putting this indomitable woman in her "place." The incantational prose is spellbinding, as only the half-asleep reader could acquiesce in the story's depiction of "the necessity of death before the vitalistic resurrection."[13] Lawrence's own glorification of the savage element is meant as a corrective to the "white," mechanistic consciousness of modern civilization; but it is also a vendetta against willful females, whose representative awaits a knife in the heart as the story ends.

In fact, the woman wonders if the Indians view her as a human being at all, or rather as "some giant, female white ant" (*CSS*, II, 558). Lawrence's proclivity for the insect image after 1916 or so has already been discussed (see chapter four). Clearly, if an offender is viewed as an insect rather than as a person, then a logical—indeed necessary—way to rid oneself of the pest is through extermination. Most of the leadership works refer to people as ants, and *Studies in Classic American Literature* is no exception: the final version of the essay on Cooper's Anglo-American (or "White," as Lawrence now called them) novels refers to the masses as "a myriad ants" (*SCAL*, 41).

The movement into violence during Lawrence's leadership period is steady, culminating in the bloodbaths of *The Plumed Serpent*. This movement parallels the movement westward from England, which gave Lawrence license for discord, even murder; in 1921 he explained to a friend in Ceylon that the expanded version of *The Fox*, with its destruction of Banford, would show that Lawrence was "not really drawn Buddhawards, but west" (*CL*, II, 678). Lawrence seems to have been fascinated by the deliverance of blows, and dwells on the subject at great length in his essay on Dana, only one version of which exists. He discusses the episode in *Two Years Before the Mast* involving the flogging of a mate by the ship's captain. Lawrence applauds the flogging and scoffs at Dana for being sickened by it. To Lawrence, the fact that Dana vomits indicates that Dana's solar plexus has suffered an outrage at this toning of the mate's ganglia! (*SCAL*, 118). Only those readers familiar with Lawrence's plexus-and-ganglion theories from other works of the leadership period can understand Lawrence's meaning here. The emphasis here as elsewhere is on corporal punishment to activate the centers of independence and pride. Dana's reaction indicates that he is a womanly creature, whose love for his fellow human is "largely pity, tinged with philanthropy. The inevitable saviourism. The ideal being" (*SCAL*, 122). Dana might as well be one of those "female-saviours" whom Lawrence lambastes in his 1922 essay on Hester Prynne, those who cannot bear to see anyone suffering pain but who destroy others by their all-encompassing love. To fight the domination of women such as Hester, Lawrence advocates a hard slap in the face.[14]

Where the tone of the 1917–18 literature essays is mystical, that of the later versions is flippant, showing a movement from anger at the status quo toward a state of devil-may-care; where the first versions are relatively pacific, the final ones are positively bellicose. The essay on Benjamin Franklin, for instance, contains a reworking of Franklin's list of virtues in accordance with Lawrence's own evolving creed. Under RESOLUTION, Lawrence changes Franklin's dictum, "Resolve to perform what you ought; perform without fail what you resolve," into "Resolve to abide by your own deepest promptings, and to sacrifice the smaller thing to the greater. Kill when you must, and be killed the same: the *must* coming from the gods inside you, or from the men in whom you recognize the Holy Ghost" (*SCAL*, 11, 17). Lawrence's "resolution" is the guiding principle of his leadership period. Between 1921 and 1924 Lawrence's characters no longer merely fulminate against the Magna Mater; instead they resort to physical means of combat, answering the call to blood sacrifice.

The connection between a psychological motivation—a fear of the "devouring mother"—and a political creed involving a repudiation of democracy is not stated explicitly in Lawrence's literature essays. Nevertheless, the connection rides beneath the surface of these essays and explains their characteristic movement. To Lawrence, what is called by the name democracy in political parlance is called incest in works of psychology; underlying both phenomena is the merger of self and other, and the loss of individual integrity. He explains that, having escaped from the domination of their parent continent, the American settlers mistook freedom for democracy and began to pursue their destructive desire for oneness. Lawrence sees in Crèvecoeur's works a recognition of otherness in the animal kingdom, but finds Crèvecoeur incapable of giving this principle any credence in the human realm. Benjamin Franklin, the quintessential American, is the primary spokesman for this ideal of democracy: "It did not seem to matter at all to him that he himself was an intrinsic being. He saw himself as a little unit in the vast total of society"

(*SM*, 46). In the final version of his essay on Franklin, the images that come to Lawrence's mind when he thinks of Franklin's creed are those of domesticity and enclosure: kitchen gardens (as opposed to dark forests); barbed wire fences, corrals, and paddocks. He concludes that Americans are still in thrall to Europe, for the son's escape "from the domination of his parents" is not complete, and will never be complete, so long as Americans believe that they are servants of humankind and part of a whole.

But it is Whitman who elicits from Lawrence the most passionate response to the democratic ideal. The 1920 revision of the essay on Whitman (the first version is lost) faults the poet for his emphasis on merging with others. Obviously the very thought disgusted Lawrence, for he compares this process to the breakdown of tissue into mucous slime (*SM*, 259). The final version of the essay, now hostile to Whitman, repudiates the love of comrades that Lawrence had once admired in Whitman's poetry as a herald of the life to come. Lawrence now calls Whitman a great "post-mortem poet, of the transitions of the soul as it loses its integrity" (*SCAL*, 170). And these are the transitions: the merging into the womb of woman; the merging of men in comradeship; the merging of humans under the banner of democracy, which spells death to the individual (p. 169). The essay on Whitman ends with a plea for what Lawrence calls a "true democracy," one which includes the worship of society's best selves (p. 177). Many of the essays on classic American authors end this way: after discussing the failure of American democracy, they promulgate the ideal of leadership; after discussing the will to dominate flaunted by women, they promulgate the means of staying single. The two subjects are inextricably related: Lawrence specifies that the American Eagle is a Hen-Eagle, shrieking, "We are the masterless" (*SCAL*, 5).

Lawrence firmly believes that woman cannot be masterless, for at least two reasons: first, she is not capable of knowing or expressing anything on her own (*SM*, 145); second, because "unless a woman is held, by man, safe within the bounds of belief, she becomes inevitably a destructive force" (p. 92). Lawrence seems unaware of the logical extension of his position on woman's proper province: women who do not know or express anything on their own are no longer people but robots. Further, he seems unaware of the inconsistency of his views on this subject, for he complains that Priscilla in Hawthorne's *The Blithedale Romance* is a totally passive medium to Westervelt and thus a monster capable of great destruction because she has no integrity, no separate being. Ironically, Lawrence also faults Whitman for reducing women to submissive creatures necessary only for sex and procreation. Yet he immediately goes on to make a statement about Whitman's poetry that implies admiration and agreement: ultimately, when a man acts "from the last and profoundest centres," his most important relationships are with other men rather than with women (*SM*, 260–61). What Lawrence means by those "centres" is left vague, but one may surmise that he means the so-called voluntary centers at the back of the body, which urge toward separation and against merger. Lawrence's first mention of the voluntary system occurs in the first essay on Cooper; though he fails to elaborate here upon this system, he does dwell at length upon the necessity for taking cognizance of the "polarity which is within us and without us" (*SM*, 86). Presumably, within us lies the polarity between the sympathetic and voluntary systems; without us, the polarity between the one and the many. "[R]esistance to the mass" (*SM*, 87) is Lawrence's psychological *and* political credo. Indeed, this essay on Cooper, the first to mention the voluntary system, is the first of the literary essays to articulate the ideal of leadership: "Some men are born from the mystery of creation, to know, to read, and to command. And some are born to listen, to follow, to obey" (*SM*, 84).

Against merger Lawrence advocates isolation; against democracy, dictatorship. The first version of the essay on Poe makes this connection clear, for after many pages of ranting about Poe's incest obsession, and his emphasis on "consuming into a oneness" (*SM*, 122), Lawrence seems gratuitously to end with a pitch for yielding precedence to a superior individual. He elaborates on this impulse to yield in his first essay on Crèvecoeur, where he explains that it accounts for the way

> the Egyptian pyramids were built, symbolic of the culminating process, the lesser life yielding and culminating, step by step, towards the apex of the God-King. In this same spirit of yielding and culminating through dark faith, or trust, our mediaeval cathedrals were erected.... In the same way Napoleon, the last great leader, attained his brief ascendancy. It is necessary, before men can unite in one great living gesture, that this impulse towards the mystical sensual yielding and culminating shall find expression. In a modern spirit of equality, we can get tremendous concerted action, ... but no culminating living oneness.... Hence we have no architecture: we have only machines. (*SM*, 60–61)

Lawrence's views on architecture in his leadership period contradict his earlier treatment of the subject in *Sons and Lovers* and *The Rainbow*. In the former novel, Paul speaks up for rounded Norman arches in opposition to the love shown by the spiritual Miriam for the pointed Gothic arch (SL, 177); in the latter novel, the rainbow shape itself stands in implied opposition to Will Brangwen's Gothic church. During the leadership period, however, pointed columns represent for Lawrence a reaching toward excellence and a culmination of society in the one superior male individual. It also represents a breaking out of constricting, womb-like enclosures associated with women and with the democratic ideal. (The relationship between democracy and architecture is made specific in *Kangaroo*, [p. 107].)

In his essay on Poe, Lawrence shows that he has thought through (some might say justified) the disparity between preserving one's isolate self and pledging allegiance to another. He explains that the true leader always recognizes and respects the otherness of his followers. Then, too, the follower becomes more truly himself in service to the leader because he gives up the false notion of his own equality or even superiority. In other words, "the highest achievement of some souls lies in perfect service" (*SM*, 130). It is a premise of these essays that no woman is capable of being a leader. L. D. Clark, among others, complains that Lawrence's essays on American literature are marred by the absence of a skeptical female voice speaking (Lawrence would say screeching) in opposition to the theory of male dominance.[15] Certainly the bulk of the major fiction of the period contains such a voice. But that voice is quickly silenced in "The Woman Who Rode Away" and can barely be heard over the roar of the major speakers in *St. Mawr*, written immediately afterward. Lawrence portrays the perfect servant in this novella *St. Mawr*: the Indian named Phoenix, employed by Louise Carrington, has just the right combination of limited intelligence and a strong feeling of attachment to his betters (*St.M*, 137). The novella also contains the perfect leader, although society does not give him his due: this is Lewis, the small and swarthy Welsh groom of Lou's stallion, St. Mawr. When Lou purchases the horse she finds that she had gotten the groom in the bargain; as one always accompanies the other, these two wild creatures are symbolically attached like a centaur. Lou recognizes in Lewis a natural aristocracy that has no place as yet in human society (p. 119). Her mother, Mrs. Witt, also admires Lewis but tries to force herself on him by proposing marriage. Mrs. Witt readily admits that "her nature [is] a destructive force" but justifies her attempts at domination by the fact that only weak males, who deserve to be dominated, will capitulate to her. Secretly she wishes to be defeated and held in check by a strong man, but inevitably she commands the male's worship (p. 95). It is from experience with her mother's ways that Lou advises Mrs. Witt "not to devour little Lewis" (p. 110). Lewis is already on the defensive, however, obviously having had numerous experiences with "devouring mothers": he explains that he avoids women because "they only want to make you give in to them, so that they feel almighty, and you feel small" (p. 120). A Celt, like Henry Grenfel in *The Fox* and Alan Anstruther in "The Border-Line," Lewis is motivated by the Celt's need for separation and singleness, as Lawrence had discussed in "The Two Principles."

Ironically, Mrs. Witt yearns to leave Europe because she cannot maintain her own singleness and separateness there. Her impetus for setting off for America is the same, in Lawrence's view, as that which drove the original settlers away from Europe to the new land: "That closeness, that sense of cohesion, that sense of being fused into a lump with all the rest—no matter how much distance you kept—this drove her mad" (p. 94). She and Lou wish to escape the "close, hedged-and-fenced English landscape. Everything enclosed, enclosed, so stifling" (p. 90), and as a stop-gap measure Mrs. Witt takes a ride across the countryside to find some breathing space. On this trip she attempts to force an intimacy with Lewis and quickly turns into a willful, hectoring bully when she is rebuffed. Although Mrs. Witt is relatively harmless—indeed, positively lovable—in comparison with other "devouring mothers" in the Lawrence canon, she shares all the traits of women as diverse as Miss Frost, Jill Banford, Harriet Somers, and Tanny Lilly: a desire to conquer others, especially those she perceives to be "little"; to make them subservient to her wishes, and to reveal their inner selves; to taunt and humiliate those who try to hold themselves apart. But she meets her match in Lewis, whose attitude toward Mrs. Witt is captured in certain often-repeated words and phrases that create variations on the theme of separation: *distant, inaccessible, refuting, far away, looking down, averted, away, out of contact, ignor[ing], staying in another world* (pp. 100–101). Mrs. Witt recognizes what she thinks of as a meanness in Lewis's spirit: "A keep-yourself-for-yourself, and don't give yourself away" (p. 101). To Lewis and to Lawrence, of course, this attitude is a response developed almost like a callus, to defend against the onslaughts of dominating females.

Lewis's desire to keep out of touch with other human beings is fully appreciated by Mrs. Witt's daughter, Lou. Perhaps it is no accident that Lewis and Louise are similarly named: they are the male and female embodiments of the principle of isolation. Lou receives her mother's news of a marriage proposal to Lewis with a feeling of repugnance. In recoil from her own marriage with Rico, Lou tells her mother, "I do so understand why Jesus said: *Noli me tangere.* Touch me not. I am not yet ascended unto the Father" (*St.M*, 117). Lawrence uses the New Testament for his own revisionist purposes. Although the biblical reference clarifies Lou's feelings in a seemingly innocuous way, Lawrence had already completed the first draft of what was to become *The Plumed Serpent,* in which society is regenerated through allegiance to a very human Father King. Lou's instinct, like Lawrence's, is "[t]o go South! Always to go South" (p. 127), and so she travels away from England and her fashionable London home to a ranch in the American Southwest. The spirit of its place is compatible with her hatred of people and her desire to kick them in the face like an untamable animal—like St. Mawr, in fact, who has seemed to her "like some living background, into which she wanted to retreat" (p. 26). Lawrence ends his novella with a long description of the landscape into which Lou has retreated (pp. 141–54), where no Christian god of love, charity, and humility rules. Lou is left alone as she wishes, wedded to a fierce spirit that reigns "like some serpent-bird" (p. 152). The serpent-bird will move to center stage in Lawrence's next novel, and will become more clearly defined as the long-deposed father who has come to regain his rightful throne.

10. Rekindling the Father-Spark:
Movements in European History and *The Plumed Serpent*

From Mexico in May 1923, when he was almost finished with the first draft of *The Plumed Serpent*, Lawrence wrote to John Middleton Murry about the relative merits of his three recently published novellas: "I think in the long run perhaps 'The Ladybird' has more the quick of a new thing than the other two stories" (*CL*, II, 703). What Lawrence had in mind by the "quick of a new thing" is probably Count Dionys's assertion of himself as "Master of the life to come. Father of the soul that would come after" (*L*, 104); the "quick" is the "father-quick" on which Lawrence expounded in *Fantasia of the Unconscious*. In that psychology treatise, as we have seen, Lawrence stresses the child's essential relationship with its father. He speaks of the "unquenched father-spark" that lies deep within each child, in the solar plexus, waiting to be fanned into a blaze of connection with the male parent (*FU*, 70). Recognizing the "father-spark" or "father-quick" was, to Lawrence, in his leadership period, the task of every individual not only in the domestic sphere but also in the political realm. Indeed, the notion of a "spark" or "quick" is bound up with Lawrence's ideal of leadership as he expressed it in his fictional works like *The Ladybird* and his essayistic writings like *Movements in European History*. Creation of the latter, a highly derivative textbook for schoolchildren, written for the Oxford Press, provided Lawrence with the opportunity systematically to find in past orders the modes of political organization that either pleased or distressed him, and therefore it helped him to formulate his own system as recorded in *The Plumed Serpent*, the crowning achievement of the leadership period.

Lawrence conceived of his history book in the summer of 1918, while reading Gibbon, who helped him to see that "one must view the species with contempt first and foremost, and find a few individuals . . . to *rule* the species" (CL, I, 561). He wrote and revised the textbook between July 1918 and November 1920; it was published in February 1921, under the pseudonym Lawrence H. Davison. In this book Lawrence praises such diverse leaders as Frederick the Great of Prussia, Luther, and Napoleon and concludes that modern Europe must unite around a single chosen leader (*MEH*, 306). In September 1924, while living in New Mexico, Lawrence was asked by the Press to write an epilogue to bring the work up to date for a new, illustrated edition (*CL*, II, 810). The editorial readers received this epilogue with disapproval and voted against its publication,[1] a reaction which Lawrence had anticipated when he noted to his bibliographer, Edward McDonald, that the piece would "make [Oxford Press] hesitate."[2] Nine months later, after the illustrated edition was published (under Lawrence's name), Lawrence continued to chafe over the omission of the epilogue. He scoffed to McDonald that the Oxford Press was "frightened to use" it and complained, "It was for the future rather than the past. But why shouldn't a history book reach both ways!"[3] This epilogue makes explicit certain ideas that had remained implicit in the body of the larger work. Here Lawrence discusses kingship as practiced in "the old days," when it entailed a sacred obligation to nations. He compares the king of old to the father in a family, except that the father, according to Lawrence, really *has* been endowed by heaven or nature with leadership, while kings have assumed title merely by heredity and have abused their rights (Kaiser Wilhelm of Germany is used as an example). But, Lawrence continues, democracy is no better as a political system. He recommends that the masses seek the truly superior few and then choose to obey them: "This is our job, then . . . : to recognise the spark of nobleness inside us, and let it make us. To recognise the spark of *noblesse* in one another, and ad our sparks together, to a flame. And to recognise the men who have stars, not mere sparks of nobility in their souls, and to choose these for leaders" (*MEH*, 317–18, 321).

Unable to find any such leaders in real life, Lawrence shortly afterward created a fantasy leader in *The Plumed Serpent*. On 3 October 1924, from his ranch in New Mexico, Lawrence wrote to Murry of his strong desire to return to old Mexico (where he had written the first draft of *The Plumed Serpent* some months earlier): "It is time to go south.—Did I tell you that my father died on September 10th, the day before my birthday?—The autumn always gets me badly. . . . I want to go south" (*CL*, II, 812). The placement of Lawrence's aside about his father's death is surely of some significance: the lack of a father is associated in Lawrence's mind with autumn and the north, and the search for a father, as well as for life and health, takes him off in a southerly direction.[4] Moreover, the seemingly offhand notation of this death is belied by the mention of its proximity to Lawrence's own birthday (his thirty-ninth). In fact, the letter to Murry begins with—was perhaps prompted by—Lawrence's reaction to Murry's news about his second wife's expecting a baby: "Frieda says every woman hopes her BABY will become the Messiah. It takes a man, not a baby. I'm afraid there will be no more Son Saviours. One was almost too much, in my opinion." What Lawrence presented to the world in his Mexican novel, a final version of which he completed a few months after writing this letter, was a Father Saviour rather than a Son Saviour—"a man, not a baby." The religion of Quetzalcoatl signifies the overthrow of the Magna Mater and the ascension of the Pater Magnus to the throne.

The role of the Magna Mater in *The Plumed Serpent* has not yet received its due, even though many note that, for all its sociological, political, and religious trappings, this novel is concerned in the main with the male-female relationship. The postures that men and women must take in the church of the living Quetzalcoatl, and that Kate Leslie and Cipriano assume in their marriage ceremony, require the woman to stoop and kneel, the man to stand erect; these ritualized positions invert the positions of the characters in works like *The Lost Girl* and are meant to correct the modern-day ascendancy of the Magna Mater that *The Lost Girl* depicts. For it is not simply woman who has assumed the power role but woman as Mary or Queen of the World: she is the real target of Lawrence's spleen in this novel. Kate has been worshiped as a queen by her previous husbands, both of them blue-eyed, ineffectual men like Basil in *The Ladybird*; now the black-eyed men, like Count Dionys in that novella, are ready to reassume their proper leadership role after pulling woman down from her pedestal. The madonna figures in the Sayula church are literally ripped down and burned in preparation for the rededication of the church to Quetzalcoatl.[5] For what is wrong with the Jesus of Mexican Catholicism is not only that he personifies meekness and death but also that he has a mother; what is right with Quetzalcoatl, among other things, is that "he has no mother, he!" (*PS*, 247).[6]

The central figure in *The Plumed Serpent*, that which initiates the action of the novel, is "the pretty white woman in a blue mantle, with her little doll's face under her crown, Mary, the doll of dolls, Niña of Niñas" (*PS*, 302)—virginal girl-child-mother, who needs no human male partner. Kate Leslie, her imposing size and sexual aura notwithstanding, is a human representation of the white Madonna: her servant Juana makes this connection when she points to Kate's feet and tells her children to "look! Look at the feet of the Niña! Pure feet of the Santisima! . . . And She, the Holy Mary, is a gringita. She came over the sea, like you, Niña?" (p. 246). In Kate's Maryhood lies one reason for Cipriano's attraction to her:

> He looked at [Kate's] soft, wet white hands over her face . . . in a sort of wonder. The wonder, the mystery, the magic that used to flood over him as a boy . . . when he kneeled before the babyish figure of the Santa Maria de la Soledad, flooded him again. He was in the presence of the goddess, white-handed, mysterious, gleaming with a moon-like power. . . . He watched [Kate] continually, with a kind of fascination: the same spell that the absurd little figures of the doll Madonna had cast over him as a boy. She was the mystery, and he the adorer, under the semi-ecstatic spell of the mystery. But once he rose from his knees, he rose in the same strutting conceit of himself as before he knelt: with all his adoration in his back pocket again. (pp. 75, 88)

The novel records both Cipriano's desire for Kate and his struggles to rise from his knees, arm thrust upward in the Quetzalcoatl salute, asserting himself as an adult male, while she, the queen dethroned, kneels or lies prone at his feet.

The purest example of the Magna Mater in *The Plumed Serpent* is the woman who commits her life absolutely to the madonna principle: Carlota, Ramón's first wife. Miss Frost was a governess in *The Lost Girl* and in this novel Carlota runs a Cuna or foundling home: both "northern" women are mother figures who live by the Christian ideal of charity that Lawrence, speaking from personal experience, termed "that cruel kindness" (*PS*, 228). Their kindness is cruel because it presumes the recipient to be a child in need of their protection (even if the recipient is an adult), robs the individual of his human dignity, and delays or stifles his maturity. Miss Frost and Carlota are but two in the long line of mother figures that includes, to name only a few, Hermione in *Women in Love*, who continually attempts to take charge of Birkin and who treats his revolutionary ideas like some sort of little-boy whim; Banford in *The Fox*, whose hospitality toward the man she regards as a younger brother ends when he threatens her domination of March; and Tanny Lilly in *Aaron's Rod*, who remarks to her would-be prophet of a husband, in front of company, that he more than most men needs to hold a woman's hand.

Carlota in her turn attempts to denigrate Ramón's efforts to bring back pre-Christian gods by reducing her husband to a child—to *her* child: "Ah, it is terrible, terrible! And foolish like a little boy! Ah, what is a man but a little boy who needs a nurse and a mother! . . . He—he—he wants to be worshipped! To be worshipped! A God! He, whom I've held, I've held in my arms! He is a child, as all men are children. And now he wants—to be worshipped—!" (*PS*, 181). Horrified by Ramón's success, Carlota asks Kate, "Could you follow Ramón? Could *you* give up the Blessed Virgin?—I could sooner die!" (p. 207). And she does die—must die, for she is the greatest enemy of the phallic mystery, and Ramón, unlike impotent Clifford Chatterley in Lawrence's last novel, refuses to be nursed and mothered. The rededication of the church to Quetzalcoatl signifies the end of Madonna worship and therefore the end of Carlota: from her deathbed Carlota accuses Ramón of murdering her, while Cipriano, Ramón's spokesman, heaps invectives on her and calls upon her to die (p. 381). At dawn—the dawn of a new era, as Lawrence would have it—she obliges.

Ramón's second wife, Teresa, provides a stark contrast to the first. A brown-skinned Indian, she parrots Ramón's philosophy of parenthood and provides Kate with a corrective to the white-northern-Christian kind of mothering: "I, if I have any children, . . . I shall try to cast my bread upon the waters, so my children come to me that way. . . . I hope I shall not try to fish them out of life for myself, with a net. I have a very great fear of love. It is so personal" (*PS*, 435). Kate's smothering relationship with her own children across the seas is only hinted at in this novel, but it is her wish to reestablish contact with them that prompts her to make plans to abandon her husband Cipriano and her new way of life.[7] Carlota herself has overprotected Ramón's sons to the point of crushing out their life spark and turning them into ninnies. One of the boys wishes to become a priest, the other a doctor—to Ramón, and thus to Lawrence, both boys would be slaves to their mother's ideal of love. In Carlota Lawrence offers a prime example of what he lambastes, in *Fantasia of the Unconscious*, as "this scorpion of maternal nourishment. Always this infernal self-conscious Madonna starving our living guts and bullying us to death with her love" (*FU*, 173).

Ramón, in contrast, refuses to bully his children with love. When they repudiate him he tells them, in disgust, "you had better say to everybody: Oh, no! we have no father! Our mother died, but we never had a father. We are children of an immaculate conception" (*PS*, 590 [Lawrence means, of course, virgin birth]). Yet if his sons should ever wish of their own accord to return to their father, Ramón will be ready to receive them, "to be a stronghold to them" (p. 392). Lawrence would have him offer protection without suffocation, authority without authoritarianism. To many readers, however, Ramón may not appear to be a good father, for he has allowed Carlota to smother the boys, retreating into himself in times of conflict with his wife (p. 187). But Ramón's unwillingness to do battle with Carlota for possession of the children is not to Lawrence the equivalent of James Houghton's evasion of parental responsibility in *The Lost Girl*. To use Lawrence's own terms, set forth in his essay called "Master in His Own House" (1928), James Houghton shows indifference; Ramón, insouciance.[8] Ramón's retreat is meant to be born of strength rather than of weakness, indicating his belief in the inviolability of each individual soul and setting an example to his children that he can only hope they will choose to follow in later years. To Cyprian's cry that only his mother has loved him, Ramón answers that "she called thee her own. I do not call thee mine own. Thou are myself" (p. 391).

Significantly, Ramón's son and Ramón's best friend are similarly named: if Cyprian is Ramón's biological son, Cipriano is his spiritual heir. Cipriano's godfather was a bishop, a Catholic father; but Cipriano believes that Ramón is better attuned to the needs of Mexico as a whole and Cipriano in particular. He explains that he worships Ramón in a sense because Ramón "can compel me to. When I grew up, and my godfather could not compel me to believe, I was very unhappy.... But Ramón *compels* me and that is very good" (*PS*, 88, 224). This compulsion is presumably "very good" because it translates into Ramón's helping Cipriano to realize the beliefs that he already possesses; that is to say, Ramón can bring out the best in Cipriano, rather than imposing something on him. When Cipriano and Ramón meet on the terrace, having convened for tea at Ramón's home, Cipriano gazes "into the other man's face with black, wondering, childlike, searching eyes, as if he, Cipriano, were searching for *himself*, in Ramón's face. Ramón looked back ... with a faint, kind smile of recognition, and Cipriano hung his head as if to hide his face" (p. 200). Sometimes at moments of great revelation between two characters, Lawrence heightens the impact of the scene by having it witnessed by a third party; in *The Lost Girl*, for instance, the pathetic confrontation between Dr. Mitchell and Alvina, when he blubbers at her knees, is watched by a matron at the hospital, and the shock value for the reader is duly increased (see chapter three). In *The Plumed Serpent*, Lawrence has Carlota and Kate witness the tender scene between Ramón and Cipriano precisely in order for them—and beyond them, the reader—to see that a new relationship has supplanted the unsatisfactory one between man and woman: as Lawrence urges in *Fan-*

tasia, "wait, quietly, in possession of your own soul, till you meet another man who has made the choice and kept it. Then you will know him by the look on his face. . . . Then you too will make the nucleus of a new society" (*FU*, 178).

The importance of the relationship betwen Ramón and Cipriano—as of that between the other blood brothers in Lawrence's works—lies in what it reacts against: the Magna Mater and her smothering love. The longing for merger and the fear of merger are the twin poles of *The Plumed Serpent*; this psychic conflict is rooted in the author's earliest experiences with his caretaker mother. The blood brotherhood of Ramón and Cipriano—a relation of men—allows Lawrence the security of merger without the threat of annihilation that he associates with woman. Indeed, the novel ends with Kate's realization that, so far as Ramón and Cipriano are concerned, "a woman is really *de trop*" (p. 486). Kate's feeling of exclusion is mitigated somewhat by the remaining lines of the novel, in which Cipriano indicates to Kate that he desires her and wants her to stay. Yet according to L. D. Clark, the final line of the novel—Kate's "You won't let me go!"—was probably not decided on until Lawrence corrected the galleys in England in October 1925; as Lawrence wrote the scene some months earlier, the concluding sentence reads, "'le gueux m'a plantée là!' she said to herself in the words of an old song."[9] Translated as "the scoundrel has jilted me," Kate's thought reiterates her feeling of exclusion, whether the French lyric refers in her mind to Ramón, who has just left the scene, or to Cipriano, who has just spoken. In *The Lost Girl*, the friendship between Ciccio and Giorgio arouses similar feelings of exclusion in Alvina, especially as the two men use French, a language that Alvina does not understand, as a secret code of communication; but Giorgio drops out of the story after Ciccio's commitment to Alvina, and Lawrence makes no political point of the love between the two men. In *The Plumed Serpent*, Ramón and Cipriano speak the language of the Quetzalcoatl movement, a language foreign to Kate, and their relationship, forming "the nucleus of a new society," is a love beyond woman.

Fantasia of the Unconscious offers an explanation of why "a woman is really *de trop*" to Ramón and Cipriano. According to the introduction to that work, in which Lawrence sets forth his major criticisms of Freudian theory, a greater urge than that toward sexual intercourse—and often in direct antagonism to it—is "the desire of the human male to build a world: . . . to build up out of his own self and his own belief and his own effort something wonderful" (*FU*, 60). During his leadership period,

10. Rekindling the Father-Spark 149

Lawrence, the self-proclaimed "priest of love" (*CL*, I, 173), preached subordination of heterosexual love—if only by a hair's breadth—to "the desire of the human male to build a world." Ramón, as founder of the Quetzalcoatl movement, has built a world animated by the patriarchal principle. The "essential quickening dark rays" that Lawrence speaks of in *Fantasia* (*FU*, 70, 73)—those that pass from father to child in the family unit, meeting the "unquenched father spark" in the child—form the basis of a religion in which the dark sun, called the Father, supersedes the Magna Mater–Mary–moon goddess of both Protestantism (à la Miss Frost in *The Lost Girl*) and Catholicism (à la Carlota). Ramón composes the hymns and stories in which, as the Mexican peasants recognize, "there spoke a new voice, the voice of a master and authority. And though they were slow to trust . . . they seized upon the new-old thrill, with a certain fear, and joy, and relief" (*PS*, 286).

A work of Lawrence's late period, the travel book *Etruscan Places*, speaks of a single idea behind "all the great old civilizations" like the Etrurian: that idea is the establishment of a king-god, "the vivid key to life" (*EPl*, 91). Such a natural aristocrat combines the sensitivity and tenderness hitherto associated with woman with the authoritativeness associated with man. Even the animals of ancient Etruria, according to Lawrence, somehow combined these attributes, like the "bull, the herd-lord, the father of calves and heifers, of cows; the father of milk" (*EPl*, 121), and the goat, "the father of milk-giving life" (p. 124). Etruscan males of the human and animal realms were therefore lords of two ways, the maternal and the paternal, like Quetzalcoatl in Lawrence's resurrected pantheon of Mexican gods. Although the masses of people in ancient Etruria were always kept in touch with the mysteries of existence, only the initiates possessed full knowledge of those mysteries. These are the bases on which Lawrence organizes his Mexican society in the leadership novel *The Plumed Serpent*.

Lawrence's recreation—or more precisely, his creation—of ancient hierarchies is the logical culmination of his leadership fiction: he aggrandizes to godhead the psychological needs of purely human characters like Rawdon Lilly in *Aaron's Rod* and Ben Cooley in *Kangaroo*, who take on maternal characteristics in their desire to be "independent of outside aid" (*AR*, 93). What Lawrence advocates in *The Plumed Serpent* is the sort of father-leadership, in all realms of life, that is shown by Don Ramón. When Ramón speaks, Kate recognizes "a certain vulnerable kindliness about him, which made her wonder, startled, if she had ever realized what real fatherliness meant. The mystery, the nobility, the inaccessibility, and the vulnerable compassion of man in his separate fatherhood" (*PS*, 206). Kate has been searching after a man worthy to take the lead in a relationship with her, and although Cipriano may seem to her at times "the supreme god-demon. . . . the Master" (p. 343), Ramón is the true Dark Master that all of Lawrence's lost girls (and boys) seek. Cipriano without Ramón is "just an instrument, and not ultimately interesting" to Kate (p. 447). Moreover Kate, who banks just as hard on her independence as Alvina Houghton does, believes that "Ramón would never encroach on her, he would never seek any close contact. It was the incompleteness in Cipriano that sought her out, and seemed to trespass on her" (p. 207). Lawrence seems not to have been fully aware of this unattractive aspect of Cipriano's personality, but his use of that key word, *trespass*, tips readers off to an unhealthy dependency problem. Incidents like the aforementioned meeting for tea, at which Ramón and Cipriano greet each other tenderly, suggests what Lawrence did not intend: that Cipriano is as dependent upon Ramón, whom he calls "my Lord," as he refuses to be on "my Lady." Herman Daleski notes that Lawrence "generally castigates a childlike dependence in adult relationships, whether between man and man or man and woman; but Cipriano's eyes are 'childlike,' and *his* dependence is apparently acceptable not only to Ramón. [The relationship] . . . is subversive of what Lawrence would seem to contend it is—an ideal relation between two men, each of whom has consummated a self and one of whom, while maintaining his independence, willingly submits to the greater soul of the other."[10] Indeed, Lawrence gives the reader no grounds for believing that Cipriano after his incarnation as Huitzilopochtli is any more of a man than he was before, when he worshiped at the feet of the Madonna. And Cipriano's crucial lack of independence does more than make Kate wary of establishing a permanent relationship with him; it also causes the reader to cast a critical eye on Ramón, who, like Miss Pinnegar in *The Lost Girl*, only *seems* to leave space.

In the first version (1919) of his essay on Cooper's Leatherstocking novels, Lawrence states that "a race falls when men begin to worship the Great Mother, when they are enveloped within the woman, as a child in the womb" (*SM*, 109). In his leadership period, Lawrence's hatred of the domineering mother type caused him to oversimplify the options open to society: he says in *Fantasia* that "it is a choice between serving *man*, or woman. It is a choice between yielding the soul to a leader, leaders, or yielding only to the woman, wife, mistress, or mother" (*FU*, 145). *The Plumed Serpent* represents the social and political corollary to Lawrence's emphasis during this period on the necessity for a father's leadership in the family. Even the supposedly just physical punishment meted out by Cipriano in his role as Quetzalcoatl's warrior aspect may be seen as a mere extension into society as a whole of the father's corporal punishment in the family group. The novel presents in fictional form the kinds of relationships that Lawrence believed would lift up the race after the cataclysmic reign of the Magna Mater: obedience of the masses to a supreme male leader; love between man and woman that is necessary for, but subordinate to, the man's larger mission in society.

Lawrence's recognition of the difficulty in establishing the prescribed relationships may have caused him to counterweight the Quetzalcoatl movement with Kate Leslie's resistance to its precepts, and to give the novel a characteristic "open" ending. Or perhaps Lawrence was unable to give his own full allegiance to the novel's strictures about sacrificing one's independence in allegiance to another (male) human being and to the mission he represents. He expresses Cipriano's attempt to dominate Kate Leslie in oral terms familiar to readers of his works:

> "You treat me as if I had no life of my own," she said. "But I have."
> "A life of your own? Who gave it you? Where did you get it?"
> "I don't know. But I have got it. And I must live it. I can't be just swallowed up." (*PS*, 406)

On the level of intimate human relationships, Lawrence's characters fight being swallowed, consumed, eaten, devoured by others; yet they also wish to merge themselves with others. One way out of this dilemma lies in connection with cosmic forces. As critic Richard Wheeler notes, Lawrence protects merger "from the threat to autonomous individuality, from what Erikson calls the 'fear of ego loss,' by submerging the self in a life force that infuses the individual with a far greater power than he can know by himself."[11] Undoubtedly Lawrence would have Kate give herself up to the larger forces embodied in her husband, for the novel suggests that losing one's small, personal identity in the god or goddess gains one a larger identity.[12] Yet Kate, like Lawrence, fears the loss of the individual self through merging with the other, whether that other is a person or a religious/political movement.

The Plumed Serpent provides a textbook case for the study of charismatic leadership and political interdependencies. Society's merging with such a leader in what one political scientist calls a "politics of passivity"[13] grows out of a crisis in legitimate authority. In the 1920s, when Lawrence wrote his novel, Mexico was at a weak and vulnerable point: Catholicism and political authority were devalued, established ideologies crumbling. This decline of orderly hierarchies created a "society without the father" (to use Alexander Mischerlich's book title). Lawrence's solution to the problem, at least in fiction, was the elevation of a leader to Super Father, a larger than life figure who gives values and ambitions to his followers. The sexual ambiguity of Don Ramón, who is somehow both father and mother, is typical of charismatic leaders; the mystery of this resolution of opposites adds to his sacredness, and hence to his power.

At least two bodies of literature are useful for an understanding of charismatic leadership. Psychoanalytic work on the early years of life reveals that problems in the pre-oedipal stages of psychological development lead to problems with a sense of self. These problems result in the need for idealizable figures who can instill in their adherents a sense of who they are. In *The Plumed Serpent*, the Mexican peasants take on a ready-made identity through participation in the cult of Quetzalcoatl. Studies of group dynamics reveal that individual patterns of behavior are accentuated in groups: a skillful leader recognizes his followers' needs and fosters and exaggerates their dependency upon him. *The Plumed Serpent* demonstrates how the crowd fuses under Ramón's influence as Ramón puts his will over the people (*PS*, 370). In totalitarianism, the leader exerts his power in all areas of life, erasing the boundaries between politics and everything else (such as family life or religion). Meanwhile the leader also is transformed by this political symbiosis: weak in some ways, he becomes stronger through his followers' dependency upon him, and their relationship is all the more vital and intimate for the mutuality of need. This kind of interdependency flowers when traditional authority patterns weaken.

Psychoanalytic research suggests that people who have been disenchanted with a parent early in childhood, through the parent's absence or dominance, may set out on a later search for idealizable leaders as replacements for these unsatisfactory parents.[14] Given the rough-and-tumble nature of politics, heroes do topple; the leader's search for followers who will love him, and the followers' search for a leader to love, are doomed to failure. Therefore persons who are fixated in the earliest (i.e., pre-oedipal) stages of psychological development are good targets of ideologies with easily distinguishable heroes and villains, a clear sense of direction, and promises for a golden future—ideologies found, for example, in "some religious cults with political components." The personality needs of D. H. Lawrence led directly to the creation of *The Plumed Serpent* and other works of the leadership period. In his novel, Lawrence created a fantasy father of heroic proportions, molded to his own specifications and subject to no vagaries of real-life circumstance. But Lawrence's insight into the dangers posed by such charismatic leadership not only prevented his aligning himself with any such figure in his own ever-changing environment; it also caused him to draw back from Don Ramón, if only slightly, in the course of the novel, and to leave behind, after its completion, the rise of a political-religious leader as a subject for his fiction.

II. Blessed are the Powerful: The Last Works

It is now a commonplace in Lawrence criticism that Lawrence repudiated the ideal of leadership after *The Plumed Serpent*, finished in January 1925 and published in 1926. It is said that he adopted instead the mode of tenderness. Yet it may be argued that Lawrence retained to the end his belief in the patriarchal ideal and gave up only the search for its embodiment in a social, political, or religious system. The works of his last phase continue to show a preoccupation with the "devouring mother" and the sustaining father.

In the fall of 1925, Lawrence stayed for two weeks in the Midlands of England, where he had his first extended visit with Frieda's children. Afterward, he sighed with relief, "I have fled again from my native land: it seems to me sunk in damp and gloom, beyond all bearing,"[1] and he complained to Dorothy Brett, "Privately, I can't stand Frieda's children. They have a sort of suburban bounce and *suffisance* which puts me off" (*CL*, II, 863). Lawrence apparently changed his mind about Frieda's children, at least about the youngest, Barbara Weekley, who, along with her sister, visited with the Lawrences in Spotorno, Italy, in early 1926 (*CL*, II, 887). There he created a novella based mainly on Barbara's life with her father after Frieda's elopement with Lawrence, and in this work he rescued Barbara from her stultifying Midlands existence much as he himself had rescued Frieda.

Lawrence entitled his novella *The Virgin and the Gipsy*, but it may be argued that the pivotal character in the work is neither the virgin nor the gipsy but rather the domineering mother figure who dictates the style of life against which the young girl, Yvette, rebels. Frieda Lawrence apparently recognized the centrality of this character, and Lawrence was unsure enough about his choice of title to write to his British publisher,

"Frieda doesn't like the title of *The Virgin and the Gipsy*, she prefers something with Granny, like 'Granny Gone' or 'Granny on the Throne.' What do you think?"[2] The Granny in question is Yvette's paternal grandmother. In real life, Ernest Weekley went to live with his parents, an unmarried aunt, and a bachelor uncle after Frieda left him; the aunt and uncle become the rector's brothers and sister in the novella, and the father disappears completely in order to give the mother full sway. Granny, we are told, is "the central figure in the house.... They called her The Mater" (*VG*, 2–3). With the wife's escape, the husband's mother reassumes her elevated position in the family. References are made to her being on her "throne" (pp. 3, 5, 18), from which she wields unlimited power. Her unmarried daughter, Cissie, has sacrificed her life to the care of the Mater, and prays often for forgiveness for her feelings of anger and resentment at this tie. The entire first chapter of *The Virgin and the Gipsy* lays the groundwork for the rest of the action—it sets forth Granny's character in detail and at length, at the same time delineating the oppressive atmosphere of the rectory where she reigns. The chapter ends with a summary statement that places Granny firmly in the camp of Lawrence's "devouring mothers": "It was not as if the Mater were a warm, kindly soul. She wasn't. She only seemed it, cunningly.... The Mater, of course, was the pivot of the family. The family was her own extended ego. Naturally she covered it with her power. And her sons and daughters, being weak and disintegrated, naturally were loyal" (p. 7).

The woman who does not allow her children and grandchildren egos of their own, but rather who engulfs them to assuage her own narcissistic needs, is marked as a "devouring mother." Lawrence draws attention to this aspect of the Mater's character by underscoring her large, even disgusting appetite: "Granny quickly slobbered her portion—lucky if she spilled nothing on her protuberant stomach" (*VG*, 10); "But she was perfectly complacent, sitting in her ancient obesity, and after meals, getting the wind from her stomach, pressing her bosom with her hand as she 'rifted' in gross physical complacency" (p. 15). Granny takes a great interest in life's activities and is praised by outsiders for that interest; but those inside the family recognize that Granny's prying into everyone's affairs robs others of their separate identities. Again, Lawrence expresses Granny's inquisitiveness in oral terms: She is "like some awful idol of old flesh, consuming all the attention" (p. 15). It is no wonder that Aunt Cissie has appetite only for a single boiled potato, since, having been consumed by her mother, she has no appetite for life. Only the rector considers himself to be sheltered rather than engulfed, and he waxes heavy under the reign of the Magna Mater (p. 11).

Granny's "insatiable greed for life" links her to the pesky toad on the grounds, snatching bees in its implacable jaws and swallowing them one by one; Yvette's calling in the gardener to kill the loathsome creature—"that'rt none goin' ter emp'y th' bee-'ive into thy guts" (*VG*, 19–20)—foreshadows the inevitable destruction of Granny herself. The reader is never allowed to forget for long what an oppressive figure Granny is, and how much Yvette wants her dead. Chapter three, concerned with Yvette's first meeting with the gipsy, concludes with the young people asking Yvette what fortune she has been told by the gipsy woman in the caravan. Yvette lists the events predicted for her, ending with "a death in the family, which if it means Granny, won't be so *very* awful" (p. 35). Yvette admires the reckless and indomitable nature of the fortune-teller and believes that such a woman "would strangle Granny with one hand" (p. 43); significantly, Yvette does not imagine the gipsy killing any person other than Granny. Granny becomes the incarnation of all the most loathsome qualities associated with the mother figures in Lawrence's own life. With her prying inquisitiveness and her belching, she begins as a caricature rather than a character; but she develops into a witch of nightmarish, fairy tale proportions:

> It was Granny whom she came to detest with all her soul. That obese old woman, sitting there in her blindness like some great red-blotched fungus, her neck swallowed between her heaped-up shoulders and her rolling, ancient chins, so that she was neckless as a double potato, her Yvette really hated, with that pure, sheer hatred which is almost a joy. . . .
> This motherly old soul, her mouth gave her away. It always had been one of the compressed sort. But in her old age it had gone like a toad's lipless, the jaw pressing up like the lower jaw of a trap. The look Yvette most hated, was the look of that lowered jaw pressing relentlessly up, with an ancient prognathous thrust, so that the stub nose in turn was forced to press upwards, and the whole face was pressed a little back, beneath the big, wall-like forehead. The will, the ancient, toad-like obscene *will* in the old woman was fearful, once you saw it: a toad-like self-will that was godless, and less than human! It belonged to the old, enduring race of toads, or tortoises. And it made one feel that Granny would never die. She would live on like these higher reptiles, in a state of semi-coma, forever. . . . [A] family!—an awful, smelly family that would never disperse, stuck half dead round the base of a fungoid old woman! How was one to cope with that? (pp. 96–97)

The only way for Yvette to cope with Granny is to get rid of her, since no one can be free while Granny lives. "Granny gone" must be the motto of this story, as Frieda recognized—a fact not without its irony in light of Lawrence's intermittent attitude toward his wife as a "devouring mother." The climax of the story comes when Yvette, hating to return inside to Granny's realm, is almost overtaken by the rampaging waters from the reservoir and is rescued by the gipsy of the novella's title. The two of them rush into the house and upstairs to higher ground, leaving Granny below to scream, to claw at the air, and then to drown. The tears that Yvette later sheds are mistakenly interpreted by the policeman as signs of her sorrow at Granny's death; in reality she is mourning the lost gipsy. Her sister Lucille weeps only with relief at Yvette's rescue, and Aunt Cissie too has a convenient moral and psychological justification for her refusal to mourn for her insufferable mistress: "Let the old be taken and the young spared! Oh I *can't* cry for the Mater, now Yvette is spared!" (*VG*, 119). The gallons of tears that the three women weep are implicitly compared to the rushing waters caused by the collapse of "an ancient, perhaps even a Roman mine tunnel" (p. 119): they mark the women's sense of release from the constricting bounds set by Granny's brand of motherhood, a release occasioned by underground—that is, primitive—modes of thinking. The death of Granny, on the most basic level, is a wish fulfillment of the first order.

Several months after completing *The Virgin and the Gipsy*, Lawrence was provided with the perfect opportunity to create a similar story. To his sister Emily he wrote that Cynthia Asquith had asked him "to do a murder story, for a murder book she has in mind." Two months later, in January 1927, Lawrence told his other sister Ada that if he didn't feel "murderous" he would not do a murder story—"unless a bluff."[3] But Lawrence had no trouble feeling murderous toward the "devouring mother" figures in his life, including the one who had produced Emily, Ada, and himself. His story "The Lovely Lady" is bluff only in that no legal murder is committed; on the psychological level, however, the story turns on the murder of the title character, a woman who bears a strong resemblance to Mrs. Morel of *Sons and Lovers* and hence to Lydia Beardsall Lawrence herself. Like her prototype and her fictional antecedent, Pauline Attenborough of "The Lovely Lady" has a favorite, older son who dies in his twenties, a victim of the mother's dominance. Richard, the second son, complains of his mother's "[p]ower to feed on other lives. . . . She has fed on me as she fed on Henry. She put a sucker into one's soul and sucked up one's essential life" (*CSS*, III, 778). Thus Pauline is perceived as yet another "devouring mother" who must die for the good of the family. She is portrayed as such a hateful witch that one must see her death as (in Julian Moynahan's words) a "deed of life," just as one must applaud Hansel and Gretel's pushing the wicked, grandmotherly hag into the oven. Where other Lawrence stories substitute "accident" (*The Fox*) or ritual ("The Woman Who Rode Away") for murder, this story uses a guilty conscience to do the willful woman in.

In a sense, the minor character of Cissie in *The Virgin and the Gipsy* moves to center stage in "The Lovely Lady." Pauline's niece Ciss, a spinsterish, pathetic woman dependent upon her aunt for sustenance, devises the trick that confounds Pauline into hearing her dead son's accusing voice. The version of the story that is read today suggests a key role for the sun in this turn of events: it is when Ciss rolls "voluptuously" with her sun-lover that she hears Pauline talking aloud to her dead son-lover (*CSS*, III, 766); the next day, when she is "hot and fierce with sunshine" (p. 773), Ciss pretends that she is Henry speaking from beyond the grave and thereby prepares the way for Pauline's decline and eventual demise. An unpublished typescript of an earlier version of the story makes the sun's role more explicit. "The sun gave one resistance, the resistance of youth. . . . Here was a new creed, for Ciss, born of the sun in her." As Brian Finney puts it, "Lawrence deliberately associates Ciss's rebellion against Pauline with the sun's insouciance."[4] The storm that accompanies Ciss and Robert's victory over Pauline, in this version, reminds one of the flood in *The Virgin and the Gipsy*, for the thunder indicates that "an ancient tightness was being broken in the atmosphere. There was a new freedom, an opening of the heart and of the whole soul."[5] In both stories, as in *Sons and Lovers*, the death of the mother figure is necessary for the child's emotional and sexual fulfillment.

The importance of the sun in "The Lovely Lady" sets that story in the context of Lawrence's increasing tendency toward myth and ritual, allegory and fable, in his works after 1921. *The Ladybird*, *The Boy in the Bush*, "The Woman Who Rode Away," *The Plumed Serpent*—these works and others describe the sun as the cosmic principle of life and offer it as a paradigm for human behavior. Lawrence crystalized his sun theories in the story "Sun," written at the Villa Bernardo in Italy in late 1925. Although usually read as a story about sexual awakening—especially in the unexpurgated version published in 1928 by Harry Crosby's Black Sun Press—or about getting in touch with the cosmos, "Sun" is just as certainly concerned with parental authority: in the first view, the sun is a lover; in the second, a god; in the third, a father. In all readings the sun replaces and supplants the inadequate male figure whom Juliet, the heroine, has left behind in America. The story is a perfect illustration of Lawrence's views on the parent's proper role in the psychological development of the child and will be discussed in chapter twelve as a summation of Lawrence's accord with postFreudian theory.

After writing "Sun," Lawrence turned his energies to other works but not necessarily to other themes. The years 1926–28 saw the creation of three versions of the novel that became *Lady Chatterley's Lover*. The versions differ in subtle ways, one from the other, with an overall movement in the direction of a hardened emphasis on the concerns that Lawrence is often thought to have outgrown after his leadership period. Certainly the often-quoted 1928 letter to Witter Bynner, about the obsolescence of the hero and the "militant ideal," lends support to the view that Lawrence changed tack in his last writing phase. In this letter, Lawrence remarks that he is "becoming a lamb at last" (*CL*, II, 1045). In fact, like his hero Jack Grant of *The Boy in the Bush*, Lawrence was a lion in lamb's clothing, as a comparison of the three versions of *Lady Chatterley's Lover* reveals.

The first and second versions, published in 1944 and 1972, respectively, fully deserve the title of *Tenderness* that Lawrence considered for the final, tougher version read today. The second and longest version, entitled *John Thomas and Lady Jane*, best reveals the desire for merger overriding the need for separation. The gamekeeper, here called Parkin, has been so wounded by his marriage to Bertha Coutts that he stiffens and hardens his spine in resistance to the appeal emanating from his unhappy lady, Connie Chatterley; she in turn, viewing Parkin from behind, realizes the man's aloneness (*JTLJ*, 27–28). But if the novel tosses around the familiar catch phrase noli me tangere, it does so only as a prelude to resurrection of the body, as in the novella of the same period, *The Escaped Cock*. Eventually Parkin streams toward Connie (p. 111), and she flows toward him. In fact, the movement of the novel is toward a melting merger of two hitherto separate identities: "If, in the beginning of time men and women had joined together in one body . . . there was no he and she. The two came together and formed one immortality, in which the I, the wearisome solitary individualistic I, disappeared and became a whole. She felt so acutely, and so achingly, the fragmentariness of the I. She was sick of single individuality" (p. 296).

The Mrs. Bolton of versions one and two of the novel (especially the latter) has "a strange dignity about her" (*JTLJ*, 75), never quite establishing with Clifford Chatterley the perverted mother-child marriage of the final version. Yet hints of Clifford's future infantile dependency upon his nurse are, in *John Thomas and Lady Jane*, to be found in the relationship between Jack Strangeways (who is absent from *The First Lady Chatterley* and from the last version)—another Jim Bricknell or Jack Middleton Murry figure—and his wife, visitors to Wragby Hall. Jack has strange ways indeed, acting "like a persistent little boy dogging his mother" (p. 54). What seems most real to his wife is "the tight string that tied her to Jack, and made her spend most of her time strangling his soul, while he, equally canny at the game, had tight strings round all her limbs and pulled them until he paralysed her. A great deal of it was mutual torment!" (p. 66). This portrait is one of the most vivid if tangential pictures of a hostile mother-child interdependency in Lawrence's fiction. The mothering role of Connie's sister, Hilda, is also mentioned in the second version of the story, even though it has nothing to do with the plot per se: Lawrence remarks that Hilda "wove a lot of importance round her little girls, round herself as mother" (p. 47), while providing no real nurturance. This casual remark coupled with the vivid portrait of Jack Strangeways shows that, for all its stress on tenderness—and this novel is very tender indeed, and a creation far superior to the work considered to be the definitive *Lady Chatterley*—*John Thomas and Lady Jane* contains considerable hostility toward the "devouring mother," who inhibits rather than fosters growth. Perhaps Parkin best pleads Lawrence's case when he asks his new lover, "But tha wunna want ter ma'e me feel sma', shall ter? Let me be mysen, an' let me feel as if tha wor littler than me!" (p. 329).

In the final version of *Lady Chatterley*, Lawrence places an even greater emphasis on infantile love relationships. Michaelis, Connie's pre-Mellors lover, appeals to her frustrated maternalism: "the infant crying in the night was crying out of his breast to her in a way that affected her very womb" (*LCL*, 24). He is frequently compared to a child (pp. 28–29, 55). Gran, the game-keeper's mother, becomes less like a real person—as she had appeared in the first and especially the second version, with the smuts upon her nose—and more like something approaching (but stopping short of) a grandmother from a fairy tale like Hansel and Gretel or like Lawrence's own *The Virgin and the Gipsy*: she becomes "that little, sharp woman" resembling Mrs. Morel and Jill Banford, a witchlike figure to be reckoned with. Most importantly, Mrs. Bolton acquires a new slant to her personality: Esther Forbes says, in her manuscript report comparing *The First Lady Chatterley* to the last, "originally [Mrs. Bolton] is a smart village gossip. She is turned into a queer thing, oozing perverted sex from every pore" (*FLC*, xvii). The charming japanned work box that

Mrs. Bolton covets in *John Thomas and Lady Jane* becomes implicitly converted into a coffin in *Lady Chatterley's Lover,* as Mrs. Bolton changes from a chirpy servant to a death-ridden mistress (*LCL,* 159). Her love and softness, seemingly positive attributes, get Clifford "by the throat. . . . She loved having his body in charge, absolutely, to the last menial offices. She said to Connie one day: 'All men are babies . . . just big babies'" (*LCL,* 103).

Clifford does behave like a child to his nurse, as the reader is often told (*LCL,* 115, 255). In his new activity at the mines, Clifford is "not aware how much Mrs. Bolton was behind him. He did not know how much he depended on her" (p. 114). So too he depends on Connie "with terror, like a child, almost like an idiot. She must be there. . . ." (p. 117). Without her he feels himself to be nothing, a cipher (p. 118), like Dr. Mitchell from *The Lost Girl* and all the real-life figures—Lawrence himself included—whom Lawrence felt to be overly dependent on "devouring mothers." In *The First Lady Chatterley,* Clifford's reaction to Connie's pregnancy reveals his sexless and perverse worship of his mother-wife: "How beautiful you are! . . . You are a virgin mother. A Madonna like a rose instead of like a lily. By God, I hope the child will be worthy of you. I'll get my paints out and try to paint you: the modern Madonna!—and I the Joseph! I shall fall into mariolatry—Mary-worship!" (*FLC,* 310). Clifford's response actually forces Connie's decision to leave him and to take a risk on any kind of life with Parkin. In the final version, Connie recognizes Clifford's "amazing dependence" on her with horror and willingly has him transfer it to his nurse, a "half-mistress, half-foster-mother" (*LCL,* 118). With Connie's final break with her husband in favor of a life with Mellors, Clifford Chatterley's degradation is complete. He casts himself into Mrs. Bolton's womb, as it were—to use the phraseology of Lawrence's 1918 "devouring mother" letter (*CL,* 1, 564)—and she, the Magna Mater, receives him with a mixture of gratification and contempt:

> And he put his arms round her and clung to her like a child, wetting the bib of her starched white apron, and the bosom of her pale-blue cotton dress with his tears. He had let himself go altogether at last.
>
> So at length she kissed him, and rocked him on her bosom, and in her heart she said to herself: "Oh, Sir Clifford! Oh, high and mighty Chatterleys! Is this what you've come down to!" And finally he even went to sleep, like a child. And she felt worn out, and went to her

own room, where she laughed and cried at once, with a hysteria of her own. . . .

After this, Clifford became like a child with Mrs. Bolton, he would hold her hand, and rest his head on her breast, and when she once lightly kissed him, he said: "Yes! Do kiss me! Do kiss me!" And when she sponged his great blond body, he would say the same. . . .

And he lay with a queer, blank face like a child, with a bit of the wonderment of a child. And he would gaze on her with wide, childish eyes, in a relaxation of madonna-worship. It was sheer relaxation on his part, letting go all his manhood, and sinking back to a childish position that was really perverse. And then he would put his hand into her bosom and feel her breasts, and kiss them in exaltation, the exaltation of perversity of being a child when he was a man.

Mrs. Bolton was both thrilled and ashamed, she both loved and hated it. Yet she never rebuffed nor rebuked him. And they drew into a closer physical intimacy, an intimacy of perversity, when he was a child stricken with an apparent candour and an apparent wonderment, that looked almost like a religious exaltation: the perverse and literal rendering of: "except ye become again as a little child." While she was the Magna Mater, full of power and potency, having the great blond child-man under her will and her stroke entirely. (pp. 316–17)

Lawrence may have intended Clifford Chatterley's paralysis to symbolize the "emotional or passional paralysis, of most men of his sort and class today," as he explains in "A Propos of *Lady Chatterley's Lover*" (*LCL*, 358); but, like Maurice Pervin's blindness in "The Blind Man," the handicap also represents reversion or regression to an infantile dependency upon the mother figure.

The other characters of Lawrence's last novel also undergo change in their course through three versions of the story. Oliver Mellors has a "kind of protective authority" (*LCL*, 91–92) in both the first and second versions but he is definitely more of a leader in the third. He becomes, in fact, more like Lawrence himself, a man of nature conversant with things of the mind. Several readers have noted that Mellors is almost an anagram for Morel; consistent with this change in name from Parkin to Mellors is an infusion of facts from Lawrence's own early life: Mellors's first two loves (the Parkin character has had none before his marriage) are clearly modeled on Jessie Chambers and Helen Corke; the gamekeeper who replaces Mellors when he loses his job is Joe Chambers, not Albert Adam, as in the first and second versions. For all Mellors's desire to come into "tender touch" with Connie, he refuses to lose "his pride or dignity or his integrity as a man" (*LCL*, 302); he is, in short, a much less vulnerable figure than the Parkin with two missing teeth, who sits with Connie near Felley Mill, opened and exposed to the challenging keeper of the grounds (*JTLJ*, 370). Indeed, a comparison of the earlier incident in which Mellors stands outside Lady Chatterley's bedroom window with the corresponding incident in the second version shows the move toward a reemphasis on singleness and isolation—not to the degree found in the leadership period, in novels like *Aaron's Rod*, but marked nonetheless. As Parkin waits futilely for his new lover to come out to meet him he feels the thread of his desire break, at least temporarily, and decides that a "man must not *depend* on a woman" (*JTLJ*, 139). Mellors, however, realizes that he's got to stick to, and accept, his aloneness and isolation (*LCL*, 155). Further, Mellors has a certain combative and hostile bearing about him in *Lady Chatterley's Lover*. His manner toward Connie's sister, Hilda, changes in proportion to her own change in character from an innocuous if misguided woman to an Amazon from whose dominion Connie is glad to be free (p. 275). Ultimately Mellors becomes so heated about the Bertha Couttses and Cliffords of the world that he would like to shoot them, justifying their deaths as "the tenderest thing you could do for them" (p. 304). Such a sentiment—certainly a most dangerous redefinition of tenderness—is a hallmark of Lawrence's leadership period and clearly lingers on into the last works.

As for Connie Chatterley, she alters in several ways from the first version of the story to the last, not the least of which is in her changing concerns about relinquishing her power as "your ladyship" and becoming a slave (*LCL*, 144–45). In their night of passion before Connie's trip abroad, Connie does become "a passive, consenting thing, like a slave, a physical slave" (p. 267); the next day, Hilda accuses Connie of having a "slave nature" (p. 274). The weight of the novel rests on Connie's relinquishing of her ladyship and becoming subservient to the lord who is Mellors. As Lawrence says in "A Propos of *Lady Chatterley's Lover*," "[t]he sense of having a potential creator and lawgiver, as father and husband, is perhaps essential to the day-by-day life of a man, if he is to live full and satisfied" (*LCL*, 342). Even the Parkin of the first *Lady Chatterley* is very worried about Connie's throwing her superior social status up to him after their marriage (*FLC*, 289); the Mellors of the final version has developed a more aggressive stance that not only ensures his lover's capitulation but also elicits the admiring remark from her own father, "You set fire to her haystack all right" (p. 307).

Connie Chatterley, of course, has been as instrumental in helping the pheasant breeder "break out of his shell" into new life as he has been in her salvation. This final novel, urging tenderness as the mode of leadership (*LCL*, 285–87), seems to reconcile power and love as no previous work had done. Keith Sagar maintains that "the old phallic awareness and the old phallic insouciance" (a phrase Lawrence used in reference to this novel) are "clearly a rejection of the power principle which had dominated *The Plumed Serpent*,"[6] and Martin Green sees the novel as "a return to the old faith in matriarchalism."[7] However, an undertone of misogyny exists even in *Lady Chatterley's Lover*, undercutting the prophet's message. The scene in which Connie and Mellors copulate in the rain has elicited John Stoll's most telling criticism of the novel; his remarks apply to the leadership works in general, with their praise of predatory animals:

> Instead of overcoming the perverse will to power, Lawrence tends to glorify and relate it integrally to the sexual bond as a manifestation of the life principle, the vital self. The cumulative effect of such incidents reflects the degeneration of the vital self into mere animalism and the inversion of tenderness to potential cruelty. In this way, he subverts his thesis, and it is impossible to accept the author's last word on the sexual relationship.[8]

Keith Sagar also recognizes that Mellors's heavy dialect and four-letter-word vocabulary match "the element of bullying which, despite the emphasis on tenderness, and the numerous episodes of real tenderness, characterises Mellors' treatment of Connie."[9] Blatantly feminist criticism of the Kate Millett sort is not the only indictment of dangerous equivocations in D. H. Lawrence's stance toward women.

The novella of this late period, known today as *The Man Who Died*, shows a similar antagonism toward women: its quasi-biblical style and fabulistic mode do not conceal Lawrence's emphasis on staying clear of the "devouring mother." The man who has come back to life confronts the Mary Magdelene figure, here called Madeleine, whom he asks for shelter; but he immediately reconsiders his request, knowing that to live in Madeleine's house would be to capitulate to the power that comes to the bestower of charity or patronage (*MD*, 176). Later he meets Madeleine again, and insists to her that he must go to his Father rather than returning to his earthly mother (p. 179). Continually he repeats that he must not be touched (the noli me tangere refrain), that there must be no trespass, that he must remain alone, alone in "his intrinsic solitude" (p. 184).

The perfect mate for this man awaits him in the temple of Isis. With the priestess of Isis, through sex, the man who died learns "the great atonement, the being in touch" (*MD*, 208). For all its tenderness, however, *The Man Who Died* contains a great deal of hostility toward the mother. The goddess herself is "not Isis, Mother of Horus. It was Isis Bereaved, Isis in Search" (p. 188)—that is, the goddess defined not as mother but as seeker of the phallus with its "inward sun" to touch her womb. The man who died praises the goddess as "greater than the mother unto man" (p. 195). The priestess in the temple has renounced her own mother in favor of obeisance to Isis and this mother is presented, though indirectly, in a distinctly unfavorable light: she loves to exert control (p. 190) and shows her imperiousness even in her "short and determined" stride (p. 199). The man who died knows that the priestess's mother will oppose her care of him, although the priestess is determined not to allow her mother to thwart her (p. 201). Yet the mother does win out in a way, as Banford wins out in *The Fox* even though she is dead, forcing the intruder who seeks shelter on her property to light out for other territory. *The Man Who Died* ends with the movement apart rather than together, and with a significant indication that the priestess is desirous of having her own inviolate space once again: "And even she wanted the coolness of her own air around her. . . ." (p. 210).

An essay of the period, called "The Risen Lord," helps to explain one impetus behind the creation of *The Escaped Cock*. Lawrence intended "The Risen Lord" for an Everyman series on "A Religion for the Young," although he believed (incorrectly, as it turned out) that the journal would be unwilling to entertain his opinions on the subject (*CL*, II, 1171). In this essay Lawrence discusses three images of Christ: as a child on his mother's lap, as a man crucified on the cross, and as a god resurrected from the dead. He laments that the vast majority of Christians are stuck at the first stage, worshiping the infantile Jesus, even though the Christchild, enthroned in the lap of the Mother, is obviously only "a preparatory image, to prepare us for Christ the Man" ("RL," 571). The matter is of utmost importance to Lawrence, for he was never prone to disconnect religious beliefs from the manner in which one conducts one's life, nor religious images from self-image; he maintains that "where the Madonna-and-Child image overwhelms everything else, the man visions himself all the time as a child. . . . sheltered in the arms of an all-sheltering mother" (pp. 571–72). World War I brought a new image of self and Christ to those who had known its horrors, for the carnage could not be soothed away by woman. Their new image of Christ, then, was of Christ Crucified, beyond the protection of the mother.

Naturally enough, says Lawrence, the postwar woman was loath to relinquish her self-image as Madonna, since it "gave her the greatest significance; and the greatest power" ("RL," 572). Lawrence sees that image as dangerously outdated: the mother figure is not to be trusted for protection and support. But neither does he advocate Christ Crucified. Rather, for the hopeful postwar young and the new era he hopes they will inaugurate, Lawrence posits the Risen Lord, risen in the whole of His flesh, even in parts hitherto unmentionable. The essay culminates in a paean to the life of the body rather than of the spirit; indeed, here Christ's resurrection represents the triumph of the body *over* the spirit. Yet an important motif underlying the stress on tenderness and touch in this essay is its implicit repudiation of two of the tenderest images in Christianity: the infant Jesus on his mother's lap and the crucified Christ on his mother's lap. Lawrence is firm in his belief that full genitality can be achieved only through disassociation from the mother, and that the ascendancy of woman as evidenced by the popularity of the Madonna must give way to ascendancy of man in his new image of resurrected Christ.

Lawrence's repudiation of the mother-child relationship also figures importantly in his short stories of the last period, including "The Blue Moccasins," written during the summer of 1928 and published in 1929. The central figure in this story is a spinster, Miss M'Leod, who has set her life's course in rebellion against "that image of tyranny, her father" (*CSS*, III, 827). At the age of forty-five she meets Percy Barlow, a twenty-two-year-old soldier referred to by the narrator as a boy (p. 828). Barlow confides in Miss M'Leod that he has in effect been turned out of his house by his stepmother: as he is attracted to his confidant because of her age—"He looked up to her immensely: 'She's miles above me'" (p. 828)—Miss M'Leod in turn loves the "orphan" in Percy Barlow. She yearns to mother him, first, and then to marry him. Lawrence draws the reader's attention to their great disparity in age by having Miss M'Leod insist that she is too old to marry Barlow and by having Barlow retort that she is not too old. The constellation of an older woman and a young soldier and the repartee between them about whether or not she is old enough to be his mother (in this story it is phrased as "It wouldn't be right for you to marry an old thing like me" [p. 828]) are reminiscent of both *The Fox* and "You Touched Me," stories of the leadership period.

The blue moccasins of the title are the central symbol of the story. Miss M'Leod has purchased them from her Indian guide on a trip to New Mexico before her marriage. The moccasins symbolize the subordination of men to women, as the narrator makes clear when he remarks that the guide was Miss M'Leod's "subordinate. In her independence she made use of men, of course, but merely as servants, subordinates" (*CSS*, III, 827). After her marriage Miss M'Leod hangs the moccasins in her husband's room, as a tacit sign of her dominance over him; the shoes are associated with the giver in her Mother Mary role by their blue color, like "the sacred blue colour, the turquoise of heaven" (p. 837) of her "forget-me-not blue eyes" (p. 840). Indeed, Miss M'Leod is very like a virgin mother, with her ivory-white skin and hair—marriage hardly touches this woman, so that others have difficulty thinking of her as Mrs. Barlow (p. 831). At the age of fifty-seven, after several years of marriage, Miss M'Leod acts like a "devouring mother" to her son-husband: rather than nurturing him she "manage[s] him with perfect ease" (p. 832).

Percy Barlow's liberation from this relationship occurs when he wins a part in an amateur production and plays leading man to a young widow in a romance called "The Shoes of Shagput." The shoes are none other than Miss M'Leod's moccasins, commandeered by Percy for his leading lady. He plays a Moor, with darkened face; she, an Eastern houri with veil and moccasins. In the course of the play, the heroine kicks off her shoes as a sign to the hero that he might approach her, crying, "Away, shoes of bondage, shoes of sorrow!" This "stage bit" parallels and even initiates the real-life attraction between Barlow and the widow and signifies Percy's freedom from bondage to his mother-wife. The actors find their true natures in these stage roles—they are no longer Percy and Alice but the Moor and the harem girl. Thus the story moves in the direction of Lawrence's writing career, toward fables like *The Virgin and the Gipsy*, *John Thomas and Lady Jane*, and *The Man Who Died*, in which the individual gives up his small personal identity and gains a greater one by "losing" himself in large, impersonal forces.

Miss M'Leod reacts to this play with fury and scorn. She demands her moccasins back in the middle of the second act, and during intermission rebukes her husband for the use to which he has put them (an earlier, rejected ending to the story has her returning the shoes to Percy).[10] Her punishing remarks practically force Percy down on top of the low pupil's desk of the church schoolroom used as a dressing room, and Alice too sits low on what Lawrence calls the "infants' bench" (*CSS*, III, 840–41). Miss M'Leod has changed from a fifty-seven-year-old lady into a "risen viper of [a] little elderly woman" (p. 838), much as Banford changes from a hostess to a witch crouched by the fire when Grenfel challenges her dominance in *The Fox*. But Percy Barlow regrets ever having put Miss M'Leod on a pedestal, looking up to her "as if she was God" (p. 842), and letting himself be kept childish and small. The third act of the play to which the actors dart back is clearly to be the third act or resurrection of Percy Barlow's life, in which he forms a new allegiance with the more appropriate woman. The audience is impatient to get on with the performance, having been caught up in the turn of events on the stage; so too the reader in tune with Lawrence "loses" himself in the events and characters of the fiction and feels a sense of liberation from the "devouring mother" and her false, infantilizing offer of security.

Yet another late story, entitled "Mother and Daughter," focuses again on the mother-child relationship and points to the necessity for a father's rule. Through the force of her will, "seeking whom she might devour, and devouring him" (*CSS*, III, 806), the mother, Miss Bodoin, thwarts her daughter's romances until finally she is vanquished by a man of authority, a "sly old fox [who] knew what he was about" (p. 825); this man steals the child from her mother, takes over the property, and establishes himself as a tribal patriarch. The daughter's hesitation at giving herself up to this dangerous yet thrilling creature is overcome in the familiar Lawrentian manner: "he used all his will, looking back at her heavily and calculating that she must submit" (p. 822). Written some time between November 1928 and February 1929, this late story presents in capsule form the major concerns of Lawrence's important leadership novel, *The Plumed Serpent*. In "Mother and Daughter," the Ramón figure, Arnault, is physically an unlikely marriage candidate for the heroine, Virginia Bodoin: he is sixty years old, gray-haired, and fat. Yet he is a powerful antagonist to Virginia's dominating mother, and in the course of the story he succeeds in overthrowing the matriarchal ideal that she represents.

Lawrence knew perfectly well the technical meaning of the term *matriarchy*, referring to the inheritance of name and property through the mother's line, since he had read Frazer's *The Golden Bough* by 1917. An essay entitled "Matriarchy," written shortly before "Mother and Daughter," shows Lawrence's familiarity with the concept as well as his firsthand knowledge of its practice by a modern American Indian tribe. As Lawrence (following Frazer) understands it, matriarchy does not require the subordination of male to female, a common misconception;[11] on the contrary, it frees the male from domestic responsibilities and allows him to achieve his full manhood. In a matriarchy, Lawrence explains, marriage and the home are of primary consideration to the woman. The man gathers "with other men, to fulfill his deeper social necessities, ... profound social cravings which can only be satisfied apart from women." Lawrence goes so far as to recommend that modern civilized societies return to this principle of matriarchy, so that men and women will again know their proper places: for the woman, the home; for the man, the communion of men, where males have traditionally "educated one another, by immediate contact, discussed politics and ideas, and made history" ("M," 552).

Without using the term *matriarchy*, Lawrence had expressed the same ideas in *Fantasia of the Unconscious*, where he credits *The Golden Bough* with giving him "hints" and "suggestions" for his arguments (*FU*, 54). In a chapter he calls a "semi-digression" from his discussion of child-consciousness, Lawrence contends that "a woman should stick to her own natural emotional positivity. But then man must stick to his own positivity of *being*, of action, *disinterested*, *non-domestic*, *male* action, which is not devoted to the increase of the female. . . . It is not woman who claims the highest in man. It is man's own religious soul that drives him on beyond woman, to his supreme activity" (*FU*, 135).[12] According to Lawrence, the "question of all time" reduces to this: "Man, the doer, the knower, the original in *being*, is he the lord of life? or is woman, the great Mother, who bore us from the womb of love, is she the supreme Goddess?" (*FU*, 133). In the present day, Lawrence believes, the second alternative receives the affirmative. Lawrence's most patriarchal novel, *The Plumed Serpent*, is matriarchal in the technical sense that Ramón's second wife, Teresa, is in charge of the woman's domestic realm while her husband busies himself in revamping Mexico. Yet the weight of this novel and Lawrence's other works is on the evils of matriarchalism in the loose sense, defined as the rule of women, and the implication is always that woman's rule in the home ruins males for their larger work (indeed, in the essay "Enslaved by Civilization," Lawrence complains that children are by and large educated first by their mothers and then by school mistresses, who are unqualified "to form the foundation of a *man*" since they consider men "mostly grown-up babies" ["EC," 578]).

His sentiments in "Matriarchy" notwithstanding, Lawrence's beliefs on the subject of a mother's rule in the home are made clear in his story "Mother and Daughter," in which Arnault's power lies in the fact that "his whole consciousness was patriarchal and tribal. And somehow, he was humble, but he was indestructible" (*CSS*, III, 820). He recognizes that Virginia has led an unsatisfactory life because she has been kept her mother's daughter: Virginia's father has been summarily dismissed—as Mrs. Bodoin had no doubt summarily dismissed him—in the first paragraph of the story, in the mere phrase, "since the effacement of a never very important husband" (p. 805). Virginia Bodoin has never achieved a satisfactory love relationship because she is married to her mother, like Banford and March in *The Fox*. Although she lives for two years with a lover, he backs out of the relationship finally because Vinnie and her mother have reduced him to nothingness, eating his marrow (p. 806) by lavishing him with gifts that he can feel only as charity. A second marriage possibility has been urged on Virginia by her mother because the man is five years younger than Virginia and therefore to be treated like a mere boy—kept in his place, "the eternal boy" (p. 813). These motifs are common to the works of the leadership period and obviously were not abandoned by Lawrence after 1925. Eventually Virginia shows some of her dead father's opposition to Mrs. Bodoin. Her contempt for her bossy mother is likened to David's pebble that vanquishes Goliath (p. 817): as in "The Lovely Lady," a "murder" is committed in self-defense by a small and seemingly helpless figure—a fictional incarnation of David Lawrence—against an evil giant, symbolic of the parent. What finally destroys Mrs. Bodoin is Virginia's attraction to the Armenian merchant whom she has met through business. Virginia obviously sees in this man salvation from the "devouring mother."

Arnault in turn is attracted to Virginia because of her gorgeous home, which offers this foreigner security and prestige in alien territory. He seeks to rescue this lost girl from her mother and to assert himself as the proper authority: "He was in love with Virginia. He saw, first and foremost, the child in her, as if she were a lost child in the gutter, a waif with a faint, fascinating cast in her brown eyes, waiting till someone would pick her up. A fatherless waif! And he was the tribal father, father through all the ages" (p. 820). When Virginia commits herself to Arnault her mother sarcastically remarks to her, "You're just the harem type, after all" (p. 826). These sentiments are the same as those that Kate Leslie entertains about Teresa's marriage to Ramón in *The Plumed Serpent*. But if Kate feels that she cannot bear Ramón's "pasha satisfaction" and Teresa's "harem" mentality, she also admits to herself that she envies Teresa and begins to question whether Teresa is not the greater woman (*PS*, 452, 449). Similarly, "Mother and Daughter" ends on a note of pity for Mrs. Bodoin, who has never been the "harem type."

It is ironic and sad that Lawrence's patriarchal ideal—the Great Father—requires the same abnegation of individual personality as the mother-worship it replaces—the same envelopment of the smaller soul by the larger, the same losing of one's soul in order to gain it. The effects are presumably different, but the differences are hard sometimes for the reader to ascertain. Jeffrey Meyers, in his reading of "Mother and Daughter," understandably concludes that Virginia has merely exchanged "her deadly existence with her mother for a kind of death-in-life with the horrible yet attractive Arnault,"[13] and Lydia Blanchard remarks that Virginia's marriage to "a comic Armenian. . . . is obviously not in her own interest."[14] Meyers and Blanchard trust the tale rather than the artist: Lawrence's depiction of the patriarch Arnault is fraught with the same ambiguities that surround the savior males in his other works, with the result that readers are as uncomfortable with Lawrence's notion of the Great Father as he would have them be with that of the Great Mother. Lawrence meant to show that, like the male-spark itself, a father's love is less showy than a mother's but deeper and more important to the child's development. In trying to ignite this father-spark, Lawrence let the blaze get out of hand. To paraphrase Lady Chatterley's father, Lawrence, by setting fire to the haystack, burns down the barn.

Lawrence's very last creation, the book called *Apocalypse*, includes a note of reverence for the Magna Mater as Lawrence finds her in the Book of Revelation. Wistfully he looks back in time to the wonder-woman, the Great Mother robed by the sun, standing with a child back in the childhood of history, when matriarchy was the ruling principle. The admiration seems out of keeping with Lawrence's views on the Magna Mater expressed elsewhere, except when one recalls that Lawrence first became interested in writing on Revelation during the 1923–1924 period when he was working on his novel *Quetzalcoatl*. In that novel, Cipriano seeks to make of Kate Leslie the pagan goddess Malintzi, "essential to the scheme of power and splendour, which must have a queen" (*A*, 120). It is only in Judaism and Christianity that woman has become either Virgin Mary or Whore of Babylon; Lawrence wishes to have in his Mexican pantheon a magnificent mother-queen to stand by the side of the warrior-king and ensure the continuance of his pagan religion.

Two months before his death, Lawrence revised and corrected the typescript of *Apocalypse* and produced his final statements on the ideal of leadership. In *Apocalypse* he remarks that if a man's country "mounts up aristocratically to a zenith of splendour and power, in a hierarchy, he will be all the more fulfilled, having his place in the hierarchy." He lambastes democracy for its *bullying* that substitutes for power, and for its fragmentation: "Modern democracy is made up of millions of frictional parts all asserting their own wholeness." Most important in terms of the relationship between the "devouring mother" and the ideal of leadership, Lawrence describes the democratic ideal as a chaotic battle between the force of love, which in its binding together annihilates the individual self, and the recoil into separation, which abrogates the force of love (*A*, 147). The only true release from this warfare comes, so Lawrence asserts, from "the willingness to give the response to the heroic" (p. 71)—the acceptance of the nobility of the natural aristocrat or leader, and the giving of homage to this leader. This response would "re-establish the living organic connections, with the cosmos, the sun and earth, with mankind and nation and family" (p. 149). The hierarchical ordering of family and country, based on a patriarchal ideal of leadership, constitutes Lawrence's final message in *Apocalypse* and his final prescription for the salvation of humankind.

12. The Symbolic Father and the Ideal of Leadership

Although the works of D. H. Lawrence's leadership period are commonly read in terms of the political power of superior male individuals, the central character in these works is the same domineering mother who figures so importantly in *Sons and Lovers*. The antagonistic female, opposed to her husband's search for a male leader, plays such a prominent role in the fiction published between 1922 and 1926 that all critics must deal with her; and in fact, almost in spite of themselves, many of the critics who eschew the biographical approach to Lawrence's works do suggest the overwhelming importance of biographical matters, especially those concerning Lawrence's wife and mother, for understanding Lawrence's ideal of leadership. For example, by way of explaining Aaron Sisson's attitude toward his predatory wife in *Aaron's Rod*, Mary Freeman, who disdains biography, notes in passing that "Lawrence's mother, having been dominant, predisposed him to see all women as dominant, insidiously if not overtly."[1]

Ernest Tedlock establishes the female's opposition—in *Aaron's Rod* and elsewhere—as Frieda Lawrence's, and sees it as "the major challenge" to Lawrence's urge toward leadership. That this opposition may have originated with Lawrence's mother, and that it may have been the source of that urge as well as the challenge to it, is suggested by Tedlock's remark that "the conflict of the boy's dependence with the man's independence," and the guilt over betrayal of mother-love, are implicit in all of Lawrence's work.[2] This assumption of a mother fixation is at the center of a frankly biographical study, Daniel Weiss's *Oedipus In Nottingham* (1962). But Weiss's strictly oedipal approach, in the tradition of Murry's *Son of Woman*, is used mainly to explain *Sons and Lovers*. In contrast, the comprehensive study by John Stoll entitled *The Novels of D. H. Lawrence: A Search for Integration* (1971) attempts to combine and transform the Freudian approach (exemplified by Weiss) and the Jungian, or vitalist, approach (exemplified by Tedlock). Biographical and psychological matters are not brought in to "explain away" Lawrence's ideas. Yet underlying this study is an assumption of Lawrence's conflicting attitudes toward woman in her Magna Mater role, and this assumption places the contradictions inherent in Lawrence's "leadership phase," to use Stoll's term, in the continuum of Lawrence's life.

The assumption behind the present work is that D. H. Lawrence's ambivalence toward the "devouring mother" was the prime motivating factor behind the works of his leadership period. *Fantasia of the Unconscious* most clearly identifies the relationship between Lawrence's fear of woman and his strictures about leadership by man; every other work of the period is likewise concerned with the question not of which man is to lead the masses, but of whether man has the courage to lead woman. In the Eden that Lawrence's works tentatively define or suggest, man fulfills his "primal need, the old-Adamic need" (as Lawrence expresses it in *Apocalypse*) to be the master. This need may conflict with Lawrence's deeply held conviction that man and woman must maintain their integrity in the love relationship, but it is nevertheless present at the same time.

The effect of Rupert Birkin's famous description in *Women in Love* of the ideal marriage as a star polarity is counteracted in that novel by the stress on male dominance. The same contradiction can be found in the novels on leadership, although the male-female issue is masked by the sociopolitical concerns and by a general misanthropy that were characteristic of these years in Lawrence's life. In *Aaron's Rod*, Rawdon Lilly speaks of the masses as insects to be exterminated and then immediately extols the worth of the individual soul (*AR*, 272). While this contradiction has stimulated commentary on Lawrence's ambivalence toward humanity,[3] what frequently passes notice is that Aaron Sisson's flight from his wife is directly connected with his search for the superior male leader, and that the only such leader offered by this novel is continually engaged in warfare with his own wife. Lawrence himself was in constant conflict with, and flight from, the Magna Mater, and his embrace of the dark gods at this time signifies not so much an acceptance of his own coalmining father as it signifies a last-ditch effort, through acceptance of a fantasy father, to escape the smothering embrace of woman.

Certain features common to the fiction of the leadership period combine to suggest a pattern of pre-oedipal concerns and conflicts:

~ the male protagonists are often smaller and/or younger than their female lovers or antagonists;
~ attention is drawn to the disparity in size by repetition of the words *small* and *little* in reference to the man;
~ attention is drawn to the disparity in age by such devices as repetition of the phrase "old enough to be your mother";
~ the women are potential or actual mothers, narcissistically absorbed in their pregancies or children;
~ the women demand the men's acknowledgment of dependency on them, yet they often chafe at the burden of this dependency;
~ when crossed or left out, the women refer to their lovers/antagonists as babies or children and characterize their behavior as willful, obstinate, or perverse;
~ the women attempt to make the men feel small;
~ they manipulate and force allegiance, by playing on guilt or making subtle threats to cut off sustenance;
~ the men wish to establish a homeplace and to connect with nurturing women;
~ the men also chafe at their dependence upon women since it makes them vulnerable to domination and bullying;
~ emphasis is placed on the men's stiffening their backbones in opposition, or generating power "at the tail";
~ the men subjugate the women or attempt to do so;
~ the reversal of power roles is often indicated by a change in physical position: the men stand erect, the women kneel;
~ the men decide that the women are bad and must die if the men are to live;
~ a turn toward violence is taken;
~ animal images connect the human and nonhuman realms and give sanctions for violence;
~ there is a recoil from connection into separation, singleness, and aloneness;
~ the men pledge allegiance to a nurturant male as an escape from the domination of women.

Many of the above motifs, it should be noted, are to be found as well in works with female protagonists, like *The Lost Girl*, a fact suggesting that Lawrence saw the struggle for independence as a universal rather than a gender-specific phenomenon.

That Lawrence himself had difficulty separating from the mother-figure is evidenced by the tension between the desire for merger and the need for independence that informs all his work; this difficulty was a wound that stimulated his art but that also resulted in the shrill excesses of his leadership period. Lawrence's relations with Lydia Beardsall Lawrence were no doubt troubled and even pathologized; the almost hysterical stress on singleness in his leadership period suggests an unresolved conflict over this issue of separation. His treatises on psychology reveal that Lawrence was well aware of the connection between his feelings of having been smothered as a child and his battle cry for space and fresh air as an adult. In fact, the developmental process that he sets forth in these treatises, and the crises in this process that he records throughout his writings, are in accord with the almost three decades of work on the "separation-individuation" phase of psychological growth conducted by psychoanalyst Margaret Mahler and her associates, mainly through observation of children. Mahler's findings shed light on the excesses of Lawrence's leadership period.

In *The Psychological Birth of the Human Infant*, Mahler delineates the phases constituting the child's growth into what might be called personhood. The first birth experience is the obvious one, the biological. The second birth experience occurs in stages between five and thirty-six months, when the child separates from the mother and achieves a sense of self. This psychological birth is the separation-individuation phase of personality development. Separation refers to the child's awareness of differentiation from the mother; individuation refers to his or her feelings of autonomy. The phase succeeds and grows out of the symbiotic phase, in which the relationship of dual unity with the mother is "the primal soil from which all subsequent human relations form."[4]

Within a certain range, there are several potential children within each child; the child is to a degree created out of the mother's own psychological makeup and therefore reflects her personality. If a mother's attachment to her baby in the very earliest stages is formed primarily out of her own narcissistic, parasitic needs rather than out of regard for her child, then differentiation—the first subphase of separation-individuation—can set in almost vehemently, with the child's pushing and arching away from the mother. Conversely, if the mother overvalues the child's sedentary, vegetative behavior, the child may fail to invest libidinally in motor functions, in order to remain dependent and hence rewarded; the differentiation subphase will in this case be delayed.

The development of motor functions, culminating in the ability to stand and walk, allows the child a great step forward psychologically as

12. The Symbolic Father 177

well as physically. In the so-called practicing subphase of separation-individuation, occurring from 10–12 months to 16–18 months of age, the child's point of view changes, literally and figuratively. The world lies open before him or her, and the threats of object loss—the disappearance of the mother—are compensated for by the pleasures of discovery and mastery as well as of escape from engulfment by the mother. The child still needs the mother, and she the child, but both must let go if the child is to become an individual. Not coincidentally, "it is the rule rather than the exception that the first unaided steps taken by the infant are in a direction away from the mother or during her absence" (p. 73).

In the third, "rapprochement" subphase, the child fears being left too much on his or her own and makes great demands on the mother to restore the symbiotic status quo. Having already witnessed the child's movements toward separation, the mother may become confused by these demands and resentful, or she may more actively resist separation. This crisis in the child's development, like all such crises, requires great adaptiveness and sensitivity on the part of the mother. The end of the rapprochement subphase, at around eighteen months of age, is characterized by the rapidly alternating or even simultaneous desires to push the mother away and to cling to her. Observers of child behavior can see in this ambivalence the "roots of many uniquely human problems and dilemmas—problems that sometimes are never completely resolved during the entire life cycle" (p. 100).

The last subphase, occurring in roughly the third year, is the consolidation of individuality and the beginning of object constancy. The mother is kept in mind even when absent; and her "good" and "bad" elements are united into one image. In a state of object constancy, the mother is not rejected or supplanted by another if she is not providing satisfaction. This fourth subphase is also marked by the development of such complex cognitive functions as speech, fantasy making, and reality testing. Each child shows his or her distinctive way of adapting to problems and crises in this period, depending upon the nature of the mother-child relationship, the innate endowment, and the accidents and circumstances of life.

Lawrence clearly delineates these crises in the practicing and rapprochement subphases of the psychological birth process in his short story called "Sun," written in late 1925, thirty years before the stages were officially observed and named. At the beginning of the story, Juliet is an inadequate mother, one who keeps her child dependent upon her and then chafes at his dependence: "The child irritated her, and preyed on her peace of mind. She felt so horribly, ghastly responsible for him: as if she must be responsible for every breath he drew. And that was torture to her, to the child, and to everyone else concerned" (*CSS*, II, 529). After only a few hours in the sun, however, Juliet begins to change her ideas about mothering and comes home from sunbathing in the nude with a different attitude toward her child:

> "Mummy! Mummy!" her child came running toward her, calling in that peculiar bird-like little anguish of want, always wanting her. She was surprised that her drowsed heart for once felt none of the anxious love-anguish in return. She caught the child up in her arms, but she thought: He should not be such a lump! If he were in the sun, he would spring up.
>
> She resented, rather, his little hands clutching at her, especially at her neck. . . .
>
> She had had the child so much in her mind, in a torment of responsibility, as if, having borne him, she had to answer for his whole existence. . . .
>
> Now a change took place. She was no longer vitally interested in the child, she took the strain of her anxiety and her will from off him. And he thrived all the more for it. (pp. 531–32)

Juliet has learned how *not* to be a "devouring mother." She is capable of protecting and sheltering her son when he needs her, as when she prevents him from falling against the thorns (p. 535). But otherwise she leaves him to his own devices, to grow apart from her. At first the child is afraid, having come to depend upon his mother: Juliet must firmly loosen his grasp upon her neck—and his grasp upon her own life—and urge him into independence by such devices as rolling an orange away from her across the tiled terrace; she rewards the boy for toddling after the fruit, and eases his fear in doing so, by calling him in to the safety of her presence with the orange as a token of his courageous effort (p. 531).

Eventually, like his mother, the boy becomes "another creature, with a peculiar, quiet, sun-darkened absorption. Now he played by himself in silence, and she hardly need notice him. He seemed no longer to know when he was alone" (*CSS*, II, 536). Even the presence of a snake in their Eden cannot disrupt their idyllic relationship with the cosmos or each other: "Some stillness of the sun" in Juliet keeps panic at bay and puts the incident in perspective. As the story progresses, the child moves, with Juliet's encouragement, physically and emotionally farther away from his mother, while still maintaining a connection with her; when he needs to run back to her for momentary support, she is there for him. And she, in turn, has no need to find emotional fulfillment in her child. Although her marriage is a failure, she finds sexual stimulation in a vital, animalistic Italian peasant.[5]

In short, Juliet lets go of her role as the smothering, overprotective mother and allows her boy successfully to undergo what Mahler, years later, would call the separation-individuation phase of childhood. The story is almost a textbook case of a turning point in a child's psychological development.

According to Mahler, conflicts over separation and separateness throughout the first few years of life are so crucial and intense that they can be "reactivated (or can remain peripherally or even centrally active) at any and all stages of life" (pp. 4–5). In Lawrence's case, the conflicts were probably always peripherally active. The facts of Lawrence's earliest years provide some clues as to the origins of his pre-oedipal conflicts. Mrs. Lawrence was disappointed in her husband and found little satisfaction in her marriage. She looked to her sons for emotional—and later, even financial—sustenance. Lawrence was sickly from birth, and his mother did not expect him to live three months; as an adult he stated that he had nearly died of bronchitis barely two weeks after he was born. His eldest brother, George, has reported that Lawrence was petted and spoiled from the beginning, and that their mother "poured her very soul into him."[6] Obviously the young Lawrence required and received a great deal of maternal care. Evidence suggests, however, that the robust second brother, Ernest, and not the sickly "Bert," was the mother's favorite child. One can only speculate on the development of self-esteem by the youngest boy, who continually looked to his mother for bolstering and who may have found that bolstering inadequate to his needs for both nurturance and independence. Early on, Lawrence may well have developed a rage against his mother and, in defense against his aggressive impulses, split the love object into "good" and "bad" mother, reserving his hostility for the latter. This rage against the "bad" mother lasted well beyond the period when object constancy might be expected to have been achieved. Indeed, it appears in one guise or another throughout the Lawrence canon, as well as in biographical accounts of Lawrence's stormy existence with Frieda and others, with its abrupt transitions of mood.

By his adult years Lawrence was convinced that women tend to engulf or devour their loved ones. His logic faltered when he placed woman securely in the domestic realm (as in the essay "Matriarchy") and then blamed her for becoming overly involved in her children; or when he attributed to woman the innate, biological urge toward connection (as in his treatises on psychology) and then blasted her for her unwillingness to let go. Yet Lawrence had a clear desire to merge with the caretaker mother himself. On the one hand he extolled the value of intimacy in his works; on the other he saw intimacy as a life-threatening merger and was driven to extoll separation and even the violence he saw as necessary to attain it.

During the leadership period, this conflict between the desire for merger and the need for separation moved to center stage in Lawrence's life and art. At this time Lawrence was especially vulnerable and powerless: feeling his autonomous self threatened by the exigencies of illness, war, and indebtedness, he lashed out at those within easy reach—his physical battles with Frieda are legendary—and took revenge in his art on those whom he could or would not touch in life, achieving a kind of separation in the process and, paradoxically, maintaining a kind of dependency. Henry Grenfel feels caught in Jill Banford's web in the first versions of *The Fox*, the image being particularly apt in terms of what Lawrence saw as the female's stress on interconnectedness;[7] the final version of *The Fox* shows Grenfel's dubious (even to Lawrence) solution to the problem of entrapment: killing off Banford to restore autonomy to the self and a hierarchical order to the world. The same repulsion from the female web is found to underlie the three so-called leadership novels—*Aaron's Rod*, *Kangaroo*, and *The Plumed Serpent*—as well as the Lawrence corpus as a whole.

Lawrence's ideal of leadership, developed in reaction to the female web, can be defined as the domination of the male as symbolic father. In this metaphor of paternalism, *father* is aggrandized beyond his natural role in the family, and *leader* is likewise imbued with a greater emotional power than he normally possesses.[8] Intimacy and distance are thereby combined in one figure. Lawrence's urge toward the paternalistic leader may be attributed partly to the economic conditions in which he grew up, with his father absent from the home during the day working in the coal mines (and during most evenings drinking in the pubs with his cronies), and partly to the emotional climate in which he was raised, with the mother effectively eliminating the father as a presence in the family and taking sole charge of the home and of her sickly youngest son. Early in Lawrence's search for the ideal society he was extremely wary of the charismatic, paternalistic leader: in a 1915 letter to Ottoline Morrell he wrote of the organization of their Rananim and warned, "We must go very, very carefully at first. The great serpent to destroy, is the Will to

Power: the desire for one man to have some dominion over his fellow man. Let us have *no* personal influence, if possible—nor personal magnetism, as they used to call it, nor persuasion—no 'Follow me'—but only 'Behold'" (*CL*, I, 312). By the time of the leadership period, however, Lawrence had committed himself to the idea if not to the reality of a man of personal magnetism who calls others to follow him. Lilly and Count Dionys articulate this ideal in *Aaron's Rod* and *The Ladybird*, calling it the power mode of relationships; Ben Cooley offers himself as such a leader in *Kangaroo* but is ultimately repudiated by the Lawrence character as being too smothering—that is, maternal; finally, Don Ramón incarnates the paternalistic ideal of leadership in *The Plumed Serpent*, a mystical novel about a fantasy Mexico.

Although Lawrence never found a leader in contemporary life worth attaching himself to—for what leader could measure up to Lawrence's demands for him to be an idealized father—he certainly had aggrandized notions of his own wisdom and leadership abilities. Many have remarked that the notion of Lawrence attaching himself to a group as either leader or follower is ridiculous, given his iconoclastic, cranky personality; Paul Delany states that Lawrence never sought "to assemble any body of initiates over whom he might exercise total control. His temperament was too open and volatile for him to become the master of a cult." But Delany overstates his case, for if Lawrence did not try to exercise total control he certainly did try to assemble a body of initiates whose disagreements with him he tended to regard as betrayals. Here is Delany himself on this subject:

> When he found . . . disciples he became euphoric, convinced that they would be "unanimous" with him in action; but his elation would be replaced by an equally profound rage and depression when the views of his followers diverged in any way from his own. Those who were acclaimed as disciples were, before too long, anathematized as heretics and cast forth. . . . [W]hen he quarreled with one intimate, he was led to demand more support and sympathy from each of those who remained—who were then all the more likely, under this increased strain, to draw the line against his encroachments.[9]

Cecil Gray, a musician friend of the Lawrences during the last years of the war, argued that Lawrence shared with Hitler "the same dark, passionate, fanatical power, the same capacity for casting spells,"[10] and Bertrand Russell went so far as to declare that Lawrence's ideas about blood-consciousness led "straight to Auschwitz."[11]

D. H. Lawrence never actually attached himself to real-life dictators nor became a dictator himself. But he sought and created fantasy leaders in his fiction. His antidemocratic notions link him with other, widely disparate British and American writers of the period—Yeats, Lewis, Eliot, and Pound[12]—and place him in a certain intellectual tradition originating, perhaps, with the ancient Greeks. In July 1915 Lawrence read a book on early Greek philosophy and wrote to Bertrand Russell, who had lent him the book, "You must drop all your democracy. You must not believe in 'the people'.... There must be an aristocracy of people who have wisdom, and there must be a Ruler: a Kaiser: no Presidents and democracies. I shall write out Herakleitos, on tablets of bronze" (*CL*, I, 352). Of course Lawrence was familiar with similar nineteenth- and twentieth-century thinkers: among them, Carlyle, with his cult of the hero; Ruskin, with his idea of the paternal state; Nietzsche, with his Superman (the emblem of Zarathustra, prophet of the Superman, is a plumed serpent). With such thinkers Lawrence believed that the hero is the chief determinant of the course of history. He wrote to Dollie Radford, in late 1916, "I firmly believe that the pure desire of the strong creates the great events, without any action: like the prayer of the saints.... What the world needs to learn, today, is to give due honor to those who are finer in spirit, and to know the inferiority of those who are mean and paltry in spirit" (*CB*, I, 406, 409). Eric Bentley states that Carlyle and Nietzsche, in their later work, "shriek, bully, and exaggerate because no one will listen."[13] So, too, Lawrence in his leadership period harangued and assaulted his readers and produced the works for which he earns no laurels. At times the carelessness, even disorder, of his language seems symptomatic of a psychological breakdown. The subject matter makes many readers uncomfortable, especially as it gives voice to antisocial urges that Lawrence expressed as early as 1915, when he wrote, "Sometimes I wish I could let go and be really wicked—kill and murder—but kill chiefly. I do want to kill. But I want to select whom I shall kill. Then I shall enjoy it."[14] Surely Lawrence had been driven bellicose, if not mad, by the banning of *The Rainbow* and the wartime persecution perpetrated on him by what he saw as mob rule and mass taste.

Gradually Lawrence carried his ideal of male leadership to an extreme in the decade between 1915 and 1925; it was from this extreme, and not from the basic issue, that Lawrence later turned away. The extreme is human sacrifice. What one finds in the leadership works, time and time again, are ruminations about the dark gods' requirements of blood. In *The Lost Girl*, Lawrence states that "the gods who had demanded human sacrifice were quite right, immutably right. The fierce, savage gods who dipped their lips in blood, these were the true gods" (*LG*, 315). And in *Kangaroo* he adds, "to be pure in heart, man must listen to the dark gods as well as to the white gods, to the call of blood-sacrifice as well as to the eucharist" (*K*, 273). Human sacrifice of one sort or another occurs in *The Fox*, *The Captain's Doll*, *The Plumed Serpent*, and "The Woman Who Rode Away." But psychic as well as physical sacrifice occurs just as frequently, and the misogyny implicit in both kinds of sacrifice is emphasized in *The Plumed Serpent*, when Kate Leslie is instructed to submit totally to her husband Cipriano: "Was this the knife to which she must be sheath?" (*PS*, 388). Keith Sagar notes that Kate's "marriage to Cipriano is seen by the novel as equivalent to the death of the woman who rode away."[15] In *The Lost Girl*, too, Alvina's sexual contact with Ciccio spells her annihilation: "And he killed her. He simply took her and assassinated her" (*LG*, 202). Later, as Mrs. Marasca, Alvina realizes that "it was *his* will which counted. Alvina, as his wife, must submit" (p. 289). Ultimately she makes the firmest possible commitment when she says to her husband, "I love you, even if it kills me" (p. 337).

In his later works Lawrence renounced the call to blood-sacrifice; the phallus as the source of regeneration replaces the dark gods, and erection equals resurrection in such stories as "Sun," *Lady Chatterley's Lover*, and *The Man Who Died*. But the basic, even desperate, belief in male dominance occupied him to the very last. Although after 1925 Lawrence no longer embodied either his destructive urge or his leadership ideal in sanctioned religious or political systems, in his fiction the phallus always demands annihilation in the sense of complete capitulation of woman to man. Lawrence did not repudiate the "lead on I follow, *ich dien* sort of business" (*CL*, II, 1045) in 1927, his statement notwithstanding. He had let go of the quasi-religious, philosophical, and political belief in the necessity for death before resurrection, emphasizing instead the physical cycle of tumescence and detumescence; but this emphasis on the life force cannot quite overshadow the same urge to destroy the Magna Mater that had marked—and marred—his earlier works.

One factor militating against acceptance of Lawrence's tribal patriarchy is his arbitrary distinction between "bullying" and power or leadership. His use of animals is intimately associated with this distinction. As early as 1915, in the posthumously published essay "The Crown," Lawrence had set up a dichotomy between wild, often dangerous, animals and domesticated animals, assigning to them the respective modes of power and love. Animals appear continually in the fictional works, as trope and as symbol; in fact, the first novel is entitled *The White Peacock*, the bird figure embodying the vanity and spirituality of modern woman. But the peacock itself plays a small part in this early novel, and Lawrence makes it carry a symbolic burden too great for it to support. Not until 1921 did animals become the controlling symbols in Lawrence's fiction, and accordingly he then gave his works animal titles. Especially in *The Fox, Kangaroo,* and *The Plumed Serpent,* human power struggles seem to gain the sanctions of the wild state, in which animals kill—but do not murder. Similarly, male dominance is seen as the "natural" state; often what females do is "bully"—that is, self-consciously exert their wills—and what males do is "lead." And the feminine, bullying will, for all Lawrence's talk of a rainbow reconciliation of opposites, or a star polarity, needs to be eliminated.

Lawrence confuses the issue when he assigns the wolf as totem to Gerald Crich in *Women in Love,* for although Gerald recognizes the need for a man of new values to save the modern world, he is himself a bully with a machine mentality. Yet Lawrence's ultimate judgment is against that form of bullying accomplished through the ideal of love, or "spiritual incest" as he calls it. Women do not alone ascribe to this ideal—Walt Whitman, with his "merging," refutes such a simpleminded notion—but they are the primary offenders. The Eden that Lady Chatterley and her lover enjoy in the woods is not only a paradise of uninhibited sexuality; it represents an escape for Connie from "the strange dominion and obsession of *other women.* How awful they were, women" (*LCL,* 262), and an escape for Mellors from the "ghastly female will" of Bertha Coutts (p. 289). The animal of Lawrence's last two novels—the cock—is as little a real animal as the peacock of the first: it is clearly the phallus, liberated from the demands of spiritual love and ready to conquer the world.[16]

In the fiction of his leadership period, and even afterward, Lawrence's overreaction to the "devouring mother" caused him to create leaders who themselves act as "devouring mothers," fostering their followers' dependence upon them and tolerating no deviation from strict adherence to their tenets. In the heterosexual love relationship, the capacity for intimacy as Lawrence depicts it leads most often not to mutuality but to exploitation of one by the other, a situation that he deplored in the mother-child relation. Occasionally Lawrence does portray a strong (as opposed to domineering) mother—Juliet in "Sun" comes to mind—but it is the sun, the male principle or "father-spark," that has taught Juliet how to parent. Instinctual good mothering seems to abound for Lawrence only in the wild animal kingdom, among she-wolves, for instance (*EP,* 623–24). The one human mother who seems to live by she-

12. The Symbolic Father 185

wolf principles is Mrs. Barlow in the play *Touch and Go* (1920), but she is too sketchily drawn, and her son too weak, for her to exemplify model motherhood. On the whole the animal kingdom provided Lawrence with role models for fathers rather than for mothers, especially in his leadership period, with its foxes and plumed serpents (its kangaroo, large of foot and thigh, shows promise of wise fatherhood, but its smothering pouch is suspiciously maternal). Although Lawrence credited both male and female children with a "father-spark," he was largely unwilling to credit females with the ability to use theirs wisely. Unfortunately, the rigidity of Lawrence's mother-father roles led to a dangerous idealization of particular males.

Yet if Lawrence's solution to the problem of maternal domination is suspect, his analysis of the problem is no less significant and the problem itself is no less real. Because of his particular family constellation in its particular Victorian setting, Lawrence was preoccupied with the parent-child relation. Indeed, it is more central to his canon than the male-female sexual relation for which he is commonly known. But Lawrence's statements on good parenting have value beyond autobiography or cultural biography. As we have seen, psychoanalytic thinking since Freud has emphasized the early dependence of the child upon the mother and the centrality of the pre-oedipal conflict between dependency and autonomy to the child's psychological development. Although the extremes of father worship to which Lawrence was led are abnormal, the basic urge toward the father is normal indeed. Margaret Mahler's work with children suggests that during the practicing subphase of separation-individuation, the child's world expands to include other people besides the mother, most notably the father. When the mother is overprotective and unable to let go, the father is in an ideal position to "rescue" the child, for the father stands outside the mother-child symbiosis but not so far outside as to be unfamiliar and frightening. Even if the mother does not feel the need to live through her children, having enough life and independence of her own, a strong father figure is still desirable—in fact, necessary—in providing the child a way to get beyond the primary caretaker: he aids the child in achieving a sense of autonomy. Sensing the difference between the parents, very young children (so Mahler has found) often show fear at their mothers' playful attempts to seize them for games or fondling, yet will seek and enjoy similar romping with and handling by their fathers. The object of the fear is interpreted as engulfment by the "devouring mother" (p. 118). Some children resolve the rapprochement crisis not so much by coming to terms with the mother as by turning to the father, who is less ambivalently loved; this solution is only temporary, however, since the relationship with the mother must eventually be faced and separation struggles with her resolved (p. 129).

Research into the role of the father in the pre-oedipal years is relatively recent, but it demonstrates conclusively the importance of the father to early childhood development. In Ernest Abelin's terms, children possess a "father thirst"[17]—a desire and need for connection with their fathers. Lawrence terms this psychological reality the "father-spark" and gives it a physical basis in *Fantasia of the Unconscious*. The movement in Lawrence's writing culminating in the patriarchal ideal of leadership shows what can happen when the father thirst is not slaked early in life: the thirst may be quenchable only by a flood that threatens the very life it is supposed to save. The matter of a father's role in the child's early development and subsequent life course bears as well on the controversial issue of D. H. Lawrence's homosexual tendencies (as suggested in the suppressed prologue to *Women in Love*[18] and certain remarks of Frieda Lawrence and others[19]). One psychoanalyst, Charles Socarides, pinpoints the nuclear conflict of homosexuality as the wish to merge with the mother versus the dread of ego dissolution that this merger signifies; the homosexual has never progressed adequately from the mother-child symbiotic unity to separation-individuation. Socarides states that "[i]n all homosexual cases [female as well as male] there is an insatiable yearning for the father which the patient may have suppressed or repressed for years. . . . This yearning is a plaintive cry for the father whom the patient unconsciously feels to be his only source of help in his fight against the phenomenon of engulfment and merging with the mother. The importance of the father to the child's psychological development cannot be overestimated."[20]

Lawrence's letters and literature, the memoirs about him by friends and enemies, and psychological studies of the mother-child relation in general—all of these underscore the importance of the "devouring mother" figure for understanding D. H. Lawrence's life and art. Because the connection between this figure and Lawrence's patriarchal ideal of male leadership is most clearly manifested in the works of Lawrence's middle years—his leadership period—these works offer important keys to the Lawrence canon; far from being anomalies, they are as deeply concerned with personal power relationships as the earlier and later works. The urge to leadership and the eventual embrace of the dark gods may be seen as facets of Lawrence's pre-oedipal, ambivalent relationship with his mother, which Joseph Rheingold terms "the most basic of all human conflicts."[21]

In a sense, Lawrence demythologizes the institution of motherhood by debunking the notion of unadulterated and wholly beneficial maternal devotion. His demythologizing of motherhood leads naturally to a reassessment and revaluation of fatherhood, freeing the male to assume parenthood of his children and to show his nurturant side without being considered "womanish." Lawrence's own tender yet firm ways with children have been documented by many who knew him, but Tom Brangwen's relationship with his stepdaughter Anna, in *The Rainbow*, stands out as perhaps the single depiction of a meaningful father-child relationship in Lawrence's fiction. In his leadership period, Lawrence stressed the importance of the father in the family constellation, as an alternative to the mother and her smothering love. Readers who wish to make instructive use of Lawrence's rage against women may view his homicidal fantasies as symbolic murder of the "bad" or "devouring" mother,[22] and his worship of the dark gods as recognition of the father's importance in the child's development of an autonomous self.

For both the mother and the father, good parenting as Lawrence forcefully and helpfully defines it includes the wisdom and the self-control to leave the child adequate space or growing room, while still providing nurturance. Lawrence's lifelong emphasis on striking the proper balance between protectiveness and respect for the integrity of each individual tempers somewhat the shrill excesses of his leadership period, and remains the emphasis that ensures his works' lasting value.

Notes

1. Clytemnestra's Victory

1. George Ford, *Double Measure: A Study of the Novels and Stories of D. H. Lawrence* (New York: Holt, Rinehart & Winston, 1965), p. 115.

2. Harry T. Moore, "Bert Lawrence and Lady Jane," in *Lawrence and Women*, ed. Anne Smith (London: Vision Press, 1978), p. 182. William Barr, "*Aaron's Rod* as D. H. Lawrence's Picaresque Novel," *D. H. Lawrence Review* 9 (Summer 1976): 213–25.

3. John Middleton Murry, *Son of Woman: The Story of D. H. Lawrence* (New York: Jonathan Cape & Harrison Smith, 1931), p. 254.

4. Introduction, *The Letters of D. H. Lawrence*, ed. Aldous Huxley (London: William Heinemann, 1932), p. x.

5. Harry T. Moore, *The Life and Works of D. H. Lawrence* (New York: Twayne, 1951), p. 242.

6. F. R. Leavis, *D. H. Lawrence: Novelist* (London: Chatto & Windus, 1955), pp. 30–69.

7. Mary Freeman, *D. H. Lawrence: A Basic Study of His Ideas* (Gainesville: University of Florida Press, 1955), p. v.

8. Eugene Goodheart, *The Utopian Vision of D. H. Lawrence* (Chicago: University of Chicago Press, 1963); Ernest Tedlock, *D. H. Lawrence: Artist and Rebel* (Albuquerque: University of New Mexico Press, 1963); George Ford, *Double Measure*; Keith Sagar, *The Art of D. H. Lawrence* (Cambridge: Cambridge University Press, 1966).

9. Harry T. Moore, *The Priest of Love: A Life of D. H. Lawrence* (New York: Farrar, Straus, & Giroux, 1974), p. 444.

10. See Ford, *Double Measure*, p. 19; Sagar, *Art of D. H. Lawrence*, p. 168; Martin Green, *The Von Richthofen Sisters: The Triumphant and the Tragic Modes of Love* (New York: Basic Books, 1974), pp. 152, 346.

11. Witter Bynner, *Journey with Genius: Recollections and Reflections Concerning the Lawrences* (New York: John Day, 1951), p. 293; Green, *The Von Richthofen Sisters*.

12. David Cavitch, *D. H. Lawrence and the New World* (New York: Oxford University Press, 1969), p. 193.

13. Harold G. McCurdy, "Literature and Personality: Analysis of the Novels of D. H. Lawrence," *Character and Personality* 8 (March, June 1940): 314–15. For McCurdy's complete discussion of this issue, see "Psychological Analysis of Literary Productions as a Revelation of Personality" (unpublished Ph.D. dissertation, Duke University, 1938).

14. Daniel Weiss, *Oedipus in Nottingham: D. H. Lawrence* (Seattle: University of Washington Press, 1962), p. 109.

15. Ford, *Double Measure*, p. 47.

16. Moore, *Priest of Love*, p. 62.

17. Erich Fromm, *The Heart of Man, Its Genius for Good and Evil* (New York: Harper & Row, 1964), p. 97.

18. More recent influential studies of the pre-oedipal phase have de-emphasized anatomy and focused instead on "separation-individuation" as observed in the behavior of young children. See Margaret Mahler, Fred Pine, Anni Bergman, *The Psychological Birth of the Human Infant* (New York: Basic Books, 1975).

19. Sigmund Freud, "On Female Sexuality," in *The Complete Psychological Works*, Standard Edition, 24 vols., ed. James Strachey (London: Hogarth Press, 1959–1974) 21 (1961): 237.

20. Joseph C. Rheingold, *The Mother, Anxiety, and Death: The Catastrophic Death Complex* (Boston: Little, Borwn, 1967), pp. 126, 152, 106–7, 18. See also Rheingold's *The Fear of Being a Woman: A Theory of Maternal Destructiveness* (New York: Grune & Stratton, 1964). A provocative literary study of this subject is Ellen Moers's "Female Gothic: The Monster's Mother," *New York Review of Books* 21 (March 21, 1974): 24–28. Moers studies *Frankenstein* as a "phantasmagoria of the nursery," constructed around the "motif of [Mary Shelley's] revulsion against newborn life, and the drama of guilt, dread, and flight surrounding birth and its consequences."

21. The Huxley edition of Lawrence's letters (p. 458) transcribes the word as *unto*. Jung himself, in the edition that Lawrence probably read (New York: Dodd, Mead, 1916), uses the phrase "return again into" or variants thereof, as on pp. 266, 427.

22. Herbert Howarth, "D. H. Lawrence From Island to Glacier," *University of Toronto Quarterly* 37 (1967–68): 222.

23. Paul Delany, *D. H. Lawrence's Nightmare: The Writer and His Circle in the Years of the Great War* (New York: Basic Books, 1978).

24. The widespread nature of this polarizing habit of mind during World War I, and its ramifications for modern literature, are discussed by Paul Fussell in *The Great War and Modern Memory* (New York: Oxford University Press, 1975).

25. Yet Lawrence seems not to have borne the grudge against the Meynells that he bore against other hostesses. His one portrait of the family, in "England, My England," is of a family branch, not of the main stock—though it, too, shows Lawrence's preoccupation with the "devouring mother" and will be discussed in chapter five.

26. Huxley, ed., *Letters*, p. 234.

27. Delany, *D. H. Lawrence's Nightmare*, p. 72.

28. The infamous incident in which Frieda smashed a dinner plate over her husband's head in Cornwall—which was transmuted in *Women in Love* into Hermione's bashing Birkin over the head with a piece of lapis lazuli—was caused, so Catherine Cornwall surmises, by the old argument about Frieda's desire to see her children. See Carswell, *The Savage Pilgrimage: A Narrative of D. H. Lawrence* (London: Chatto & Windus, 1932), p. 76.

29. The letter referring to Frieda as a "devouring mother" contains as well a reference to the engulfing landscape: "I find the Midlands full of the fear of death—truly. . . . Last evening at dusk I sat by the rapid brook which runs by the highroad in the valley bed. The spell of hastening, secret water goes over one's mind. When I got to the top—a very hard climb—I felt as if I had climbed out of a womb" (*CL*, I, 556).

30. Quoted in Peter L. Irvine and Anne Kiley, "D. H. Lawrence: Letters to Gordon and Beatrice Campbell," *D. H. Lawrence Review* 6 (Spring 1973): 15.

31. Lawrence's need for mothering also seems to have been the common denominator of many business or literary relationships. Of Lawrence in his Croydon years, during which time his mother died, Ford Madox Ford writes, "I cannot say that I liked Lawrence much. . . . He had so much need of moral support to take the place of his mother's influence that he kept one in a constant state of solicitude. He claimed moral support imperiously—and physical care too." See Ford, *Portraits from Life* (Boston: Houghton Mifflin, 1937), p. 85. Shortly after Lawrence left England he decided to take business matters in his own hands: in January 1920 he broke with his agent, J. B. Pinker, and with Pinker's "grinning patronage" (*CL*, I, 544). Lawrence explained the break to his American publisher, Ben Huebsch: "I want to act now for myself. . . I don't like this vague, half-friendly, in-the-air sort of business. It leaves me irritated and dependent" (*CL*, I, 613). Yet Lawrence was still dependent on publishers, and he soon complained to Huebsch that Huebsch was as dominating as the rest (*CL*, I, 618). Recognizing Lawrence's extreme touchiness on the subject, a friend advised a publisher's agent that "if you don't want to lose Lawrence's friendship, you must be very careful never to let him guess that you are doing anything for him" (*CB*, I, 492).

32. Rheingold, *The Mother, Anxiety, and Death*, p. 105.
33. Carswell, *Savage Pilgrimage*, p. 7.
34. Hillis Miller, "D. H. Lawrence: The Fox and the Perspective Glass," *Harvard Advocate* 137 (December 1952): 27.
35. Bertrand Russell, *Autobiography*, 2 vols. (Boston: Little, Brown, 1951) 1:15.
36. Mark Gertler, *Selected Letters*, ed. Noel Carrington (London: Rupert Hall-Davis, 1965), p. 162.
37. Letter to Ottoline Morrell, unpublished. Quoted by Delany, *D. H. Lawrence's Nightmare*, p. 229. For an interesting assessment of Katherine Mansfield herself in terms of aggression and orality, see Brigid Brophy, *Don't Never Forget* (New York: Holt, Rinehart & Winston, 1966), pp. 255–62.
38. Letter 1194, Gerald M. Lacy, *An Analytical Calendar of the Letters of D. H. Lawrence* (Ann Arbor: University Microfilms, 1971). Quoted by Delany, *D. H. Lawrence's Nightmare*, pp. 281–82.
39. Here, as throughout, I disagree with Martin Green, *The Von Richthofen Sisters*, who believes that "Lawrence was in effect living Bachofen," p. 84.
40. J. J. Bachofen, *Der Mythus von Orient und Okzident*, ed. Manfred Schroeder (Munich: Ch. Becksche Buchhandlung, 1926), pp. 14 f. Quoted by Erich Fromm in *The Forgotten Language: An Introduction to the Understanding of Dreams, Fairy Tales, and Myths* (New York: Holt, Rinehart & Winston, 1951), pp. 208–9. Fromm writes extensively of Bachofen in essays composed between 1932 and 1969 and collected in *The Crisis of Psychoanalysis: Essays on Freud, Marx, and Social Psychology* (New York: Holt, Rinehart & Winston, 1970). See especially "The Crisis of Psychoanalysis," "The Significance of the Theory of Mother Right for Today," and "The Theory of Mother Right and Its Relevance for Social Psychology." Bachofen's work supports Fromm's own emphasis on the importance of the pre-oedipal, pre-genital mother fixation in the development of children of both sexes. I should note here that Fromm, like Bachofen, underplays the mother's ambivalence toward the child and the potentially destructive nature of the mother-child bond; he attributes the widespread image of the possessive mother to the patricentricity of modern society. See, for example, *The Crisis of Psychoanalysis*, p. 130.
41. The phrase is Robert Lindner's, "The Equivalents of Matricide," *Psychoanalytic Quarterly* 17 (October 1948): 453–70.
42. Eliseo Vivas, *D. H. Lawrence: The Failure and the Triumph of Art* (Evanston: Northwestern University Press, 1960).

2. Lawrence's Pollyanalytics

1. For an incisive but not unsympathetic analysis of Lawrence's theories, see James C. Cowan, *D. H. Lawrence's American Journey: A Study in Myth and Literature* (Cleveland: Case Western Reserve University Press, 1970), pp. 15–24. Other critics discussing the psychological treatises are John Carey, "D. H. Lawrence's Doctrine," in *D. H. Lawrence: Novelist, Poet, Prophet*, ed. Stephen Spender (London: Weidenfeld & Nicolson, 1973); Frederick J. Hoffman, "Lawrence's Quarrel with Freud," in *Freudianism and the Literary Mind*, 2d ed. (Baton Rouge: Louisiana State University Press, 1957); John Middleton Murry, *Son of Woman: The Story of D. H. Lawrence* (New York: Jonathan Cape & Harrison Smith, 1931); Philip Rieff, "The Therapeutic as Mythmaker: Lawrence's True Christian Philosophy," in *The Triumph of the Therapeutic: The Uses of Faith After Freud* (New York: Harper & Row, 1966); William York Tindall, *D. H. Lawrence and Susan His Cow* (New York: Columbia University Press, 1939).
2. *David Eder: Memoirs of a Modern Pioneer*, ed. J. B. Hobman (London: Victor Gollancz, 1945), p. 119.
3. Groddeck had a clinic in Baden-Baden, and Lawrence went to Baden-Baden in the last week of April 1921; however, there is no record of any firsthand acquaintance with

Groddeck, nor any mention of Groddeck in Lawrence's works. Yet one of Groddeck's key beliefs, enacted at his clinic, was the value of massage for the cure of physical and emotional ills. The massage scene in *Aaron's Rod* (and similar scenes in other works) may well have received inspiration from Groddeck.

4. See Trigant Burrow, "The Origin of the Incest-Awe," *The Psychoanalytic Review* 5 (July 1918): 243–54.

5. See Margaret Mahler, Fred Pine, Anni Bergman, *The Psychological Birth of the Human Infant* (New York: Basic Books, 1975).

6. See Elizabeth Janeway, *Man's World, Woman's Place: A Study in Social Mythology* (New York: Dell, Delta, 1971).

7. John Stoll, *The Novels of D. H. Lawrence: A Search for Integration* (Columbia: University of Missouri Press, 1971), p. 206.

3. In Flight from Matriarchy

1. Graham Hough, *The Dark Son* (London: Gerald Duckworth, 1956), pp. 90–91.

2. *The Letters of D. H. Lawrence*, ed. James T. Boulton (Cambridge: Cambridge University Press, 1979) 1:234n.

3. Keith Sagar, *The Life of D. H. Lawrence* (New York: Pantheon, 1980), pp. 62, 49.

4. Jessie Chambers [E. T.], *D. H. Lawrence, a Personal Record* (New York: Knight Publications, 1936), pp. 190–92.

5. *The Frieda Lawrence Collection of D. H. Lawrence Manuscripts, A Descriptive Bibliography*, ed. E. W. Tedlock, Jr. (Albuquerque: University of New Mexico Press, 1948), p. 44. This manuscript is now housed in the special collections of the Morris Library at Southern Illinois University in Carbondale. A typescript of this manuscript is appended to the new Cambridge edition of *The Lost Girl*, ed. John Worthen, pp. 343–58.

6. Sir Compton Mackenzie, *My Life and Times: Octave Five* (London: Chatto & Windus, 1966), p. 171. For a detailed history of the composition of *The Lost Girl*, see John Worthen's introduction to the Cambridge edition, pp. xix–xxxii.

7. Miss Pinnegar voices (and Mr. May implies) the conventional view that Alvina is morally lost. Alvina realizes that by her relationship with Ciccio she has cut herself off from society, and that she has lost one aspect of her self in order to gain another. See pp. 217, 225–26, 228, 306, 314, 316, 175.

8. In Lawrence's introduction to "Memoirs of the Foreign Legion," by Maurice Magnus, the prototype for Mr. May, Lawrence writes of Magnus's mother that "M—— adored her, and she him. Part of his failings one can *certainly* ascribe to the fact that he was an only son, an adored son, in whose veins the mother imagined only royal blood." In *Phoenix II: Uncollected, Unpublished and Other Prose Works by D. H. Lawrence*, ed. Warren Roberts and Harry T. Moore (New York: Viking Press, Compass Books, 1970), p. 360.

9. Harry T. Moore, *The Priest of Love: A Life of D. H. Lawrence* (New York: Farrar, Straus, & Giroux, 1974), p. 32.

10. L. D. Clark, *The Minoan Distance: The Symbolism of Travel in D. H. Lawrence* (Tucson: University of Arizona Press, 1980), p. 65.

11. Moore, *Priest of Love*, p. 31.

12. In fact, the original title for this chapter, in the holograph manuscript of May 1920, was "The Decline and Fall of Manchester House" (*LG*, 361). Obviously Lawrence had in mind Gibbon's *Decline and Fall of the Roman Empire*, a work which he read in the formative stage of his leadership period.

4. Sanctions from the Animal World

1. This 1918 "Fox," a twenty-two page unpublished draft, is now in the George Lazarus collection in England, but it was made available to the public in 1959 by Harry T. Moore in

A D. H. Lawrence Miscellany (Carbondale: Southern Illinois University Press, 1959). Moore reproduced the holograph manuscript and provided a not totally accurate printed transcript as well.

2. *Letters of D. H. Lawrence*, ed. Aldous Huxley (London: William Heinemann, 1932), pp. 480–81. No manuscript or typescript of this second, revised version appears to be extant.

3. This journal is now publicly available only in the British Library copy. The corrected proof sheets from *Hutchinson's Story Magazine* were owned by the late Mr. John E. Baker, Jr., who kindly answered my questions about them in a two-year correspondence before his untimely death in November 1977. Thanks to his widow, Mrs. Dudley Baker, I have examined photocopies of four of the eight galley pages; damage to the material prevented further copying. The proof sheets are part of the Baker holdings auctioned by Christie's in New York in April 1979. According to Mr. Baker's privately printed catalog of his twentieth-century literature collection (Desbarats, Ontario, 1977), p. 17, the *Hutchinson's* proofs show "10 revisions (deletions and additions), 20 words, and 13 typographical corrections in Lawrence's hand."

4. Diary listing, in *The Frieda Lawrence Collection of D. H. Lawrence Manuscripts: A Descriptive Bibliography*, ed. E. W. Tedlock, Jr. (Albuquerque: University of New Mexico Press, 1948), p. 89.

5. This Taormina, Sicily, manuscript is now owned by the Humanities Research Center at the University of Texas in Austin.

6. Lawrence may well have had his eye on *The Dial* when he revised *The Fox* in 1921, for the magazine had already printed his work in seven out of its fifteen previous issues.

7. F. R. Leavis, *D. H. Lawrence: Novelist* (London: Chatto & Windus, 1955), p. 256.

8. Quoted in *D. H. Lawrence: The Critical Heritage*, ed. Ronald P. Draper (London: Routledge & Kegan Paul, 1970), p. 196.

9. To George Ford, in *Double Measure: A Study of the Novels and Stories of D. H. Lawrence* (New York: Holt, Rinehart & Winston, 1965), p. 102, *The Fox* shows Lawrence daydreaming of himself as the savior of women; to Peg Brayfield, in "Lawrence's 'Male and Female Principles' and the Symbolism of 'The Fox,'" *Mosaic* 4 (Spring 1971): 41–51, Lawrence is quite critical of Grenfel's attempts to rescue March. Julian Moynahan, in *The Deed of Life: The Novels and Tales of D. H. Lawrence* (Princeton: Princeton University Press, 1963), p. 208, describes the murder of Banford as a "deed of life," to inspire admiration; but Keith Sagar, in *The Art of D. H. Lawrence* (Cambridge: Cambridge University Press, 1966), p. 117, sees it rather as evidence of Lawrence's "withering vision."

10. See Ernest Tedlock, *D. H. Lawrence: Artist and Rebel* (Albuquerque: University of New Mexico Press, 1963), p. 119.

11. Edmund Bergler, "D. H. Lawrence's *The Fox* and the Psychoanalytic Theory on Lesbianism," *Journal of Nervous and Mental Disease* (Baltimore, 1958), reprinted in Moore, *A D. H. Lawrence Miscellany*, pp. 49–55.

12. In the Taormina manuscript, after Grenfel kills the marauding fox he says that he will go out to see if the *dog*-fox is creeping about: this suggests that Lawrence conceived of the slaughtered fox, at least subconsciously, as female. He caught the error himself and corrected it to *she*-fox, but the slip of the pen attests to his confusion about this critical detail.

13. Hillis Miller, "D. H. Lawrence: *The Fox* and the Perspective Glass," *Harvard Advocate* 1937 (December 1952): 26.

14. Ford, *Double Measure*, pp. 101–2.

15. According to the corrected proof sheets of the *Hutchinson's Story Magazine* version of *The Fox*, Lawrence made his changes when he got ready to publish the story in 1920, not when he revised it in 1919.

16. John B. Vickery, "Myth and Ritual in the Shorter Fiction of D. H. Lawrence," *Modern Fiction Studies* 5 (Spring 1959): 80. Vickery makes Frazer's single example into an universal principle by stating that "significantly enough, during harvest season the man who hits the last corn with his sickle is called the Fox and during the evening dances with all the

girls." See Sir James Frazer, *The Golden Bough: A Study in Magic and Religion*, 12 vols. (London: Macmillan, 1925–1930), 8 (1925): 296–97.

17. Frazer, *Golden Bough*, 7:131–70.

18. Ibid., 8:297–98.

19. Quoted in Vickery, "Myth and Ritual," p. 81. No citation given.

20. Erik Erikson, in *Childhood and Society* (New York: W. W. Norton, 2d ed. 1963), p. 251, relates "primitive religions, the most primitive layer in all religions, and the religious layer in each individual" to the conflict between basic trust and mistrust that arises in the oral stage of psychological development, centering on the mother.

21. Miller, "D. H. Lawrence: *The Fox* and the Perspective Glass," p. 27.

22. Joseph C. Rheingold, *The Mother, Anxiety and Death: The Catastrophic Death Complex* (Boston: Little, Brown, 1967), pp. 132–33.

23. Kingsley Widmer, *The Art of Perversity: D. H. Lawrence's Shorter Fictions* (Seattle: University of Washington Press, 1962), p. 62.

24. Erikson, *Childhood and Society*, p. 253.

25. Eugene Goodhart, *The Utopian Vision of D. H. Lawrence* (Chicago: University of Chicago Press, 1963), p. 86; Moynahan, *Deed of Life*, p. 208. More praise for the "deed of life" can be found in Tedlock, *Artist and Rebel*, p. 119; Widmer, *Art of Perversity*, pp. 62–64; Leavis, *D. H. Lawrence: Novelist*, pp. 264–65; G. B. Crump, "*The Fox* on Film," *The D. H. Lawrence Review* 1 (Fall 1968): 241. Condemnation for the deed was voiced early on by Alyse Gregory in *The Dial* in January 1924, her review being reprinted in Draper, ed., *D. H. Lawrence: The Critical Heritage*, p. 219. Other "deed of death" views can be found in Sagar, *Art of D. H. Lawrence*, p. 117; Ian Gregor, "*The Fox*: A Caveat," *Essays in Criticism* 9 (January 1959): 15; Leo Gurko, "D. H. Lawrence's Great Collection of Short Stories—What Holds It Together," *Modern Fiction Studies* 18 (Summer 1972): 181; Mark Spilka, *The Love Ethic of D. H. Lawrence* (Bloomington: Indiana University Press, 1955), p. 199. This view is implied in Ronald P. Draper, "The Defeat of Feminism: D. H. Lawrence's *The Fox* and 'The Woman Who Rode Away,'" *Studies in Short Fiction* 3 (Winter 1966): 192–98. E. F. Shields, in "Broken Vision in Lawrence's 'The Fox,'" *Studies in Short Fiction* 9 (Fall 1972): 353–63, questions the aesthetic, rather than the moral or psychological, validity of Banford's death.

26. Robert Lindner, "The Equivalents of Matricide," *Psychoanalytic Quarterly* 17 (October 1948): 453–70.

27. Erikson, *Childhood and Society*, p. 253.

28. Monroe Engel, in "The Continuity of Lawrence's Short Novels," *Hudson Review* 11 (Summer 1958): 201, goes too far when he asserts that "a peculiar state of disorder" is suggested by the fact that March and Banford are known by their surnames.

29. Catherine Carswell, *The Savage Pilgrimage: A Narrative of D. H. Lawrence* (London: Chatto & Windus, 1932), p. 207.

30. Quoted in Harry T. Moore, *The Priest of Love: A Life of D. H. Lawrence* (Farrar, Straus, & Giroux, 1974), p. 264.

31. Richard Aldington, *Life for Life's Sake: A Book of Reminiscences* (New York: Viking Press, 1941), p. 235.

32. John Middleton Murry, *Reminiscences of D. H. Lawrence* (London: Jonathan Cape, 1933), p. 91.

33. Frieda Lawrence, *Not I, But the Wind . . .* (New York: Viking Press, 1934), p. 92.

34. Harry T. Moore, *The Intelligent Heart: The Story of D. H. Lawrence* (New York: Farrar, Straus, & Young, 1954), p. 240.

35. D. H. Lawrence, *The Quest for Rananim: D. H. Lawrence's Letters to S. S. Koteliansky, 1914–1930*, ed. Geoge Zytaruk (Montreal: McGill–Queen's University Press, 1970), p. 177. Zytaruck corrects Harry T. Moore's dating of this letter in the *Collected Letters*.

36. Zytaruck, ed., *Quest for Rananim*, p. 91.

37. Ford, *Double Measure*, pp. 182, 198.

38. As Catherine Carswell tells the story (*Savage Pilgrimage*, p. 110), Lawrence's relationship during this period with Middleton Murry also reflects the dependency-and-betrayal

motif. In January 1919 Murry assumed editorship of the *Athenaeum*, and thus he was in a position to help his friend in the time of his great need for literary support. Instead, in the months to follow, Murry refused many of Lawrence's articles and used the pages of his journal to denigrate Lawrence's work.

39. Ottoline Morrell, for example, must have gained a measure of relief in noting the Frieda aspects of her own portrait as Hermione Roddice in *Women in Love*: Edward Nehls has revealed that in Lady Ottoline's copy of the novel there is a marginal annotation next to the lapis lazuli scene, in which Hermione smashes Birkin over the head with the stone wielded in her left hand, that reads, "Frida [sic] was left-handed!" Reported in Moore, *Priest of Love*, p. 271.

40. Mabel Dodge Luhan, *Lorenzo in Taos* (London: Martin Secker, 1933), p. 68.

41. Martin Green, *The Von Richthofen Sisters: The Triumphant and The Tragic Modes of Love* (New York: Basic Books, 1974), p. 342.

42. Dorothy Brett, *Lawrence and Brett: A Friendship* (Philadelphia: J. B. Lippincott, 1933), p. 89. Witter Bynner, in *Journey with Genius: Recollections and Reflections Concerning the Lawrences* (New York: John Day, 1951), p. 8, says that the name was Red Wolf.

43. Ford Madox Ford, *Portraits from Life* (Boston: Houghton Mifflin, 1937), pp. 76–77.

44. Hilda Doolittle [H. D.], *Bid Me to Live (A Madrigal)* (New York: Grove Press, 1960), p. 84.

45. And/or an early title for *Women in Love*. See the conjectures of Lawrence scholars George Zytaruk, "What Happened to *Goats and Compasses*?", the *D. H. Lawrence Review* 4 (Fall 1971): 280–85; Charles Ross and George Zytaruk, "*Goats and Compasses* and/or *Women in Love*: An Exchange," the *D. H. Lawrence Review* 6 (Spring 1973): 33–46; and Keith Sagar, "*Goats and Compasses* and *Women in Love* Again," the *D. H. Lawrence Review* 6 (Fall 1973): 303–8.

5. Over the Border

1. This is the suggestion of the anonymous writer who provided the introduction to Lady Cynthia Asquith, *Diaries 1915–1918* (London: Hutchinson, 1968), p. xviii.

2. This attitude probably figures as well in the well-known tale "The Rocking Horse Winner," which Lawrence later wrote for inclusion in Lady Cynthia's collection of stories called *The Ghost Book*.

3. Lawrence may have taken his name from Lord Basil Blackwood, who was killed in battle on 3 July 1917. Lady Cynthia's diary is full of references to Basil, whom she saw often; after his death, she noted that a friend consoled her with the words, "of course, he adored you with his whole being." Diary entry, 10 July 1917, *Diaries 1915–1918*, p. 319.

4. L. P. Hartley, foreword to *Diaries 1915–1918*, p. x.

5. The Count is responding to Lady Daphne's quotation from an unnamed poem by Swinburne, which happens to be his "Garden of Proserpine." This poem is an appropriate if unconscious choice on Daphne's part, considering the Persephone-Hades mythological substratum of the story. Lawrence was very fond of Swinburne, calling him "the last fiery spirit among us" (*CL*, I, 474).

6. See Ernest Tedlock, *D. H. Lawrence, Artist and Rebel* (Albuquerque: University of New Mexico Press, 1963), p. 122.

7. Sandra Gilbert finds a submerged and subversive narrative structure built on a revitalizing trip to the underworld in the entire *Birds, Beasts and Flowers* volume of which "Snake" is a part. She argues that because this volume is more cohesive than the novels of 1920–22, it provides a better link than they between Lawrence's middle-period social novels and his late-period mythologies. See her essay, "D. H. Lawrence's Uncommon Prayers," in *D. H. Lawrence: The Man Who Lived*, ed. Robert B. Partlow, Jr., and Harry T. Moore (Carbondale: Southern Illinois University Press, 1980), pp. 73–93.

8. William York Tindall, *D. H. Lawrence and Susan His Cow* (New York: Columbia University Press, 1939), pp. 149–54.

9. John Stall, *The Novels of D. H. Lawrence: A Search for Integration* (Columbia: University of Missouri Press, 1971), p. 133.

10. As Kenneth Inniss points out, in *D. H. Lawrence's Bestiary: A Study of His Use of Animal Trope and Symbol* (The Hague: Mouton, 1971), pp. 44–45, the swan was to Lawrence a symbol of reduction to the elements of darkness. In *The Fox*, March paints swans on porcelain.

11. Lady Cynthia Asquith, *Remember and Be Glad* (New York; Charles Scribner's Sons, 1952), p. 140.

12. Lawrence's story "Glad Ghosts" suggests this desire once again; in it, the Lawrence figure sires a child by the Cynthia figure. Lawrence wrote of this story, "I promised Cynthia Asquith a ghost story for a collection she is making. How will she swallow 'Gay Ghosts' [an early title for the story]?" (*CL*, II, 882).

13. Asquith, *Diaries*, p. 133.

14. "D. H. Lawrence From Island to Glacier," *University of Toronto Quarterly* 37 (1967–68): 222.

15. See Evelyn J. Hinz, "D. H. Lawrence and 'Something Called *Canada*,'" *The Dalhousie Review* 54 (Summer 1974): 240–50.

16. Richard P. Wheeler, "Intimacy and Irony in 'The Blind Man,'" *The D. H. Lawrence Review* 9 (Summer 1976): 240–41.

17. Paul Delany, *D. H. Lawrence's Nightmare: The Writer and His Circle in the Years of the Great War* (New York: Basic Books, 1978), p. 372.

18. W. S. Marks, III, "The Psychology of Regression in D. H. Lawrence's 'The Blind Man,'" *Literature and Psychology* 17 (1967): 181.

19. Ibid., p. 190.

20. Harry T. Moore, *The Priest of Love: A Life of D. H. Lawrence* (New York: Farrar, Straus, & Giroux, 1974), p. 221.

21. Ibid., p. 302.

22. Helen Corke, *D. H. Lawrence: The Croydon Years* (Austin: University of Texas Press, 1965), p. 12.

23. Frieda Lawrence, *The Memoirs and Correspondence*, ed. Ernest W. Tedlock, Jr. (New York: Knopf, 1964), p. 341.

24. Mabel Dodge Luhan, *Lorenzo in Taos* (London: Martin Secker, 1933), pp. 71, 74.

25. Frieda Lawrence, *Not I, But the Wind* . . . (New York: Viking Press, 1934), p. 57.

6. "The Italian Brutal Way"

1. Lady Cynthia Asquith reports that Lawrence and Frieda went to the opera with her at Covent Garden and sat in the box lent by Lady Cunard. *Remember and Be Glad* (New York: Charles Scribner's Sons, 1952), p. 142.

2. *The Quest for Rananim: D. H. Lawrence's Letters to S. S. Koteliansky, 1914–1930*, ed. George Zytaruck (Montreal: McGill–Queen's University Press, 1970), p. 91.

3. See Nicholas Joost and Alvin Sullivan, *D. H. Lawrence and the Dial* (Carbondale: Southern Illinois University Press, 1970), p. 60.

4. Letter to Thomas Seltzer, 8 October 1921. In D. H. Lawrence, *Letters to Thomas and Adele Seltzer*, ed. Gerald M. Lacy (Santa Barbara: Black Sparrow Press, 1976), pp. 26–27.

5. And even then it was technically Frieda's. Dorothy Brett tells the story in *Lawrence and Brett: A Friendship* (Philadelphia: J. B. Lippincott, 1933), p. 63: "'Mabel,' you tell me, 'has offered me the Ranch. She wants to give it to me, but I won't accept it. I hate presents of all kinds and I hate possessions. She has offered it to Frieda. I told Frieda she could do as she liked, so she has accepted it.'"

6. In a letter of 22 September 1922, Lawrence writes of Mabel Dodge, "The drawback is, of course, living under the wing of the '*padrona*.' She is generous and nice—but still, I don't feel free. I can't breathe my own air and go on my little way" (*CL*, II, 718).

7. *The Letters of D. H. Lawrence*, ed. Aldous Huxley (London: William Heinemann, 1932), p. 102.

8. *Ottoline at Garsington: Memoirs of Lady Ottoline Morrell 1915–1918*, ed. R. Gathorne-Hardy (London: Faber & Faber, 1974), p. 37. Quoted in Paul Delany, *D. H. Lawrence's Nightmare: The Writer and His Circle in the Years of the Great War* (New York: Basic Books, 1978), p. 113.

9. The controversy over the nature of the lovemaking practices of Lawrence's heroes was initiated by G. Wilson Knight in "Lawrence, Joyce and Powys," *Essays in Criticism* 11 (1961); 403–17, and taken up over the years by numerous other critics. One critic who discusses Lawrence's use of anal intercourse in terms of his psychological theories is Frank Kermode, in *D. H. Lawrence* (New York: Viking Press, 1973), pp. 76–77: in *Women in Love*, "[m]etaphysically Lawrence is saying . . . that the source of resistance to the evil male surrender to the solar plexus, the lapse into the hated mother, was in the lumbar ganglia; separateness once established and venerated, the 'immemorable magnificence' of that love act was possible. It is not like the intentions of most novelists, and the method is therefore totally idiosyncratic."

10. Keith Sagar, *D. H. Lawrence: A Calendar of His Works* (Austin: University of Texas Press, 1979), pp. 119–20.

11. Jim Bricknell may also be based in part on John Middleton Murry, whom Lawrence in his 1918 "devouring mother" letter accused of a similar childish dependence upon *his* mother figure. Katherine Mansfield's desertion of Murry for another man, in 1915, had caused him to seek out Lawrence at his Greatham Cottage, where Lawrence set about revivifying him. According to Delany (*D. H. Lawrence's Nightmare*, p. 62), the incident is recorded in the chapter "Low-Water Mark" in *Aaron's Rod*, with Murry as the sickly Aaron. However, Murry is less like Aaron, who has abandoned his wife, than like Jim, who has himself been abandoned. The parallel between Jack and Jim is made stronger by the fact that Katherine Mansfield's telegram to Murry after only six days with her new lover caused Murry immediately to leave Lawrence and his friendship and to return to London to meet Mansfield. Thus, like Jim, Murry had hardly been a day with a male friend when he reestablished contact with a woman via the telegraph. See also Murry's autobiography, *Between Two Worlds*, in which he states that he recognizes in his own behavior "an unconscious urge towards a peculiar intensity in my personal relations. . . . Only when I was surrounded by the safety and warmth of an intimate personal affection could I breathe freely. . . ." (London: Jonathan Cape, 1935), pp. 326–27. Murry admitted that his "capacity for love" may have been "largely a desire for protection"; see Frieda Lawrence, *The Memoirs and Correspondence*, ed. Ernest W. Tedlock, Jr. (New York: Knopf, 1964), pp. 281–82. In *Katherine Mansfield: The Memories of L. M.* [Ida Baker] (New York: Taplinger, 1972), p. 83, Baker says that "unconsciously [Murry] leaned on her strength. . . . Her love became imbued with the tenderness of mother-love, with which her heart has always been full."

12. Eliseo Vivas, *D. H. Lawrence: The Failure and the Triumph of Art* (Evanston: Northwestern University Press, 1960), p. 23.

13. Graham Hough, *The Dark Sun* (London: Gerald Duckworth, 1956), p. 111.

14. Letter 1194 in Gerald M. Lacy, *An Analytical Calendar of the Letters of D. H. Lawrence* (Ann Arbor: University Microfilms, 1971). Quoted by Delany, *D. H. Lawrence's Nightmare*, pp. 281–82.

15. In *The Lost Girl*, Alvina rides beside Ciccio on the tram and clings "to Ciccio's dark, despised foreign nature. She loved it, she worshipped it, she defied all the other world. Dark, he sat beside her, drawn in to himself, overcast by his presumed inferiority among these northern industrial people, and she was with him, on his side, outside the pale of her own people" (*LG*, p. 215).

7. A Lesson in Disillusion

1. Frank Kermode, *D. H. Lawrence* (New York: Viking Press, 1973), p. 105.

2. Harry T. Moore, "Bert Lawrence and Lady Jane," in *Lawrence and Women*, ed. Anne Smith (London: Vision Press, 1978), p. 182.

3. Paul Delany, *D. H. Lawrence's Nightmare: The Writer and His Circle in the Years of the Great War* (New York: Basic Books, 1978), p. 264.

4. Roundtable on "D. H. Lawrence and the Cult of the Hero," held in the Durham County Library as part of "D. H. Lawrence Fifty Years Later: Perspectives on Society," co-sponsored by the Duke University Office of Continuing Education and the Durham Public Library with funding from the North Carolina Humanities Committee, 28 October 1980. Panelists included James B. Reston, Jr., John Cell, Alan Stern, and this author. Remarks are taken from a videotape of the proceedings.

5. See, for example, James Cowan, "D. H. Lawrence and the Resurrection of the Body," in *Healing Arts in Dialogue, Medicine and Literature*, ed. Joanne Trautmann (Carbondale: Southern Illinois University Press, 1981), pp. 55–70.

6. See Erich Fromm's exploration of J. J. Bachofen's theories of Mother Right and the connection between matriarchalism and democracy in "The Significance of the Theory of Mother Right and its Relevance for Social Psychology" in *The Crisis of Psychoanalysis* (New York: Holt, Rinehart & Winston, 1970).

7. Ferdinand Tönnies, *Gemeinschaft and Gesellschaft* (Leipzig, 1887), trans. Charles P. Loomis as *Community and Association* (London, 1955). This distinction is discussed in Malcolm Bradbury, *The Social Context of Modern English Literature* (New York: Schocken, 1971), pp. 9–14.

8. Kermode, *D. H. Lawrence*, p. 110.

9. Susan Sontag explores the traditional conceptions about tuberculosis that connect the disease with frustrated passion in "Illness as Metaphor," *New York Review of Books* 24 (January 26, 1978): 12–16.

10. George Ford, *Double Measure: A Study of the Novels and Stories of D. H. Lawrence* (New York: Holt, Rinehart & Winston, 1965), p. 127.

11. James Reston, Jr., *Our Father Who Art in Hell* (New York: Times Books, 1981), pp. 97–98.

12. L. D. Clark, *The Minoan Distance: The Symbolism of Travel in D. H. Lawrence* (Tucson: University of Arizona Press, 1980), p. 258.

8. The Outlaw Hero

1. A discussion of the manuscripts and typescripts of *The Boy in the Bush* may be found in Harry T. Moore's preface to the Viking Compass Edition, pp. xi–xviii. Also see Charles Rossman, "*The Boy in the Bush* in the Lawrence Canon," in *D. H. Lawrence: The Man Who Lived*, ed. Robert B. Partlow, Jr., and Harry T. Moore (Carbondale: Southern Illinois University Press, 1980), pp. 187–89.

2. Harry T. Moore, *The Priest of Love: A Life of D. H. Lawrence* (New York: Farrar, Straus, & Giroux, 1974), p. 43.

3. George Ford, *Double Measure: A Study of the Novels and Stories of D. H. Lawrence* (New York: Holt, Rinehart & Winston, 1965), p. 18. However, to Ford, the leadership novels (by which he means only *Aaron's Rod*, *Kangaroo*, and *The Plumed Serpent*) "represent a deviation from the typical preoccupations of the rest of [Lawrence's] fiction"—a position with which I disagree.

4. A letter to Mollie Skinner after her brother's death in 1925 shows Lawrence clearly identifying with Jack Grant. See M. L. Skinner, *The Fifth Sparrow* (London: Angus and Robertson, 1973), p. 158.

5. Jessie Chambers [E. T.], *D. H. Lawrence, A Personal Record* (New York: Knight Publications, 1936), pp. 85–86.

6. Ibid., p. 88.

7. Paul Delany, *D. H. Lawrence's Nightmare: The Writer and His Circle in the Years of the Great War* (New York: Basic Books, 1978), p. 314.

8. Letter 1177, Gerald M. Lacy, *An Analytical Calendar of the Letters of D. H. Lawrence* (Ann Arbor: University Microfilms, 1971). Quoted by Delany, *D. H. Lawrence's Nightmare*, p. 280.

9. See Robert Lindner, "The Equivalents of Matricide," *Psychoanalytic Quarterly* 17 (October 1948): 453–70.
10. The Australian novelist Katherine Susannah Prichard objected to the scene for this reason (*CB*, II, 275).
11. Herman Daleski, *The Forked Flame: A Study of D. H. Lawrence* (Evanston: Northwestern University Press, 1965), chapter four.
12. Moore, preface, *Priest of Love*, p. xv.
13. D. H. Lawrence, preface to *Black Swans* by M. L. Skinner, in *Phoenix II: Uncollected, Unpublished, and Other Prose Works by D. H. Lawrence*, ed. Warren Roberts and Harry T. Moore (New York: Viking Press, Compass Books, 1970), p. 295.
14. Catherine Carswell, *The Savage Pilgrimage, A Narrative of D. H. Lawrence* (London: Secker & Warburg, 1951), p. 199.
15. Chambers [E. T.], *D. H. Lawrence*, pp. 219–22.

9. The American Experience

1. Lawrence had an exaggerated vision of the influence of his theories on orthodox psychoanalysis. In 1919 he told Ben Huebsch that the "new science of psychology" to be found in his essays on American literature was at that moment being grafted by psychoanalysts onto Freudian theory in order "to solidify their windy theory of the unconscious" (*CL*, I, 596).
2. George Ford, *Double Measure: A Study of the Novels and Stories of D. H. Lawrence* (New York: Holt, Rinehart & Winston, 1965), p. 47.
3. See W. S. Marks, III, "The Psychology of the Uncanny in Lawrence's 'The Rocking-Horse Winner,'" *Modern Fiction Studies* 11 (Winter 1965–66): 387–89.
4. D. H. Lawrence, *Letters to Thomas and Adele Seltzer*, ed. Gerald M. Lacy (Santa Barbara: Black Sparrow Press, 1976), p. 93.
5. See Dorothy Brett, *Lawrence and Brett: A Friendship* (Philadelphia: J. B. Lippincott, 1933), p. 82:

you say suddenly, "How I hate these people who write books from their armchairs; men who . . . . just sit at home and write about everything second-hand, never having seen an Indian or a tiger. . . . They are afraid to meet life, to experience it for themselves." Frieda stitches away silently. I look up and say:
"Didn't Fenimore Cooper know Indians?"
"No, never," you say abruptly. "I doubt if he ever saw one. Haven't you read my Essays?"

6. Mabel Dodge Luhan, *Lorenzo in Taos* (London: Martin Secker, 1933), p. 45.
7. Lacy, ed., *Letters to Thomas and Adele Seltzer*, p. 93.
8. Letters 1181, 1177, Gerald M. Lacy, *An Analytical Calendar of the Letters of D. H. Lawrence* (Ann Arbor: University Microfilms, 1971). Quoted in Paul Delany, *D. H. Lawrence's Nightmare: The Writer and His Circle in the Years of the Great War* (New York: Basic Books, 1978), p. 280.
9. Harry T. Moore, *The Priest of Love: A Life of D. H. Lawrence* (New York: Farrar, Straus, & Giroux, 1974), p. 375.
10. Luhan, *Lorenzo in Taos*, pp. 194–96. See also Brett, *Lawrence and Brett*, p. 87.
11. The fragment is published only in *The Princess and Other Stories*, ed. Keith Sagar (London: Penguin Books, 1971), pp. 15–21.
12. Luhan, *Lorenzo in Taos*, p. 219, n. 10. To add insult to injury, the story was typed on a typewriter borrowed from Mabel. See Brett, *Lawrence and Brett*, p. 107.
13. E. W. Tedlock, Jr., *D. H. Lawrence: Artist and Rebel* (Albuquerque: University of New Mexico Press, 1963), p. 180.
14. As reported by John Evans (Mabel Dodge's son), Lawrence gave the following premarital counseling: "He said for me to be always alone. Always separate. Never to let Alice

know my thoughts. To be gentle with her when she was gentle, but if she opposed my will, to beat her." See Luhan, *Lorenzo in Taos*, p. 85.

15. L. D. Clark, *The Minoan Distance: The Symbolism of Travel in D. H. Lawrence* (Tucson: University of Arizona Press, 1980), p. 281.

10. Rekindling the Father-Spark

1. See James Boulton's introduction to D. H. Lawrence, *Movements in European History* (Oxford: Oxford University Press, 1971), pp. xii–xiv.

2. D. H. Lawrence, *The Centaur Letters*, ed. Edward D. McDonald (Austin: University of Texas Press, 1970), p. 16.

3. Ibid., p. 20.

4. Several years earlier Lawrence had remarked, "When one walks, one must travel west or south. If one turns northward or eastward it is like walking down a *cul-de-sac*, to the blind end" (*TI*, 145). Probably the one place Lawrence truly wished to stay in was Higher Tregerthen on the coast of Cornwall, during World War I; his eviction as a probable spy makes the following letter to Katherine Mansfield seem both ironic and poignant: "Really, one should find a place one can live in, and stay there. Geographical change doesn't help one much. And people go from bad to worse. I think I shall be staring out from Higher Tregerthen when I am a nice old man of seventy" (*CL*, I, 465).

5. In *Sons and Lovers*, the young Paul and his sister burn the doll, called the Missus, that stands in for the mother. An interesting sidelight on the subject of doll-burning is provided by an August 1924 letter to Clarence Thompson, one of the hangers-on at Mabel Dodge's ranch: "I burned that hideous Indian doll—seriously set fire to her. She was too ugly . . . I feel it is a new phase altogether. The old idols put in the kitchen stove, like that doll" (*CL*, II, 805).

In *Lorenzo in Search of the Sun: D. H. Lawrence in Italy, Mexico, and the American Southwest* (New York: Bookman Associates, 1953), p. 39, Eliot Fay notes that the Pueblo Indians of Taos had been converted by the Spaniards to Catholicism and records Lawrence's interest in their ceremony, on the patron saint's day, of taking from the village chapel the statue of the Virgin Mary and carrying it joyfully through the streets.

6. According to tradition, Quetzalcoatl does indeed have a mother—a virgin mother, to boot! Laurette Sejourne, *Burning Water: Thought and Religion in Ancient Mexico* (London and New York: Thames and Hudson, 1956), p. 56. Quoted in James Cowan, *D. H. Lawrence's American Journey: A Study in Literature and Myth* (Cleveland and London: Case Western Reserve University Press, 1970), p. 107.

7. According to L. D. Clark, the first draft of *The Plumed Serpent*, produced in the summer of 1923, has Kate renouncing "mother love for her children and something in the western continent strengthens her against returning to it." Clark adds, "Hence she is fulfilling for Lawrence what he craved both from Frieda and from the memory of his mother." *The Minoan Distance: The Symbolism of Travel in D. H. Lawrence* (Tucson: University of Arizona Press, 1980), p. 288.

8. In *Phoenix II: Uncollected, Unpublished, and Other Prose Works by D. H. Lawrence*, ed. Warren Roberts and Harry T. Moore (New York: Viking Press, Compass Books, 1970), p. 548: "Insouciance means not caring about things that don't concern you; it also means not being pinched by anxiety. But indifference is inability to care; it is the result of a certain deadness or numbness. And it is nearly always accompanied by a pinch of anxiety. Men who can't care anymore, feel anxious about it. They have no insouciance. They are thankful if the woman will care. And at the same time they resent the woman's caring and running the show. The trouble is not in the woman's bossiness, but in the men's indifference."

9. L. D. Clark, *Dark Night of the Body: D. H. Lawrence's The Plumed Serpent* (Austin: University of Texas Press, 1964), p. 47. Clark believes that the French lyric is an inappropriate closing line because, "suggesting desertion, it is a long way from the circumstances."

10. Herman Daleski, *The Forked Flame: A Study of D. H. Lawrence* (Evanston: Northwestern University Press, 1965), p. 239.
11. Richard P. Wheeler, "Intimacy and Irony in 'The Blind Man,'" *The D. H. Lawrence Review* 9 (Summer 1976): 250.
12. Other twentieth-century British romanticists point to the archetypal significance of individual identities and thereby reaffirm the authenticity of the self. Robert Graves's White Goddess poems are a case in point. See Robert Langbaum, "The Mysteries of Identity: A Theme in Modern Literature," in *The Modern Spirit* (New York: Oxford University Press, 1970), pp. 164–84.
13. For the discussion that follows I am indebted to Professor Alan Stern of The University of North Carolina at Chapel Hill, who participated in a roundtable on "D. H. Lawrence and the Cult of the Hero," devised by this author and held in October 1980 as part of the series "D. H. Lawrence Fifty Years Later: Perspectives on Society."
14. See Alan J. Stern and John Rhoads, "Regulation of Self-Esteem in Some Political Activists," *The Annual of Psychoanalysis*, VIII (New York: International Universities Press, Inc., 1981), 288.

11. Blessed are the Powerful

1. D. H. Lawrence, *The Centaur Letters*, ed. Edward McDonald (Austin: Humanities Research Center, 1970), p. 24.
2. D. H. Lawrence, *Letters to Martin Secker, 1911–1930* (Buckingham: Martin Secker, 1970), p. 70.
3. Quoted in Brian H. Finney, "A Newly Discovered Text of D. H. Lawrence's 'The Lovely Lady,'" *The Yale University Library Gazette* 49 (January 1975): 248.
4. Ibid., p. 251.
5. Ibid.
6. Keith Sagar, *The Art of D. H. Lawrence* (Cambridge: Cambridge University Press, 1966), p. 192.
7. Martin Green, *The Von Richthofen Sisters: The Triumphant and the Tragic Modes of Love* (New York: Basic Books, 1974), p. 350.
8. John Stoll, *The Novels of D. H. Lawrence: A Search for Integration* (Columbia: University of Missouri Press, 1971), p. 246.
9. Sagar, *Art of D. H. Lawrence*, p. 195.
10. *The Frieda Lawrence Collection of D. H. Lawrence Manuscripts: A Descriptive Bibliography*, ed. Ernest W. Tedlock, Jr. (Albuquerque: University of New Mexico Press, 1948), p. 68.
11. Compare Sir James Frazer, *The Golden Bough: A Study of Magic and Religion*, 12 vols. (London: Macmillan, 1925–30) 2 (1926): 271, n. 2: "The system of mother-kin, that is, of tracing descent through females instead of through males, is often called the matriarchate. But this term is inappropriate and misleading, as it implies that under the system in question the women govern the men. Even when the so-called matriarchate regulates the descent of the kingdom, this does not mean that the women of the royal family reign; it only means that they are the channel through which the kinship is transmitted to their husbands or sons."
12. Compare Frazer, *Golden Bough* 6 (1927): 211: "In point of fact the great religious ideals which have permanently impressed themselves on the world seem always to have been a product of the male imagination. Men make gods and women worship them."
13. Jeffrey Meyers, "Katherine Mansfield, Gurdjieff, and Lawrence's 'Mother and Daughter,'" *Twentieth Century Literature* 22 (December 1976): 452.
14. Lydia Blanchard, "Mothers and Daughters in D. H. Lawrence: *The Rainbow* and Selected Shorter Works," in *Lawrence and Women*, ed. Ann Smith (London: Vision Press, 1978), p. 96.

12. The Symbolic Father

1. Mary Freeman, *D. H. Lawrence: A Basic Study of His Ideas* (Gainesville: University of Florida Press, 1955), p. 253, n. 5.

2. Ernest Tedlock, *D. H. Lawrence: Artist and Rebel* (Albuquerque: University of New Mexico Press, 1963), pp. 128, 166.

3. See, for example, Keith Sagar, *The Art of D. H. Lawrence* (Cambridge: Cambridge University Press, 1966), p. 109.

4. Margaret S. Mahler, Fred Pine, and Anni Bergman, *The Psychological Birth of the Human Infant* (New York: Basic Books, 1975), p. 48. Subsequent quotations from the work appear parenthetically in the text.

5. It is interesting to speculate about the extent to which the characters in the story "Sun" are modeled on the family of Martin Secker, Lawrence's British publisher at the time. From the Villa Bernarda Lawrence wrote to Secker about Secker's wife Rina and his eighteen-month-old son Adrian, who were visiting in Sportorno: "Rina usually comes with Adrian in the afternoon. She is much better now, was very *nervosa* at first. . . . Adrian is not 'in the pink' but the scarlet. He is very bonnie, and growing fast, and perfectly happy and chirpy here. . . . When Rina can leave the boy for a few hours with her mother, and get a good walk in the hills with us all, she will be perfectly happy all right." These remarks suggest at least a partial resemblance between Rina and Adrian and the mother and child in "Sun"; by extension, the implied comparison between Secker himself and the character of the husband, Maurice, is distinctly unflattering. But—had he been asked—Lawrence probably would have explained patiently to Secker, as he had explained about Compton Mackenzie's relationship to Lawrence's story "The Man Who Loved Islands," that Secker's family "only *suggests* the idea—it's no portrait." Lawrence obviously had an interest in these people and inquired about "Rina and the boy" to the end of his life. See D. H. Lawrence, *Letters to Martin Secker, 1911–1930* (Buckingham: Martin Secker, 1970), pp. 68, 88.

6. Harry T. Moore, *The Priest of Love: A Life of D. H. Lawrence* (New York: Farrar, Straus, & Giroux, 1974), p. 12.

7. The female web is discussed by Carol Gilligan in *In a Different Voice: Psychological Theory and Women's Development* (Cambridge, Mass.: Harvard University Press, 1982).

8. For a discussion of paternalism see Richard Sennett, *Authority* (New York: Knopf, 1980). Technically Lawrence's ideal of leadership should be termed paternalistic rather than patriarchal, since in a patriarchy the leader is related to his followers by blood ties.

9. Paul Delany, *D. H. Lawrence's Nightmare: The Writer and His Circle in the Years of the Great War* (New York: Basic Books, 1978), pp. 301, 205.

10. Cecil Gray, *Musical Chairs* (London: Home & Van Thal, 1948), pp. 130–31.

11. Bertrand Russell, *Autobiography*, 2 vols. (Boston: Little, Brown, 1951), 2:13.

12. See John Harrison, *The Reactionaries: Yeats, Lewis, Pound, Eliot, Lawrence, A Study of the Anti-Democratic Intelligencia* (New York: Schocken, 1967).

13. Eric Bentley, *A Century of Hero-Worship*, 2d ed. (Boston: Beacon Press, 1957), p. 162.

14. D. H. Lawrence, *Letters*, ed. Aldous Huxley (London: William Heinemann, 1932), p. 237.

15. Sagar, *Art of D. H. Lawrence*, p. 167.

16. The poetry of Lawrence's leadership period, collected in *Birds, Beasts and Flowers*, by and large escapes the onus of being an inferior Lawrence production, even though the work concerns the nonhuman realm that usually allowed Lawrence the freedom to act less than human. Sandra Gilbert explores the connection between the ideal of leadership and the overall success of this poetry in *Acts of Attention: The Poems of D. H. Lawrence* (Ithaca: Cornell University Press, 1972), pp. 128–29.

17. See "The Role of the Father in the Preoedipal Years," report of the annual meeting of the American Psychoanalytic Association, April, 1977, in the *Journal of the American Psychoanalytic Association* 26 (1978): 143–61.

18. In *Phoenix II: Uncollected, Unpublished, and Other Prose Works by D. H. Lawrence*, ed.

Warren Roberts and Harry T. Moore (New York: Viking Press, Compass Books, 1970), pp. 92–108.

19. Moore, *Priest of Love*, pp. 59–63.

20. Charles W. Socarides, *The Overt Homosexual* (New York: Grune & Stratton, 1968), p. 226.

21. Joseph C. Rheingold, *The Mother, Anxiety, and Death: The Catastrophic Death Complex* (Boston: Little, Brown, 1967), p. 18.

22. Carolyn G. Heilbrun reinterprets the murder of Clytemnestra in this fashion in *Reinventing Womanhood* (New York: W. W. Norton, 1979), p. 154. Marina Warner demythologizes the Virgin Mary in a similar fashion and for similar reasons in *Alone of All Her Sex: The Myth and Cult of the Virgin Mary* (New York: Knopf, 1976).

Index

Aaron's Rod, 90–103; Bolshevist, 20; characteristics of leader, 111; devouring mother, 140; fear of entrapment, 112; female domination, 109, 123, 173; flippant attitude, 105; hatred of domesticity, 117; hero, 107; homosexuality, 98; infantile dependency, 160; isolation, 163; leadership ideal, 6, 181; as leadership novel, 6–7; lumbar ganglion, 121; merits, 5, 115; maternal characteristics of male, 149; misanthropy, 174; mother figure, 145; motif of communication, 105–6; nursing, 131; picaresque quality, 92–93, 100, 104; repulsion for female web, 180
Abelin, Ernest, 186
Acts of Attention, 202 n.16
Adam, 126
Aldington, Richard, 57; description of M. Radford, 62
Alone of All Her Sex, 203 n.22
Also Sprach Zarathustra, 104
America, 18, 71–73, 127–28, 140
Americans, 77
anal stage, 96
animals, 15, 76, 77–78, 119–22, 141, 149, 183–85
Apocalypse, 171–72, 174
"A Propos of *Lady Chatterley's Lover*," 162, 163
Asquith, Lady Cynthia, 10, 71–74, 75, 80, 85, 157, 196 n.1
Asquith, John, 72–73
Authority, 202 n.8

Bachofen, J. J., 20
Baker, John E., 193 n.3
Barrie, Sir James, 85
Bennett, Arnold, 37
Bentley, Eric, 182
Bergler, Edmund, 50, 59
Birds, Beasts and Flowers, 69, 202 n.16
Black Sun Press, 158
Blackwood, Lord Basil, 195 n.3
Blake, William, 78
Blanchard, Lydia, 171

Blavatsky, Elena, 23, 77
"The Blind Man," 25, 83–87, 88, 121, 162
The Blithedale Romance, 131, 137
blood brotherhood, 85, 91, 111, 147–48
"The Blue Moccasins," 166–67
Book of the It, 23
"The Border-Line," 79, 140
The Boy in the Bush, 79, 104, 115–126, 129, 158, 159
Brett, Dorothy, 125, 154
Briffault, Robert, 20
Brown, Hilda, 58
Browning, Robert, 35
"bullying," 7, 15, 171–72, 183–84
Burns, Robert, 45–46
Burrow, Trigant, 24
Bynner, Witter, 7
Byronic hero, 119
Bystander, 48

Canaan, Mary, 114
The Captain's Doll, 48, 60–61, 71, 79, 88, 109, 183
cardiac plexus, 25, 32, 40–41
Carlyle, Thomas, 182
Carswell, Catherine, 16, 61–62, 65, 68, 72–73, 84–85, 125, 194 n.38
Carswell, Donald, 85–86
Carswell, John, 85–86
Carter, Vivian, 48
Cavitch, David, 7
Cecil, Lord David, 62
cervical ganglion, 33
cervical plexus, 33
Cezanne, Paul, 76
Chambers, Alan, 46, 118
Chambers, Jessie, 38, 118, 125, 132, 162
Childhood and Society, 9–10
"Children of Adam," 76
Clark, L. D., 46, 139, 148
Clarke, Ada Lawrence, 15, 57, 157
Collings, Ernest, 15
Communism, 19, 106
Conrad, Joseph, 64
Cooper, James Fenimore, 119, 129, 132–33, 135, 138, 150, 199 n.5

Corke, Helen, 89, 162
Crèvecoeur, Hector St. John de, 128, 136, 138
Crosby, Harry, 159
"The Crown," 183
Cullen, Flossie, 37–38, 45

Daleski, Herman, 122, 150
Dana, Richard Henry, 135
dark gods, 35, 45–47, 108, 110, 118–19, 121, 174, 183–84, 186–87
"Daughters of the Vicar," 11
Davison, Lawrence H. *See* D. H. Lawrence
The Decline and Fall of the Roman Empire, 64, 192 n.12
Deerslayer, 132
Delany, Paul, 12, 85, 105, 107, 118, 181
democracy, 19–20, 30, 136, 139
D. H. Lawrence: A Composite Biography, 60
D. H. Lawrence and Human Existence, 9
D. H. Lawrence: Novelist, 6
The Dial, 49, 92, 193 n.6
Dodge, Mabel, 13–14, 67, 89, 103, 108, 127, 132–34
Doolittle, Hilda. *See* H. D.
Dostoevsky, Fyodor, 131
Double Measure, 9

Education of the People, 15, 27–32, 56, 120–21, 129
Eliot, George, 12
Eliot, T. S., 20, 182
England, My England, 61–62, 71, 77, 81–89
The English Review, 17, 76, 86, 127, 130
"Enslaved by Civilization," 169
Erikson, Erik, 9–10, 56–57, 151
The Escaped Cock, 6, 159, 165, 184. See also *The Man Who Died*
Etruscan Places, 149
Evans, John, 199 n.14
Eve, 30

Fantasia of the Unconscious, 27, 29–35; blood brotherhood, 147–48; cosmology, 126; on father's role, 40; father-quick, 142; father-spark, 31, 186; flippant attitude, 30, 105; husband and wife, 107; ideal wife, 123; on maternal bullying, 38, 42, 146, 150–51, 174; matriarchy, 169; on mother worship, 42–43; "Southern" mode of love, 41; sympathetic mode, 97; on teeth, 67; theories, 128; title, 22
fascism, 19, 102
father, absence of, 39–40, 86, 128, 141, 143–44; and leadership ideal, 36, 117–19, 149–50, 152–53, 177, 181; role in child's development, 32, 185–87. *See also* paternalism
father-quick, 36
father-spark, 31–32, 36, 142, 149, 171, 184–86
"father thirst," 186
Finney, Brian, 158
The First Lady Chatterley, 160–61, 162–63
The Flying Fish, 69
Forbes, Esther, 161
Ford, Ford Madox, 68, 190 n.31
Ford, George, 5–6, 8, 64, 116, 130–31
The Fox, 48–70; animals, 66–67, 68–69, 184; and "Blue Moccasins," 166; class consciousness, 61–62; death, 64–65, 109, 112, 119, 122, 135, 158, 180, 183; ending, 51, 56, 66–67; expanded from short story, 71; female entrapment, 63–64, 180; Grenfel as fox, 69; Grenfel's need for security, 53; hero, 76, 77–78, 107–8, 140; history, 48, 57–58, 71; hospitality, 49, 54–55, 61, 145; "ideal" woman, 16; as inverted Genesis story, 77–78; and *The Ladybird*, 76; "long tail to," 48; maternal domination, 41, 160, 167, 169–70; oedipal view, 51; paired women, 11–12, 55; pre-oedipal nature, 50, 51–54; prototype, 57–66, 67–70, 122; revenge, 13, 55–56, 70; similarities to "You Touched Me," 81–83; similarities to "Monkey Nuts," 87; triumph of Banford, 57, 165
Franklin, Benjamin, 127, 136–37
Frazer, Sir James, 23, 52, 168
Frederick the Great, 143
Freeman, Mary, 6, 173
Freud, Sigmund: D. H. Lawrence's disagreements with, 23–24, 27, 29, 30–31, 32, 34–35, 148; D. H. Lawrence's ideas in accord with, 97; D. H. Lawrence's "improvement" on, 199 n.1; "on Female Sexuality," 9; on female space, 94; on mother's hostility, 10; on "oceanic state," 83
Fromm, Erich, 9
Fussell, Paul, 190 n.24

Garnett, Edward, 14
Genesis, 76–77, 79
Gibbon, Edward, 65, 119, 192 n.12
Gilbert, Sandra, 195 n.7, 202 n.16
Gilligan, Carol, 202 n.7
"Glad Ghosts," 196 n.12
Goats and Compasses, 69

The Golden Bough, 52, 168–69
Goodheart, Eugene, 6, 56
Graves, Robert, 22, 201 n.12
Gray, Cecil, 62, 181
The Great War and Modern Memory, 190 n.24
Green, Martin, 7, 67, 164
Grenzleute, 79
Groddeck, George, 23, 191 n.3

H. D., 68
Hamlet, 17–18
Hardy, Thomas, 12
Hartley, L. P., 75
Hawthorne, Nathaniel, 76–77, 127–38 passim
Heilbrun, Carolyn, 203 n.22
Herakleitos, 182
hero, 6, 69, 76, 107–8, 119–20, 123, 126
Hitler, Adolf, 181
Hocking, William Henry, 118
homosexuality, 118, 187
"The Horse-Dealer's Daughter," 82, 88
Hough, Graham, 37
The House of Ellis, 115
Howarth, Herbert, 11, 80
Huebsch, Ben, 190 n.31, 199 n.1
Hutchinson's Story Magazine, 48, 71
Huxley, Aldous, 5
hypogastric plexus, 33

In a Different Voice, 202
incest, 10–11, 24–25, 27, 33–34, 35, 44–45, 113, 136
Indians, 44, 102–3, 104, 132–34, 199 n.5, 200 n.5
Inniss, Kenneth, 196 n.10
The Insurrection of Miss Houghton, 38, 46. See also *The Lost Girl*
intimacy, 180

James Tait Black prize, 37
Jarrett-Kerr, Father Martin, 8
Jesus, 86, 117–18, 141, 144, 165–66
John Bull, 127
John Thomas and Lady Jane, 159–61, 162–63, 166. See also *Lady Chatterley's Lover*
Jones, Jim, 109–10, 113
Jung, Carl, 10–11, 83

Kangaroo, 104–14; animals, 69, 184; architecture, 110, 139; break with Europe, 105–6, 113–14; critics, 5, 6–7, 104; dark gods, 108, 110, 121, 183; devouring mother, 106–7, 111, 140; difficulties in writing, 115; ending, 123; fears of entrapment, 112–13; flippant attitude, 105; leadership ideal, 109, 110–11, 181; maternal characteristics of leader, 110–11, 149; on mob rule, 127; motif of communication, 105–6; "nightmare" chapter, 109, 122; politics, 106, 109–10; rejection of socialism, 20, 111; repulsion from female web, 180; search for father, 109, 110–11; snake, 77
Kermode, Frank, 104, 112
King, Emily Lawrence, 157
Koteliansky, S. S., 16, 63, 64, 65, 91, 105
Kundalini, 77–78

The Ladybird, 71–86 passim; animals, 69, 75–78; expanded from short story, 48, 73; hero, 73–75, 79–80; as inverted Genesis story, 76, 79; D. H. Lawrence's view of, 142; leadership ideal, 6, 80, 181; outdated creed of gentility, 101; sun, 158; symbolic father, 80, 86–87; worship of Magna Mater, 75, 144
Lady Chatterley's Lover, 159–64, 265; ending, 123; escape from female domination, 163, 184; hero, 162–64; incest, 24; infantile dependency, 146, 159–62; as inverted Genesis story, 79; isolation, 162–63; misogyny, 163–64; resurrection, 183; sex, 96, 163–64; tenderness, 6, 163–64
Lambert, Cecily, 58–62, 65, 67, 121
Lambert, Nip, 60–61, 67, 121
Lawrence, D. H.: and America, 18–20, 71–72, 127; on animals, 67–69; on architecture, 138–39; on charity, 81, 145–46; on democracy, 28, 143; desire for children, 14; education theories, 27–30, 34, 109; on Freud, 23–24, 27, 29, 30, 34–35, 148, 199 n.1; on the "hero," 125; homosexuality, 118; illness, 14–16, 66; on incest, 10–11, 20, 24, 27, 33–34, 36, 130; insect image, 64–65, 75–76, 135; intimacy, 88–89; on Jesus, 144; as leader, 181–82, 183; on maternal destructiveness, 10–11; misanthropy, 119, 135, 174–75, 182; models for characters in "The Blind Man," 85–86; need for support, 57, 61, 190 n.31; as "outlaw," 119, 132; pairing of women in fiction, 11–12; psychology theories, 22–35, 94–98, 110–11, 128–30, 137–38, 199 n.1; on touch, 110
Lawrence, Frieda: on babies, 144; and Brett, 125; and her children, 14, 72–73, 99; dependency of husband, 15, 94, 98;

as devouring mother, 16–17, 82, 157; elopement with D. H. Lawrence, 8, 12, 154; fights with husband, 122, 125; isolation in Australia, 108; on D. H. Lawrence's fear of women, 89; on D. H. Lawrence's homosexuality, 186; D. H. Lawrence's "incest" with, 45; and leadership ideals, 173; model for Banford and March, 53, 66–67; model for Harriet Somers, 107; model for Isabel Pewin, 85–86; separations from husband, 58, 93, 113, 125; on *The Virgin and the Gipsy*, 154–55
Lawrence, George, 179
Lawrence, John Arthur, 8, 32, 86, 118, 143–44, 180
Lawrence, Lydia Beardsall: D. H. Lawrence's dependency, 15, 66; D. H. Lawrence's relations with, 7, 32–33, 176, 179–80; illness of, 37, 105; and leadership ideal, 173; model for "Lovely Lady," 157
Lawrence, William Ernest, 179
Lazarus, George, 192
leader, charismatic, 151–53
leadership ideal: in *Apocalypse*, 171–72; and architecture, 138–39; carried to extreme, 182–83; distinguished from bullying, 183–84; father's role, 180–81; first stirrings, 13; relationship to devouring mother, 35–36; supposed repudiation, 154
leadership period: animals, 78; defined, 5–6; and devouring mother, 174, 185, 187; violence, 135–36; vocabulary, 90, 128–29, 140
Leavis, F. R., 6, 49
Lewis, Wyndham, 182
Look! We Have Come Through!, 14
The Lost Girl, 37–47; blood brotherhood, 148; dark gods, 45–46, 182–83, 197 n.15; death, 41, 112, 183; devouring mother, 47, 141; history, 37–39; kinds of love, 31; lack of father, 39, 147; marriage, 45–47, 79, 122–23; maternal domination, 39–46, 145, 151; need for nurturance, 107, 161; pre-oedipal motifs, 175; rule of Magna Mater, 36, 145, 149; witness to action, 147, 148
"The Lovely Lady," 157–58, 170
Lowell, Amy, 82
Luhan, Mabel. *See* Dodge, Mabel
Luhan, Tony, 133
lumbar ganglion, 25, 32, 67, 95–97, 110, 112
Luther, Martin, 143

McCurdy, Harold, 8
McDonald, Edward, 143
Mackenzie, Compton, 202 n.5
Magna Mater: in *Apocalypse*, 171; in "The Blind Man," 86; in essays on American literature, 19, 132; in *Lady Chatterley's Lover*, 161–62; D. H. Lawrence's conflicting attitudes toward, 174; in D. H. Lawrence's life, 89; in *The Plumed Serpent*, 144, 145; positive or negative aspects, 12, 55; revenge, 137, 184; in *Scarlet Letter*, 131; in *The Virgin and the Gipsy*, 155
Mahler, Margaret, 30, 176, 179, 185–86
The Man Who Died, 77, 159, 164–65, 166, 183. See also *The Escaped Cock*
"The Man Who Loved Islands," 202 n.5
"Manifesto," prologue, 3
Mansfield, Katherine: on *The Fox*, 48; on Frieda as "devouring mother," 16–17; "incest" with Middleton Murry, 11–12, 44–45, 83, 85; letter, 200; on *The Lost Girl*, 46; model for *Aaron's Rod*, 197 n.11; psychological assessment, 191
Marks, W. S., 86
"Master in His Own House," 147
matriarchalism, 7, 18–19, 20–21, 38–46, 116–17, 168–69
"Matriarchy," 168–69, 179–80
matricide, 18, 21, 55–57, 170
"Meeting at Night," 35
Melville, Herman, 119, 127, 129–30, 133
Meyers, Jeffrey, 171
Meynell family, 13, 62, 72, 80, 86
Meynell, Viola, 80
Miller, Hillis J., 16, 51, 54
Millet, Kate, 164
Milton, John, 76–77
Mischerlich, Alexander, 152
Mixed Marriage, 38, 45. See also *The Lost Girl*
Moby-Dick, 129
Moers, Ellen, 110 n.20
Monk, Violet, 58–60
"Monkey Nuts," 87–88
moon, 34, 75, 126
Moore, Harry T., 6, 8, 46, 63, 86, 87, 104
Morgan, L. H., 20
Morning in Mexico, 14
Morrell, Ottoline, 13, 16, 62, 94, 180–81, 195 n.39
"The Mortal Coil," 48, 71. See also *The Captain's Doll*
mother: "bad," 12, 131, 177–78, 179, 187; "good," 131, 177–78, 179
"Mother and Daughter," 168–71
The Mother, Anxiety, and Death, 10

mother fixation, 7; Bachofen and Fromm on, 191 n.40; in *The Boy in the Bush*, 117; cause of society's problems, 35–36; at center of critical views of D. H. Lawrence, 173; as D. H. Lawrence's central concern, 11; effect on D. H. Lawrence's theories of matriarchalism, 20; on Frieda and other women, 82; in *The Lost Girl*, 42–43; in *Sons and Lovers*, 33–34
Mother Right, 20; theory of, 198 n.6
motherhood, 187, 203 n.22
"mother-imago," 11
mother-kin, 201 n.11
The Mothers, 20
Mountsier, Robert, 17, 18, 119
Movements in European History, 81, 142–43
Moynahan, Julian, 56, 158
Murry, John Middleton: on *Aaron's Rod* and D. H. Lawrence's homosexuality, 5; C. Carswell's view of his betrayal of D. H. Lawrence, 194 n.38; "incest" with Katherine Mansfield, 11, 45; D. H. Lawrence's criticism of, 98; on D. H. Lawrence and Margaret Radford, 62; letter, 142, 143; love-thy-neighbor creed, 132; model for *Aaron's Rod*, 196 n.11; model for "The Blind Man," 84–86; model for *John Thomas and Lady Jane*, 159–60; oedipal approach to D. H. Lawrence, 173

Napoleon, 143
Nehls, Edward, 60
Nietzsche, Friedrich, 182
Noli me tangere, 15, 83, 85, 92, 120, 129, 140–41, 159, 165–66
The Novels of D. H. Lawrence: A Search for Integration, 174

object constancy. *See* mother: "good"
oedipal approach to D. H. Lawrence, 7–8, 51, 82, 173
oedipal phase, 10
Oedipus in Nottingham, 8, 173
"The Old Adam," 78
Omoo, 129, 133
oral stage, 95–96
Oresteia, 18, 20
Our Father Who Art in Hell, 110

Paradise Lost, 77–78
Paradise Regained, 78
"Parting at Morning," 35
Pater Magnus, 36, 144, 171
paternalism, 86–87, 180, 202 n.8. *See also* patriarchalism
patriarchalism, 18–19, 21, 109, 124, 148–51, 154, 169–172. *See also* paternalism
Paul Morel, 37–38. *See also Sons and Lovers*
Peoples Temple, 109–10, 113
Pinker, J. B., 48, 190
The Plumed Serpent, chapter 10; animals, 69, 77–78, 184; blood brotherhood, 132, 147–48; Christianity, 145–46; death, 112, 134–35, 183; father, 36, 86, 141, 146–47; D. H. Lawrence's repudiation, 7; leadership ideal, 6, 12, 154, 164, 181; male domination, 122–23, 168, 170; matriarchalism, 169; pre-oedipal conflicts, 147, 180; sun, 158. *See also Quetzalcoatl*
Poe, Edgar Allan, 112–13, 127, 129–30, 138–39
Pound, Ezra, 182
political movements, 19–20, 106
pre-oedipal conflicts, 9–10, 148, 153, 185, 186–87
pre-oedipal motifs in D. H. Lawrence's works, 174–76
pre-oedipal phase, 9
Prichard, Katherine Susannah, 199 n.10
"The Prussian Officer," 119
Pryse, James, 77
Psychoanalysis and the Unconscious, 23–27, 30–31, 33, 38, 95, 128
"Psychological Analysis of Literary Productions as a Revelation of Personality," 8
The Psychological Birth of the Human Infant, 176–78, 179
psychology, D. H. Lawrence's theories on, 22–36, 128–30, 138
The Psychology of the Unconscious, 9–10, 23

Quetzalcoatl, 126, 142, 144, 171. *See also The Plumed Serpent*
Quetzalcoatl (god), 144–46, 148–49, 152

Radford, Dollie, 57, 62–63, 182
Radford, Margaret, 13, 15, 57–58, 63–66
The Rainbow, 12, 14, 28, 78, 92, 127, 138, 182, 187
Rananim, 17, 47, 48, 126, 127, 133, 180
"The Reality of Peace," 64
Red Ridinghood, 120, 121
Reflections on the Death of a Porcupine, 69
Reinventing Womanhood, 203 n.22
Reston, James B., Jr., 109–10
Returned Serviceman's League, 106
Rheingold, Joseph, 10, 16, 55, 187
"The Risen Lord," 101, 165
"The Rocking-Horse Winner," 131, 195 n.2

Romulus and Remus, 29
Ruskin, John, 182
Russell, Sir Bertrand, 16, 62, 182

sacral ganglion, 33, 130
sacrifice, human, 108, 117, 136, 182–83
Sagar, Keith, 6, 164, 183
St. John, 23
St. Mawr, 69, 121, 126, 139–41
"Samson and Delilah," 88
Sartor Resartus, 104
The Scarlet Letter, 76–77, 130–31, 133, 136
Sea and Sardinia, 13, 55, 57
Secker, Adrian, 202 n.5
Secker, Martin, 30, 38, 202 n.5
Secker, Rina, 202 n.5
Secret Doctrine, 23
Seltzer, Thomas, 30, 128, 133
Sennett, Richard, 202 n.8
"separation-individuation," 176–79
serpent-bird, 141. See also *The Plumed Serpent*; snake
Seven Arts, 71
Skinner, Jack, 121
Skinner, Mollie, 113, 115, 119, 121, 123–24
snake, 76, 77–79
"Snake," 76
Socarides, Charles, 186
socialism, 20
solar plexus, 25, 31, 41, 95, 97, 112, 135, 142
Son of Woman, 5, 173
Sons and Lovers: architecture, 138–39; comparison with *The Fox*, 66; comparison with *Lady Chatterley's Lover*, 160–61; comparison with "The Rocking-Horse Winner," 131; as D. H. Lawrence's attempt at freedom from mother, 105, 107; doll burning, 200 n.5; domineering mother, 173; foreword, 93–94; like "Lovely Lady," 157–58; mother fixation, 8, 33–34; paired women, 11; woman's role, 35. See also *Paul Morel*
Sontag, Susan, 198 n.9
The Spectator, 49
"The Spirit of Place," 128
Stern, Alan, 201 n.13
Sterne, Mabel. See Dodge, Mabel
Stoll, John, 35, 78, 164, 174
Studies in Classic American Literature, 76, 111, 137 passim
sun, 34, 126, 149, 158, 184. See also father-spark
"Sun," 158, 177–79, 183, 184
Superman, 182
Swinburne, 196 n.5

symbiotic phase, 176
sympathetic mode, 26–27, 32, 34, 35, 94–95, 97–98, 110, 138
Systems of Consanguinity and Affinity, 20

Tedlock, Ernest, 6, 173–74
Tenderness, 6, 159. See also *Lady Chatterley's Lover*
tenderness, 154, 163–64
"The Theatre," 17–19
"The Thimble," 48, 71, 73–74, 75–76, 80. See also *The Ladybird*
thoracic ganglion, 25–26, 32
"Tickets, Please!," 88, 116
Tindall, William York, 77
Tönnies, Ferdinand, 111
Tortoises, 69
totemism, 52
touch, 85, 89, 165
Touch and Go, 64, 185
The Trespasser, 30
trespassing, 27, 30, 129, 150, 164–65
Twilight in Italy, 17–19, 128
"The Two Principles," 129, 140
Two Years Before the Mast, 135
Typee, 129, 133

the unconscious, 24–26
Unwin, Stanley, 31

Vickery, John, 52
The Virgin and the Gipsy, 120, 154–58, 166
Virgin Mary, 75, 144–46, 161, 165–66
A Vision, 22
Vivas, Eliseo, 21, 97
voluntary mode, 26, 32, 34, 95–98, 138
Von Richthofen, Baroness Anna Marquier, 125

"War Baby," 72–73
Warner, Marina, 203 n.22
Weekley, Barbara, 154
Weekley, Ernest, 155
Weekley, Frieda. See Lawrence, Frieda
Weiss, Daniel, 8, 173–74
Wheeler, Richard, 83, 151
The White Goddess, 22
The White Peacock, 19, 30, 37, 116, 121, 183–84
Whitman, Walt, 19, 76, 111, 137–38, 184
Widmer, Kingsley, 55
"The Wilful Woman," 134
Wilhelm, Kaiser, 143
will to power, 14, 180–81
"The Woman Who Rode Away," 14, 109, 134–35, 139, 158, 183
Women in Love: animals, 184; death, 119;

Frieda's reaction, 14; insects, 64; leadership ideal, 6, 71; mastery over animals, 121; misanthropy, 69, 93; "Moony" chapter, 126; mother-country, 105; mothering, 11–12, 107, 145; prologue, 186; publishing of, 127; relation to D. H. Lawrence's life, 13, 28, 62, 190 n.28; sex, 96; star polarity, 34, 90, 122, 174
World War I, 12, 17, 19, 101–2, 190 n.24

Yeats, William Butler, 22, 182
yoga, 77–78
Yorke, Dorothy, 65
"You Touched Me," 16, 81–83, 88, 166. *See also* "Hadrian"

Judith Ruderman is Director of Continuing Education at Duke University.

Of related interest

Confessions of a Prosaic Dreamer
Charles Lamb's Art of Autobiography
Gerald Monsman

The Elements of Chaucer's *Troilus*
Chauncey Wood

Gentle Flame
The Life and Verse of Dudley, Fourth Lord North
Dale B. J. Randall

Spenser and the Motives of Metaphor
A. Leigh DeNeef

Kinde Pitty **and** *Brave Scorn*
John Donne's Satyres
M. Thomas Hester

Accommodating the Chaos
Samuel Beckett's Nonrelational Art
J. E. Dearlove

Jl

(

I